Foreword

In 2002, the OECD Public Governance Committee launched a review of the initiatives in member countries designed to modernise government. Two Symposia were held: "The New Public Executive" (November 2003) and "Adaptive Government: New Challenges, Different Contexts, Common Values" (October 2004). The two-year review aimed to acquire a deeper understanding of the impact of reform initiatives, with a view to helping those involved with public governance policy to equip themselves for the future. This book identifies levers for reform to modernise the public sector, and presents an overview of public sector modernisation in OECD countries over the last 20 years. It defines different policy paths with the common objectives of making the public sector more responsive, transparent and efficient.

The review was led by Alex Matheson and co-ordinated by Teresa Curristine of the OECD Secretariat. Contributors include Jón R. Blöndal, Joanne Caddy, Teresa Curristine, Dirk-Jan Kraan, Dorothée Landel, Alex Matheson, Elsa Pilichowski, Michael Ruffner and Joaquin Sevilla of the OECD Secretariat, and Deok-Seob Shim, former staff member. The work was reviewed by an expert panel of government officials and academics: Sabino Cassese, Benoît Chevauchez, Hiromitsu Kataoka, Pan Suk Kim, John Murray, Christopher Pollitt, Christoph Reichard, Knut Rexed and Allen Schick. The book was edited by Teresa Curristine with the assistance of Derek Abbott.

90 0732247 0

WITHDRAWN
FROM
UNIVERSITY OF PLYMOUTH
LIBRARY SERVICES

Modernising Government

University of Plymouth Library

Subject to status this item may be renewed
via your Voyager account

http://voyager.plymouth.ac.uk

Exeter tel: (01392) 475049
Exmouth tel: (01395) 255331
Plymouth tel: (01752) 232323

OECD **{{●**

ORGANISATION FOR ECONOMIC CO-OPERATION AND DEVELOPMENT

ORGANISATION FOR ECONOMIC CO-OPERATION AND DEVELOPMENT

The OECD is a unique forum where the governments of 30 democracies work together to address the economic, social and environmental challenges of globalisation. The OECD is also at the forefront of efforts to understand and to help governments respond to new developments and concerns, such as corporate governance, the information economy and the challenges of an ageing population. The Organisation provides a setting where governments can compare policy experiences, seek answers to common problems, identify good practice and work to co-ordinate domestic and international policies.

The OECD member countries are: Australia, Austria, Belgium, Canada, the Czech Republic, Denmark, Finland, France, Germany, Greece, Hungary, Iceland, Ireland, Italy, Japan, Korea, Luxembourg, Mexico, the Netherlands, New Zealand, Norway, Poland, Portugal, the Slovak Republic, Spain, Sweden, Switzerland, Turkey, the United Kingdom and the United States. The Commission of the European Communities takes part in the work of the OECD.

OECD Publishing disseminates widely the results of the Organisation's statistics gathering and research on economic, social and environmental issues, as well as the conventions, guidelines and standards agreed by its members.

This work is published on the responsibility of the Secretary-General of the OECD. The opinions expressed and arguments employed herein do not necessarily reflect the official views of the Organisation or of the governments of its member countries.

Publié en français sous le titre :
Moderniser l'État :
La route à suivre

UNIVERSITY OF PLYMOUTH
9007322470

© OECD 2005

No reproduction, copy, transmission or translation of this publication may be made without written permission. Applications should be sent to OECD Publishing: *rights@oecd.org* or by fax (33 1) 45 24 13 91. Permission to photocopy a portion of this work should be addressed to the Centre français d'exploitation du droit de copie, 20, rue des Grands-Augustins, 75006 Paris, France (*contact@cfcopies.com*).

Table of Contents

List of Boxes

List of Figures

List of Tables

MODERNISING GOVERNMENT: THE WAY FORWARD – ISBN 92-64-01049-1 – © OECD 2005

ISBN 92-64-01049-1
Modernising Government: The Way Forward
© OECD 2005

Executive Summary

The past two decades have witnessed an influx of new ideas and initiatives in the field of public management in OECD member countries. This review seeks to acquire a deeper understanding of how some of these new ideas have worked in practice by examining selected key public management reform policy levers. Based on these findings, this review considers more generally how the understanding of public management and governance has changed over the same period with a view to helping those involved with public management policy equip themselves for the future.

The impetus for change came from the social, economic and technological developments in the latter half of the 20th century. While in many countries fiscal stress provided the trigger for reform, the underlying pressures for change came from the fact that governments were increasingly out of step with a changing society which had new and different expectations.

Government has a larger role in the societies of OECD countries than two decades ago. But the nature of the public policy problems and the methods to deal with them are still undergoing deep change. Governments are moving away from the direct provision of services towards a greater role for private and non-profit entities and increased regulation of markets. Governments' regulatory reach is also extending into new socio-economic areas.

After decades in which new government initiatives could be funded by extra revenue, fiscal stress now means that OECD member countries have reached the limits of affordability. Despite years of public sector reform, upward pressure on government expenditure remains; governments must continue to adapt to the changing needs of society, while remaining within expenditure limits.

In the past 20 years, governments have made major changes to the way they manage the public sector. Most OECD public administrations have become more efficient, more transparent and customer oriented, more flexible, and more focused on performance. However, public administrative arrangements are inextricably linked to fundamental institutions of public governance. Reformers need to be aware of the possible effects of reforms on wider governance values.

Lessons learned from key public management policy levers

Open government: Across OECD member countries, governments are becoming more open and more transparent, accessible and consultative. This phenomenon has found expression through new legislation and institutions and a wide array of policy measures. Today 90% of OECD countries have a Freedom of Information Act and an Ombudsman office and over 50% have customer service standards.

A continuing challenge for governments is to meet higher expectations of citizens for more accessible and high quality services and information. Currently, another major challenge for OECD countries in the face of the threat from terrorism is to preserve government openness while ensuring national security and effective law enforcement.

Enhancing public sector performance: Governments have become much more performance focused. The performance movement has increased formalised planning, reporting and control across many governments. Most OECD countries have introduced performance management and budgeting: 72% include non-financial performance data in their budget documentation. Thus information available to managers and policy makers has both increased and improved.

Governments should, however, be wary of overrating the potential of performance-oriented approaches to change behaviour and culture, and of underestimating the limitations of performance-based systems. Performance approaches require increased managerial flexibility. However, key challenges are to balance this flexibility with control and to integrate performance measurement systems into a particular country's traditional accountability system. Too much flexibility could lead to abuse and mismanagement; too little flexibility risks an inefficient and unresponsive public service. More attention needs to be given to keeping performance transaction costs in check and to making optimal use of social and internalised motivators and controls.

Modernising accountability and control: How governments keep control over large and complex operations has changed over the past 15 years because of technological innovations, changes in the size and structure of government, and the introduction of performance budgeting and management. The main trends in control across OECD member countries are the move from *ex ante* to *ex post* control, and the development of stronger processes of internal control. In practice there is a move from the inefficient but relative certainty of checking the regularity and legality of individual transactions to the more efficient but relative uncertainty of verifying the proper operation of systems. The challenge is to maintain control in systems that are more delegated, with more autonomous agencies and third-party providers.

Reallocation and restructuring: The need for government to set outer limits for expenditure and to reallocate within those limits has changed national budgeting from a support function to the primary vehicle for strategic management. The budget process is also frequently used as a vehicle for wider managerial reform.

The ability to change organisational structures is essential for a modern government. However, structural change – either the dismantling of existing organisations or the creation of new ones – should not be undertaken lightly. Dismantling organisations can lead to a loss of continuity, of institutional memory and of long-term capacity. The proliferation of more or less autonomous arm's-length public bodies makes collective action and co-ordination difficult. Governments should understand the structural strengths and weaknesses of their existing systems and build on their strengths.

The use of market-type mechanisms: Market-type mechanisms of various kinds have become more common across OECD member countries, although there are marked country differences in their use. These mechanisms have the potential to produce significant efficiency gains. The decision to use market-type mechanisms needs, however, to be made on a case-by-case basis, and the specific design of these instruments is critical to their successful application. It remains important to protect key governance principles, not to confuse private gain and public interest or to obscure public responsibility or accountability. Governments must protect their freedom for future action if priorities change.

Modernising public employment: The nature of public employment in OECD countries has evolved significantly. In many countries the employment arrangements of public servants have become more like those of the private sector by altering the legal status and employment conditions. Individualised employment policies have become increasingly common; these include the introduction of contracts and performance-related pay, the latter now being implemented in two-thirds of OECD countries.

The implementation of these policies tends to make a collective culture more difficult to achieve. Early reformers underestimated the complexity of introducing private sector techniques into the public service. Staying with traditional public employment arrangements, however, is not a feasible option for most countries.

Wider conclusions about public management and governance

Modernisation is dependent on context. While all governments are being affected by global trends, there are no public management cure-alls. History, culture and the stage of development give governments different characteristics and priorities. Adaptation can be assisted by learning from other governments but, unless countries are very similar indeed, learning will work better at the level of system dynamics than at the level of instruments and specific practices.

The contemporary problem is how to organise the public sector so that it can adapt to the changing needs of society, without losing coherence of strategy or continuity of governance values. Modernised governments are required to be responsive to various groups of citizens. But there is a cost in terms of capacity for collective action when the public service is differentiated and fragmented. New management approaches need to go beyond contracting and reporting to give renewed attention to connecting the public interest to individual motivation and values.

Governments must adapt to constantly changing societies. It is not a matter of one-off "reform" but of having a whole-of-government public management policy capability that enables governments to make adjustments with the total system in mind. Effective public management policies need clear problem diagnosis and outcome evaluation.

Citizens' expectations and demands of governments are growing, not diminishing: they expect openness, higher levels of service quality delivery, solutions to more complex problems, and the maintenance of existing social entitlements. Reforms to the public sector in the past 20 years have significantly improved efficiency, but governments of OECD countries now face a major challenge in finding new efficiency gains that will enable them to fund these growing demands on 21st century government. For the next 20 years, policy makers face hard political choices. Since most governments cannot increase their share of the economy, in some countries this will put pressure on entitlement programmes. These new demands on builders of public management systems will require leadership from officials with enhanced individual technical, managerial and political capacities who think and plan collectively and who can work well with other actors.

The Review

The OECD Public Sector Modernisation Review takes an overview of public sector modernisation in OECD member countries over the last 20 years in order to gain a better understanding of how past reform efforts have worked in practice.

This study was conducted by examining a selection of key public management policies. It hypothesised that certain public management policies had particular importance as "levers" on public sector behaviour. It sought to examine the trends and results of the following levers across OECD countries: open government; performance; accountability and control; restructuring organisations; the use of market-type mechanisms; and public employment/civil service. Once the study was underway, it became clear that the nature of these levers varied. Some were drivers of change, some were consequences of change, and "performance" was an aspiration influenced by several different public management instruments.

This book examines trends in the use of the six levers and how they have influenced public governance in different OECD countries. The review looks at these levers from a whole-of-government viewpoint; that is, it views governments as joined-up systems and from a governance perspective. As a result of having examined the interaction between particular public management policies and whole-of-government dynamics, this study also reflects on how the understanding of the dynamics of public management and governance has changed over the course of the reform period. Finally, it identifies challenges facing governments in the future, and seeks to help governments think about how to ensure that their public management policies are coherent, manageable, and calibrated to national circumstances.

This review is necessarily limited in scope. It examines selected aspects of reforms and focuses on selected dimensions of managing government. As a result, several important developments are not included in this review, such as: the movement of power between levels of government, the changing role of the centre, the extension and elaboration of regulation, the impact of electronic communication and information tools, new networks and relationships with stakeholders, and major developments in service delivery (*e.g.* privatisation). Furthermore, the evaluation of public sector reforms is currently hindered by gaps in the availability of data. More sustained tracking of key institutional reforms would allow for more comprehensive analysis and comparison.

Introduction

Governance: A work in progress

The 30 member countries of the OECD share core governance elements. These have emerged with the evolution of the modern state and include: democracy and citizenship; representation; a constitution; the rule of law; competitive party and electoral systems; a permanent civil service; separation of powers between the executive, the legislature and the judiciary; judicial review; and secularity.[*] Most of these elements are common to all OECD countries, but are combined in different ways. There are republics and constitutional monarchies, unitary or federal states, prime ministerial, presidential and semi-presidential systems. Legislatures may be bicameral or unicameral and possess features of the Westminster or congressional systems. Governments may operate under administrative law or common law, with a strong executive or a strong parliament, under close or distant judicial scrutiny, with a court of accounts or an auditor general. Constitutional arrangements may be set out in a written constitution or embodied in the accumulation of legislation, precedent and practice bearing on the constitutional structure. Heads of government may be directly or indirectly elected; ministers may be elected or appointed. Electoral systems may use forms of proportional representation or "first past the post" voting. Powers are differently separated, and each branch of government is differently organised.

These formal differences reflect the history of individual nations. More importantly, they signify that nations are animated and distinguished by cultural forces rooted in their past. These differences, formal and cultural, influence the organisation and operation of public administration.

The amalgamation of these core governance elements into national democratic systems has only recently gained wide international acceptance – and for less than half of the world's population. The democratic fundamentals now taken for granted (*e.g.* suffrage for more than a small proportion of the population) are relatively recent for many countries. A third of OECD member countries were under non-democratic forms of government in their recent history. The key development since the middle of the 20th century has been the spread of constitutional and democratic systems of government.

Governance is therefore a work in progress. Not only are many countries still in transition from regimes that lacked core elements of what is now considered good governance, but also the idea of governance itself is in

---

[*] Drawn from Finer (1997).

constant flux. Governance has to continue to adapt in response to such pressures as the spread of national and international commerce, the shifting of powers between levels of government, the spread of new technologies and media of mass persuasion, the permeability of national borders, the influence of globalised communities of values and interests, and the vulnerability of free societies to the threat of terrorism.

Governance and public administration

"Governance" refers to the formal and informal arrangements that determine how public decisions are made and how public actions are carried out, from the perspective of maintaining a country's constitutional values in the face of changing problems, actors and environments. Public administration is a constituent pillar of governance. Ideas of good governance emerge from assumptions about the status of individual rights to property, personal inviolability, equality and redress under the law, participation in collective decision making, and duties and obligations as the citizen of a state. At a basic level, these values are what OECD member countries have in common, but in their elaboration they reflect national culture and explain why nations are different. They explain why OECD member countries, even though they draw on common governance elements, have put them together in very different ways. An appreciation of these contextual differences is necessary to avoid the trap of seeking to prescribe universal answers to questions of governance.

Cultural differences are expressed in the public administration domain in areas such as the relative importance of social vs. formal controls, the level of compliance with laws and regulations, the standing of the public service, the disposition to use commercial agents in the delivery of services to the public, the role of unions, the capacity to find national consensus, the disposition to corporatism and the capacity to change national direction. Not only are there differences among countries in individual elements, but there are also systemic differences among groups of countries with different historical heritages.

In the period under review, many of the assumptions about the extent of direct government responsibility as a service provider have been challenged and, in some countries, radically changed. Governments have progressively withdrawn from commercial activities, ownership of industries and service provision in, for example, communications and energy and water supply. These are explicit governance changes. However, reforms undertaken ostensibly in the interests of better management have also had an impact on the distribution of power, whether this was intended or not. For example, the adoption of better accounting standards by the executive may also strengthen the role of the legislature by providing it with more accessible information on the state of public finances. In contrast, giving semi-autonomous government agencies more policy-making power could weaken parliamentary oversight.

As illustrated in the following quotation, any reform can have its advantages and its shortcomings for the system as a whole. The most appropriate approach depends on the problems and risks of the specific system:

> The irritants (of public bureaucracies) are so disparate that no remedy could be expected to be effective against all of them at once. Besides, steps taken to relieve one often aggravate another.
>
> ...depoliticizing administration may undermine executive leadership, while strengthening political executives may create openings for partisan considerations to displace professionalism.
>
> Pitting bureaucrats against each other complicates and slows the decision making process, as do measures to democratize administration, but rationalizing jurisdictions through reorganization and procedural streamlining inhibits competition and cuts back internal checks and balances.
>
> Turning functions back to the marketplace overcomes some dysfunctions, but the factors that induced people to demand governmental intervention in the first place soon generate renewed calls for public programs; markets, after all, are very seldom perfect.
>
> Contracting out public services alleviates some failings, but administering contracts has historically been the Achilles heel of government, a source of corruption and mismanagement.
>
> Policy planning and coordination and efficiency are furthered by orderly budgeting systems, but budget analysts inexpert in specialized fields often end up second-guessing skilled and experienced professionals...
>
> Decentralizing authority to field officers generally results in prompter decisions; it may also result in grossly disparate treatment of clients in identical circumstances. On the other hand, centralizing authority may advance consistency in policies but delay action as the center gets inundated by detail.
>
> One irritation is alleviated, another is intensified.

Kaufman (2001), p. 40.

Kaufman's observation also points up the interrelationships between the various components of public administration. As government makes changes in one aspect of its system, other parts will be forced to respond.

These different dimensions of public administration are not of equal importance. There is a hierarchy of values between the day-to-day activities of government and the shared values that underpin constitutions and hold societies together in the long term. One simplified way of presenting this hierarchy is as follows:

Table 0.1. **Hierarchy of values**

Short-term significance	RESPONSIVE GOVERNMENT	
	Faithfully executes policies of the day. Meets needs of client groups. Communicates and consults with them.	Current policies meet needs of citizens involved.
	RESPONSIBLE GOVERNMENT	
	Serves interests of all citizens, attends to long-term impact of policies. Does not burden future generations. Adaptive – takes "hard" resource and organisational decisions when necessary. Collective interest protected from private gain.	Takes care of the collective interest.
	LEGITIMATE GOVERNMENT	
Long-term governance significance	Constitution and law-abiding in spirit/action. Treats citizens fairly, respects individuals and communities. Sense of security maintained. Transparent decision making. Use of coercive power safe-guarded. Collective interest protected from private gain.	Maintains/builds trust in public institutions.

In addressing governance issues, as in other areas of policy making, an action to fix a short- or medium-term problem can have a long-term impact on legitimacy. For example, varying the balance between the protection of the individual and the powers of the state in response to a perceived national security emergency may reduce the confidence of the public that their rights are adequately protected. Contracts to make senior officials more sharply responsive to the government of the day might reduce their freedom to give independent professional advice and their sense of responsibility to the public interest.

An unresponsive government can be voted out of office without harm to trust in public institutions, but if the legitimacy of the institution of government is damaged, a society's ability to function is permanently impaired. There is, therefore, no clear line between governance and public management – any significant public administrative change can have governance consequences.

Why reform public administration?

The last 30 years have seen significant changes in the attitudes towards government and public administration in OECD member countries. In the decades after 1945, a model of government held sway: the monopoly, or near-monopoly, provider of utilities such as power and water supplies, of services such as health care, social welfare and education, and of transport infrastructure and services. While never universally accepted or uniformly applied, this model dominated thinking about the role of government and how best to meet the needs of citizens. In this model, government was responsible for all the steps in service provision: mandating action by declaring its policy intentions in the form of laws and regulations, providing the services needed to give effect to its policies, and financing the services from general taxation.

The traditional model of government as a comprehensive service provider is not intrinsically flawed – it provided a basis for steady and progressive recovery in post-war Europe that went hand-in-hand with unprecedented economic growth. Indeed, it continues to be the model for government in some OECD countries. However, it was increasingly seen in some quarters as having failed to adapt to political, social and economic changes. The driving forces that had inspired it – post-war reconstruction and a determination to avoid a repetition of the political, economic and social calamities of the inter-war decades – were no longer paramount.

The impetus for change came from many different sources – including the social, economic and technological developments in the latter half of the 20th century – which put pressure on all governments to adapt to new problems, new capacities and new relationships between citizens and governments. The public were increasingly concerned about the quality of the services they received and the choices available to them. Citizens were also increasingly resistant to the government's growing share of the national economy. In some countries, an expectation that taxation would decline became generally accepted across the political spectrum. Private alternatives to public services – in health, education and transport – were increasingly available and affordable.

More and more, governments became out of step with a changing society and with an educated and empowered citizenry looking to amend their social contract. In many countries, fiscal stress and financial crises provided the main trigger for widespread public sector reform. From the early 1980s onwards, it became clear that some of the open-ended, demand-driven commitments of the traditional model were leading countries into financial crisis. At the same time, in areas such as transport, communications and health, the need to respond to technological change was imposing increasing costs on government. Funding ever-expanding public responsibilities by taking an increased share of the national economy was no longer politically or economically tenable.

For some countries, financial pressure on governments coincided with the opening up of the international economy, facilitating the free movement of capital and the adoption of floating exchange rates for national currencies. Governments found that their freedom to manage the national economy and determine the size and scope of government activity was increasingly limited by international expectations. It became more difficult for governments to tackle issues generated by societal changes through increased spending. As one possible response in addressing these issues, many governments looked to reducing the size of their public sector or radically altering its structure. The direction that public sector reform took was heavily influenced by the national context of the individual country.

What has emerged from two decades of reform?

Government has a larger not a smaller role: After 20 years of reform, government is more, not less present in OECD countries, but the nature of that role has changed significantly. Society's expectations of governments have not diminished; if anything, they have increased. The nature of the public policy problems governments face, and the mix and modes of intervention, are still undergoing deep change.

There is significant change in the mix and modes of government interventions: The means used by governments to fulfil their responsibilities have altered considerably. Through privatisations many governments have not only removed themselves from several commercial enterprises (*e.g.* airlines) but have also withdrawn from ownership and provision of energy, water and communications. Governments have moved from direct provision of some services towards creating and regulating new markets.

Over the same period, the regulatory coverage of governments has increased. Government concern has spread in all directions – pollution, health, safety, corporate governance, environmental protection, data matching, protection of minorities, global terrorism, credit control, commercial law, consumer protection, product labelling, consumption taxes, means testing, illegal migration, control of the Internet, and so on. This expansion in regulation reflects the increased complexity of societies. At the same time, through technological advances, government's ability to accumulate information in these areas has increased significantly.

As governments face more new and complex problems that cannot be dealt with easily by direct public service provision, more ambitious policies require more complex interventions and collaboration with non-governmental parties.

Government expenditure has not shrunk a great deal in the OECD area: In reaction to fiscal stress, governments have sought to reduce public expenditure through cutbacks, privatisation, restructuring and other reforms. In many OECD countries, the past decade of reform has resulted in a reduction in the share of public employment compared to the total working population (OECD, 2002b, pp. 2-3; and see Table A.1 in Annex A).

Despite these changes – and contrary to the expectations of some reformers – in most OECD countries, public expenditure did not shrink greatly.

In fact, general government expenditure as a share of GDP increased slightly, on average, in the OECD area at the beginning of the 1990s (some two percentage points; see Table B.1 in Annex B). Since its pinnacle in 1993, the ratio of public spending to GDP in the OECD area has declined again to stand at around 40% in 2005.

However, in cyclically adjusted terms, general government primary outlays have remained broadly constant (OECD, 2004a). This development is largely the result of, on the one hand, increasing revenues flowing from the economic boom in the late 1990s and several one-off or transient factors (for example, the peace dividend, lower debt financing cost, privatisations and public restructuring) and, on the other hand, persistent underlying pressures on public spending.

Upward pressure on expenditure remains: The underlying pressures on public spending remain, as demands on social transfer systems intensify: spending on pensions, education and health continue in a clear upward trend and this is likely to be exacerbated by the problem of ageing populations (OECD, 2004a).

Reforms cannot substitute for hard political choices: For OECD countries, improving the cost-effectiveness and performance of their public sectors will help to reduce pressure on spending. As the past decade has shown, however, this in itself is unlikely to stem the continued upward pressure on expenditure generated by social entitlement programmes and social transfers. Public sector reform is not a substitute for the hard and, in many cases, unpopular choices that politicians have to make in some countries if long-term difficulties are to be avoided.

What has been learned about public sector modernisation?

There has been considerable change in public sector management: Over the past two decades there have been significant changes in how governments manage their public sectors. These changes have brought positive benefits: today, governments in most OECD countries are more efficient, more transparent, more customer-aware, and more focused on performance than 20 years ago.

Reality did not match the rhetoric: Nevertheless, the reality of reform has not lived up to the rhetoric. In many cases, the changes made to rules, structures and processes have not resulted in the intended changes in behaviour and culture. Indeed, in some cases reforms have produced unintended or perverse consequences, and have negatively affected underlying public sector and governance values. Many countries continue to struggle with attaining the fundamental behavioural changes that are often needed to sustain reforms over the long term and in some cases to undo the unintended effects of past modernisation initiatives.

Often, governments have adopted reform instruments or ideas from the private sector or from other governments (for example, performance-related pay) without regard for the country context and/or understanding the inherent limitations and weakness of these instruments. Furthermore, in some cases there has been a failure to view the public administration as part of a wider governance structure. It is important to see it not as a series of separate entities, but rather as a whole interconnected system: reforming one part of the system can have unintended impacts on another part.

Modernisation is context dependent: OECD countries' reform experiences demonstrate that the same reform instruments perform differently and produce very diverse results in different country contexts. This variation in reform experiences reflects the disparate institutional structures and environments that confront the reformers. A strong lesson to emerge from this review is that modernisation is context dependent. Modernisation strategies need to be tailored to an individual country's context, needs and circumstances. These differences will be reflected in the starting point from which the reforms are launched, the nature of the problems faced and the most appropriate solution to apply. Other issues that depend on context include how countries deal with accountability and control in public management, the involvement of the private and community sectors in service delivery, the use of market-type mechanisms and the line between the public and private domains.

Understanding the dynamics of the public administration system is important: Modernising government requires an understanding of the nature and dynamics of the public administration system as a whole and how it functions as part of society. Each system has its own dynamics, trade-offs and risks which reflect its unique history, culture and institutional structure. Governments need to understand the dynamics of their own system and to design reform strategies that are calibrated to the risks and dynamics of their system.

Public governance and public administration are intrinsically linked. The reform experiences of OECD countries have highlighted that a country's public administration system is part of its wider governance and constitutional structures. The practice of public administration both reflects and influences the values of governance.

Adopting a whole-of-government approach to reform is necessary: In addition to understanding the public administration system, it is important that governments take a whole-of-government approach to reform – that is, understanding and viewing both public administration and governance structures as part of an interconnected whole. Government operates in a unified constitutional setting under a common law, and its performance is influenced by the interaction of an entire body of government levers such as the accountability and budget processes, and the political-administrative culture. Thus, to be effective, reforms must be designed to change the behaviour of a variety of actors. Changes in part of the system will have an impact on others.

For example, to ensure that performance-oriented budgeting and management achieves its objectives, its introduction requires not only changes in the behaviour of managers but also of the ministry of finance and politicians in the legislature and the executive, who all must use this performance information. A whole-of-government approach is needed to understand the behavioural changes required and the incentives available, both formal and informal, to achieve these changes. Therefore, consideration should be given to the potential impact of reforms on the wider national governance arrangements and the underlying attributes that support this.

Reform is continuous: The past two decades have not witnessed a diminishing of the pace of reforms, but rather the emergence of more complex problems and continuous reforms. In sum, as societies keep changing, governments must keep adapting. It is not a matter of one-off "reform" but of having a whole-of-government public management policy capability that enables governments to make adjustments with the total system in mind. Effective public management policies need clear problem diagnosis and outcome evaluation.

Before looking at the changes to the public sector in detail, it is important to remember that the rate and scope of change should not be exaggerated. While there have been many changes to public administration in the period under review, they have not been uniform across countries. Nor have OECD countries embraced reforms to the same extent or at the same pace – some have chosen and emphasised all levers of reform, others have only concentrated on a few. Some have moved with great speed in reaction to a financial crisis, while others have moved slowly along the path. For example, New Zealand and the United Kingdom began strong reform drives in the 1980s, while Germany and Japan launched managerial reforms in the 1990s.

Structure of the book

The book examines the following public management reform levers in detail. Although this book is organised into discrete chapters, it is important to remember that each of the processes discussed is often driven by, and driving, change in other areas. The review seeks to understand these changes from a whole-of-government perspective.

Chapter 1: **Open Government** discusses the growing demands for greater openness in OECD countries. It reviews the steps taken by governments to achieve greater openness, such as the introduction of freedom of information laws. It also explores the limits to openness, and identifies future challenges.

Chapter 2: **Enhancing Public Sector Performance** reviews one of the most significant attitudinal changes in public sector management in the last two decades: the move from process-driven approaches to managing for performance. This chapter briefly discusses the wider perspective on government performance before looking at the developments in performance-oriented budgeting and management in OECD countries. It identifies the trends and the strengths and weaknesses of current approaches and future challenges.

The shift in the focus of public sector management has resulted in the adoption of a range of new approaches to management, budgeting, personnel and institutional structures in pursuit of improved performance. The creation of decentralised agencies, the use of outsourcing and the privatisation of public sector service provision are examples of typical institutional changes. The focus on performance also motivated changes to public sector employment such as the introduction of contracts and performance-related pay. These trends are examined in later chapters.

Chapter 3: **Modernising Accountability and Control** examines the key elements of control systems in OECD countries. It explores the main reform trends and changes under way, for example the move from *ex ante* to *ex post* control and the challenges resulting from these changes.

Chapter 4: **Reallocation and Restructuring: The Heavy Machinery of Reform** explores the ways in which the structure of public sector organisations has adapted to the changing demands both from within the public sector and from the community at large. The chapter also examines the role of the budget as a tool of central agencies for driving structural change and resource reallocation.

Chapter 5: **The Use of Market-type Mechanisms to Provide Government Services** examines the use of market-type mechanisms to provide government services across OECD countries. The main market-type mechanisms examined are outsourcing (contracting out), public-private partnerships and vouchers. This chapter begins with a discussion of the mechanisms and an overview of the extent of their use in countries. Then the issues involved in introducing these mechanisms, both in terms of design and governance factors, are discussed as well as future challenges.

Chapter 6: **Organising and Motivating Public Servants: Modernising Public Employment** looks at changes in the nature of employment in the core public service in OECD countries, as well as issues and challenges for the future. There has been a variety of reform initiatives across countries, but this chapter concentrates on: attempts to increase managerial flexibility through the decentralisation of human resources management responsibilities; efforts to reduce public employment; the individualisation of employment contracts; accountability and the introduction of performance-related pay; and changes in the management of senior civil servants.

Chapter 7: **Modernisation: Context, Lessons and Challenges** provides a general overview of the lessons learned about the different levers of reform, and discusses the key strategic lessons, mainly the importance of context.

ISBN 92-64-01049-1
Modernising Government: The Way Forward
© OECD 2005

Chapter 1

Open Government

1. Introduction

As societies change, citizens are redefining how they relate to the government. Among the most important changes in attitudes to, and expectations of, government in the period under review is the trend towards more open government. There has been progress from a hope to a demand and even to a legal right for citizens to have access to information. OECD countries are moving from a situation where government chose what it revealed, to a principle of all government information being available unless there is a defined public interest in it being withheld.

The scope of modern government gives much more to be open about. As the complexity of societies has increased, the reach of regulation penetrates deeper into people's lives and the volume and scope of information about individuals collected by government have increased significantly. Government regulation has spread into new socio-economic areas (such as pollution, safety, consumer protection). In some countries this trend has been combined with declining public trust in government and demands from increasingly well-educated and informed citizens that their views be taken into account in policy decision making.

Both officials and politicians are under increasing pressure to take individual responsibility for their use of the power and resources at their disposal. The public increasingly demands to know what decisions have been taken by officials and who took them and, in most OECD member countries, has a legal right to that information. There is an expectation that citizens will be made aware in advance and consulted about decisions that affect them. Flowing from this is a right, given institutional form in many countries, that the citizen will be able to challenge administrative decisions and seek redress for failures of administrative process and practice.

Open government is increasingly recognised to be an essential ingredient for democratic governance, social stability and economic development. Building open government is a challenge for all countries. The principles of good governance – transparency and accountability; fairness and equity; efficiency and effectiveness; respect for the rule of law; and high standards of ethical behaviour – represent the basis upon which to build open government.

This chapter explores how governments of OECD countries have responded to the growing demands for greater openness, reviews measures for achieving open government, examines the limits to openness and identifies future challenges.

2. What is "open" government?

What does the term "open" government mean? Three characteristics appear to be most relevant when describing a government as open, namely:

- Transparency – that its actions, and the individuals responsible for those actions, will be exposed to public scrutiny and challenge;

- Accessibility – that its services and information on its activities will be readily accessible to citizens; and

- Responsiveness – that it will be responsive to new ideas, demands and needs.

As used here, "openness" both encompasses and goes beyond the more commonly used term of "transparency". It introduces two further aspects, namely "accessibility" and "responsiveness", in order to capture other qualities of the relationship between government and the wider community it serves. While these dimensions are closely interlinked, they remain distinct and may be present to differing degrees.

Each of these dimensions of "openness" has practical implications from the point of view of those outside government looking in. From the public's perspective, an open government is one where citizens, businesses and civil society organisations (CSOs) have:

- the ability to request and receive relevant and understandable information (exposure);

- the capacity to obtain services and undertake transactions (accessibility);

- the opportunity to participate in decision making (responsiveness).

2.1. Principles in practice

Over the past two decades, all OECD countries have invested in building open government. Yet their policy choices have varied considerably given their different country contexts and priorities. Each of these three dimensions of openness may be applied in practice through appropriate legislation and policies, as well as formal and informal institutional frameworks. Taken together, these measures act as "levers" for public sector modernisation (OECD, 2003f). Open government measures cannot simply be grafted onto existing government. Rather, their use over time may lead to profound systemic change within government and qualitatively different forms of governance. Many open government measures exist. They are not all of equal importance, and they are not applied to an equal degree in all countries. Nor is the process without opposition from entrenched interests. Some open government measures underpin democracy as a system of government, and may therefore be considered fundamental. Others strengthen the legitimacy and credibility of government action as a whole while some serve short-term instrumental goals, such as improving the quality of particular policies.

Laws establishing rights of access to information – as well as the institutional mechanisms to enforce these rights – are a basic building block for enhancing exposure of government to public scrutiny and therefore democratic control. Other transparency measures – such as the publication of customer service standards, performance results and "score cards" – contribute less directly to strengthening democracy and more to ensuring the credibility of government commitments. Efforts to promote administrative simplification, "plain language" drafting requirements, one-stop shops, and online services all contribute to removing barriers, reducing the transaction costs of dealing with government and making it more accessible. Finally, the use of customer complaint forms, focus groups and statutory requirements for public consultation during policy making and rule making ensure more responsive governments that listen to businesses, civil society organisations (CSOs) and citizens, and take their suggestions into account when designing and implementing public policies and services.

3. The demand for open government

This section examines the demand for more open government, the implications of falling levels of public trust and the emergence of new actors in civil society.

3.1. Restoring public trust

Increasingly, well-educated, informed and critical citizens expect high quality services, streamlined administrative procedures and to have their views and knowledge taken into account in public decision making. Their expectations are often not met. In a public opinion survey conducted in 2003 in the United Kingdom, 40% of those interviewed describe local public services as "bureaucratic" and only 5% regarded them as "open" (United Kingdom Office of the Deputy Prime Minister, 2002, p. 2). The same survey reveals a demand for more information on government services, on reasons why decisions are taken, on how public money is spent, on who to contact and on how to lodge a complaint. Other surveys indicate that many citizens recognise that freedom of information is important for exercising rights of citizenship and accessing public services (Marcella and Baxter, 2000, pp. 136-160). A similar picture holds in many other OECD countries. Governments today may be more open, but they are increasingly difficult for citizens to understand given the degree of complexity and diversity of tasks they undertake.

The steady erosion of voter turnout in elections, falling membership in political parties and surveys showing declining confidence in key public institutions give scant grounds for complacency. According to the Spring 2004 Euro-barometer survey of public opinion in the 25 European Union Member States, 19 of which are also OECD member countries, two-thirds of the respondents tend not to trust national governments. They rank third to last in a list of 15 institutions, just above big companies and political parties, but well behind the top four – namely, the army, the radio, the police and charitable or voluntary organisations (Euro-barometer, 2004, p. 10). More bad news for senior public managers comes from a recent United Kingdom survey question on public leadership which showed that only 22% of respondents regarded them as being trustworthy. The fact that this was double the level scored by national politicians (11%) is cold comfort indeed (MORI, 2003). Trust in government is a fundamental element of the democratic "contract" and its decline may have significant impacts on how people perceive, comply with and interact with the public bodies that exercise power in their name.

In response to rising public expectations, the standards of openness to which both private and public sector organisations are held have become far more demanding over the past 30 years – and this trend may be expected to continue in the future. Calls for greater government transparency and accountability have grown as public and media scrutiny of government actions increases and standards in public life are codified and raised. In many OECD countries, business associations have been among the most vocal supporters of government reforms introducing greater openness – particularly with regard to regulatory policies and administrative simplification – and in some cases have even become partners in their implementation, for example in running one-stop shops for small businesses (OECD, 2003b, p. 28). As governments contract out public services and pursue privatisation, the boundary between the public and private sectors is increasingly blurred – posing new challenges in deciding where and how to apply government standards of openness. Over two-thirds of OECD countries have adopted legislation setting out the standards of behaviour expected of public servants, while many countries also use codes of conduct and guidelines (OECD, 2000b, pp. 38-39).

3.2. More and better watchdogs

While traditional institutions for *ex post* public oversight, such as supreme audit institutions (SAIs) and Ombudsman offices, continue to shoulder the main responsibility for ensuring adherence to such standards, new and highly vocal public watchdogs have emerged in the past decade. The number, capacity and global reach of CSOs have grown apace.[1] In many areas of government activity, CSOs have evolved from well-meaning but essentially amateur lobbyists or fund-raisers into highly professional organisations engaged in policy development, research and monitoring of government performance. Scandals, public criticism and increasing competition for resources (*e.g.* funds, public attention) within the sector has meant that CSOs too have had to raise their standards of openness and accountability in order to maintain their principal assets of credibility and legitimacy. When taken together with traditional sources of independent monitoring of government performance (*e.g.* media, international organisations, rating agencies), the modern version of the "fourth estate" exercises powerful pressures, and advances vocal demands, for openness. As governments scramble to respond, what at first sight appear to be piecemeal reforms do, over time, produce a cumulative effect. Once the standards against which government openness is measured have been raised there is no non-controversial way of going back.

4. Why open government contributes to good governance

The choice of open government policies by OECD countries reflects their differing national priorities. Some countries privilege instruments that make government more open to public scrutiny (*i.e.* exposed) in the interest of fighting corruption (*e.g.* Korea, Mexico). Others focus on making government more user-friendly (*i.e.* accessible) in order to improve service delivery (*e.g.* Denmark) while yet others seek to enhance government interaction with external stakeholders (*i.e.* responsive) in order to foster better quality and more inclusive policy making (*e.g.* Canada, Finland). While diverse, all such measures may ultimately be regarded as contributing to the broader goal of strengthening public trust in government as a necessary precondition for effective public policy.

"Supply side" arguments for building open government may be couched in democratic or instrumental terms. A democratic approach will regard openness as worth pursuing given its essential role in determining the legitimacy and credibility of democracy as a form of government. An instrumental approach sees greater government openness as a means to achieve other important policy goals – such as economic growth or social cohesion. These two lines of argument will be explored briefly below.

4.1. Openness: An important democratic value

As a system of government, democracy rests upon the informed consent of citizens and their ability to exercise control over those who wield public authority on their behalf. Open government strengthens democracy by providing a bulwark against misgovernment, by exposing abuse of power, by offering greater protection to minorities through equal rights of citizenship and by providing greater opportunities for popular participation. As noted by

James Madison almost two centuries ago, "A popular government without popular information or the means of acquiring it is but a prologue to a farce, a tragedy or perhaps both" (Madison, 1822). Many government policies for greater openness explicitly acknowledge the contribution such measures make to enhancing democratic governance. Some countries have gone further still, recognising that more open government is a necessary but not sufficient condition for strengthening democracy and that achieving this goal also requires capacity building in civil society (e.g. Finland's Civil Participation Policy Programme).[2]

4.2. Openness: Its impact on economic and government performance

Comparative research undertaken by the World Bank at the global level shows that, "in those settings with high levels of transparency, effective parliamentary oversight, and high standards of corporate ethics, there was a higher rate of GDP growth over the previous three years than in countries with lower standards" (Kaufmann, 2003, p. 19).[3] Several reasons for this may be advanced. Governments have a near monopoly on certain types of information upon which market actors depend (e.g. reliable statistics on inflation, forthcoming regulations and interest rates changes). The more open, reliable and timely governments are about sharing this information, the sounder the basis for economic decision making leading to more efficient resource allocation (Stiglitz, 2002, pp. 35-37). A higher degree of openness in government decision making may contribute to a more "level playing field" for all economic agents (large or small, domestic or foreign).

The OECD work on public governance shows that greater openness has a positive impact on performance in several key areas of government operations, including regulatory governance, budgeting and expenditure management, and public sector integrity. These policy lessons have been incorporated into a number of OECD recommendations and guidelines which cover all three dimensions of government openness as defined above (see Annex C).

Provisions for openness contribute to regulatory quality by allowing those with a stake in government regulations to scrutinise and contribute to the drafting and review of regulations. "Transparency of the regulatory policy itself, as well as its institutions, tools and process is equally important for its success. Transparency encourages the development of better policy options, and helps reduce the incidence and impact of arbitrary decisions in regulatory implementation" (OECD, 2002h, p. 65).

The budget is the prime vehicle for giving effect to a country's economic and social priorities. As such, the process by which it is prepared, debated and approved is often highly contested but barely understood, and rarely amenable to participation, by a wider public (Schick, 2002). Greater openness to public and parliamentary scrutiny can help to ensure "due process" in budgeting and thus contribute to sounder public expenditure, providing that fiscal discipline is maintained (OECD, 2001a).

Open government means cleaner government. Openness in government enables effective public scrutiny which, in turn, helps to achieve and maintain high standards of integrity in the public sphere. To be effective this requires: clear standards for conflicts of interest and provisions for disclosure; review systems for public appointments, recruitment, and promotion; clear lines of accountability and reporting; transparent financial management and procurement procedures; and support from robust and professional internal and external audit (OECD, 2002f, p. 8).

5. Potential sources of opposition to open government

Opening up government to outside scrutiny and interaction can be a complex and painful process which may face opposition from a number of sources. Furthermore, the complex nature of modern government systems makes transparency more difficult. There is a legitimate and continuing debate about where the boundary lies between the public interest in confidentiality of information and the public interest in open access to government. Reservations regarding greater government openness should not be dismissed automatically as self-serving or obstructive.

5.1. *Defending the* status quo

Arguments for maintaining an element of secrecy are strong and may be held in good faith. Making decisions is easier with fewer actors. Civil servants may find it easier to give "frank and fearless advice" when they know it will not be exposed to public scrutiny. The consequences of making mistakes are lessened, and compromises may be negotiated (Stiglitz, 2002, p. 34). Less justifiably, government officials may fear that their practices will be exposed to unwelcome scrutiny. Lastly, all institutions have a burden of inertia coupled with (sometimes justified) cynicism about change, which must be overcome.

Many with a stake in the *status quo* may feel that they will lose a privileged position if government becomes more open. These may range from private businesses fearing greater competition in the supply of goods and services to government, professional civil society organisations concerned to maintain exclusive access to government policy makers, and professional associations wishing to preserve their status as sources of expert advice (MacDonell, 2003). Government officials may also resist greater openness given that, in the absence of freely available information, they may engage in rent-seeking behaviour, for example through selectively releasing information in their possession (Stiglitz, 2002, p. 35). As noted by a recent OECD report, "Vested interests are strengthened by opaque decision processes and unaccountable administrative discretion" (OECD, 2002h, p. 21).

A greater degree of openness may allow actors pursuing illegitimate or anti-social goals to operate more freely or undermine important social values (e.g. equity). For example, in the environment after 11 September 2001, openness may be deemed to be in conflict with national security and less important. An open market for government information may simply increase existing inequalities – whereby those who are better equipped (by virtue of their greater education or resources) benefit disproportionately.

The history of openness in government is recent, while the history of secrecy is centuries old. Balancing the need to protect legitimate national security concerns and to ensure public scrutiny of government activities has always been a challenge and is even more so today.

5.2. Dealing with opposition: Applying incentives, sanctions and leadership

The introduction of open government must recognise and deal with these sources of opposition. Valid objections must be met with sound alternative arguments. Employees are more likely to respond to hard data on the concrete benefits of open government than abstract appeals to democratic principles or the special nature of the public service (OECD, 2004d). Civil servants need to be convinced that open government will help them to do their jobs better and that leadership is fully committed to the process. Arguments must be supported by incentives (e.g. awards, public recognition), training (e.g. on newly introduced provisions for freedom of information (FOI) such as in Ireland and the United Kingdom), and networking and mentoring (e.g. regular meetings of ministry officials responsible for consultation in Canada). Creating change agents within government requires public officials to adopt appropriate standards of openness, rather than having them imposed from above. Effective ex ante and ex post controls, backed up by sanctions, are needed to demonstrate that open government provisions are not an optional extra, but an essential element of public service (e.g. sanctions for non-compliance with access to information legislation or non-disclosure of assets). Finally, leadership and strong commitment to open government are needed at all levels – from politicians, senior managers and front-line public officials.

6. How governments are making themselves more open

Over the past two decades, OECD countries have introduced an array of concrete legislative and policy measures to enhance government openness in the conduct of public affairs. Their experience to date demonstrates that successful implementation requires a whole-of-government perspective and an awareness that reforms introduced in one area (*e.g.* in making government more exposed) may have system-wide impacts (*e.g.* on the accessibility and/or responsiveness of government). For example, information on public service performance (*e.g.* via scorecards) can lead to higher quality and more accessible services, which may in turn place a higher premium on responsiveness. For ease of reference, reforms are presented below in terms of their most immediate impact on the three dimensions of open government discussed earlier. Effective implementation of open government requires appropriate legal frameworks, policy instruments, institutions and tools – a selection of which are described below. These are necessary but not sufficient conditions for openness in government. Achieving this goal in practice depends upon creating and nurturing a culture of openness throughout government.

6.1. Exposing government to greater public scrutiny

Governments exposed: key trends

The scope, quantity and quality of government information provided to the public has increased significantly in the past 20 years and the provision of information is now an objective shared by all OECD member countries. Maintaining quality standards for government information (*i.e.* which is relevant, timely, complete and objective), given the ever-increasing quantity available online, constitutes a challenge for the future.

Freedom of information legislation: Access to information is a precondition for public scrutiny and a basic building block for open government and is enshrined in the constitutions of some OECD countries (*e.g.* Austria, Hungary, and Poland).[4] Freedom of information (FOI) laws are the single most important means of giving substance to such basic rights, and their adoption has gathered pace in the past two decades. In 1980 only a third of (then 24) OECD member countries had legislation on access to information; by 2004 the percentage had reached over 90% – or 28 out of the current 30 countries. Figure 1.1 clearly illustrates the explosion of FOI legislation in OECD countries since the 1980s. It also underscores how very recent these laws are in historical terms, which suggests that their full impact as "levers" for systemic change in government openness has yet to be felt in many OECD countries.

Figure 1.1. **OECD countries with laws on access to information (date of first introduction)**

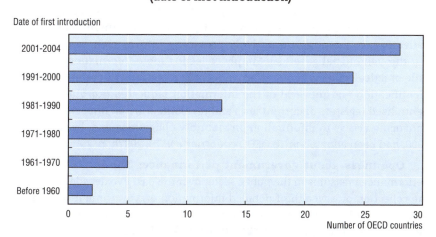

Date of first introduction

Number of OECD countries

Freedom of information legislation seeks to give the citizen a right of access to information held by government. The workload and costs of an effective regime for access to information may be reduced significantly if government publishes information extensively in the first place and limits the information which it wishes to withhold to those categories in which there is a genuine public interest in confidentiality or the protection of privacy. Where institutions comply with the letter of the law, rather than its spirit, public officials may resort to delaying tactics or to providing large bundles of information rather than the specific items requested, thus increasing the costs (and frustrations) of the system. It should be noted that the cost of FOI systems is many times smaller than government communication budgets that seek to manage the flow of information to the public.

Openness in the public realm should not endanger individual rights to privacy. All governments hold significant amounts of information on individual citizens, often of a sensitive nature (*e.g.* health records). Thus promoting openness to public scrutiny via legislation on access to information requires equally strong legal provisions setting out limits to access in the interests of individual privacy and data protection. Over 90% of OECD countries have passed legislation in this field. Exceptions to privacy legislation may be required for holders of public office where, in the interest of enhancing public scrutiny and avoiding conflicts of interest, disclosure policies require high-level officials to provide details of their private assets and pecuniary interests (OECD, 2003g, p. 5).

Efforts to provide greater access to more information will not, of itself, make government more open nor will it satisfy public demands without equivalent efforts to ensure the quality of information on offer. Legal rights on access to information are given substance by government policies on collecting, managing and actively providing information to the public (*e.g.* through official gazettes). Simply collecting more information will be of little practical value without effective records management systems to allow identification and retrieval of the information requested (*e.g.* via registers). Centralised registers of current laws and regulations are an important tool for enhancing access to information on statutory obligations and, by the end of 2000, had been adopted in 18 OECD countries (OECD, 2002h, p. 70).

Openness about government performance: The introduction of performance measures in the public sector over the past two decades has led to the collection of a wealth of detailed information on government operations. Two-thirds of OECD member countries now provide reports on their performance to the public (OECD, 2004c). Examples include publication of results obtained by the Program Assessment Rating Tool (PART) developed by the United States Office of Management and Budget and applied to all major government programmes.[5] This trend is discussed in more detail in Chapter 2.

New tools: As the uptake of new information and communication technologies (ICT) by governments and households progresses, the importance of online tools for access to government information has grown. The Internet is the medium of choice for all OECD member countries when providing a potentially vast number of stakeholders with an unprecedented degree of access to government information at marginal cost and high speed. ICT offer powerful tools for searching, selecting, and integrating the vast amounts of information held by the public administration as well as presenting the results in a form that can be readily used by citizens and businesses. As e-government advances and in order to ensure the quality, consistency and coherence of online information, some governments have issued standards for public authorities (*e.g.* Australia's Online Information Service Obligations[6]). More broadly, knowledge management tools are needed to allow governments to draw upon, update and share existing knowledge while incorporating new information from both internal and external partners.

Information on forthcoming decisions: The publication of annual reports, performance data and public accounts are an important tool for ensuring public scrutiny of past government actions. But they do not enable stakeholders outside government to monitor government actions today nor examine their plans for the future. The publication of strategic plans, legislative timetables, forthcoming projects and upcoming consultations are all important features of government openness and provide the conditions for key public stakeholders to prepare policy making by government and hence contribute more effectively.

Box 1.1. **Finland: Access to information for open policy making**

The 1999 Act on the Openness of Government Activities establishes that the moment at which preparatory documents relating to decision making are to enter the public domain will be considered on a case by case basis. The Act provides detailed provisions on the issue. According to the Act, all preparatory documents relating to decision making will, however, enter the public domain at the latest when the decision has been made.[1] Under the new Act, certain documents relating to the preparation of projects of general interest will enter the public domain as soon as they are finalised. The new Act applies to public authorities, state and municipal enterprises and the courts as well as private law organisations and private individuals performing functions involving the exercise of public authority or commissioned by a public body.

Public authorities also keep a public register of projects and legal preparatory documents of the Finnish Government. The register is both a tool for public officials and an information service for citizens. It includes data on preparatory legal documents, development and reform projects, and reports to the parliament, boards of state enterprises and agencies. All the information in the register is public, available free of charge on the Internet, and shown in the same format to both the information providers and the viewers. By placing information on upcoming policy issues in the public domain, the Act, coupled with the register, ensures greater transparency and public scrutiny of government policies and how they are prepared.

1. Holkeri (2002), p. 153. See also *www.hare.vn.fi.*

6.2. *Making government more accessible*

Accessible government: key trends

Governments are more accessible and user-friendly today than they have been at any point in history. The challenge for all OECD countries will be to meet ever higher demands from citizens and business for streamlined transactions, tailored services and ubiquitous access.

Access through administrative procedure laws: Building an open government that is accessible to anyone requires, at a minimum, provisions to ensure equal treatment. Administrative procedure laws do so by defining the basic conditions for citizens' access and establishing mechanisms for holding administrative powers accountable for their decisions. They provide guarantees for citizens in their interactions with government, uphold the rule of law and give substance to constitutional rights – for example, equality before the law, non-discrimination and due process (OECD, 1997). Administrative procedure laws and codes are typically a mixture of detailed procedural rules and general procedural principles, are found in over 70% of OECD member countries, and generally predate FOI legislation. They often include provisions to ensure that citizens who are potentially affected by administrative actions and decisions have the possibility to receive prior notice of a given decision-making process and thus defend their interests. The definition of the scope of interests to be considered varies, from a restricted focus on those whose interests will be directly affected by an administrative decision (e.g. Italy) to a wider definition also including those on whom the decision will have a substantial impact (e.g. Finland).

Enhancing access through customer charters: Over half of OECD countries have introduced citizens' charters with the aim of providing high quality, accessible and customer-centred public services (Kuuttiniemi and Virtanen, 1998). Today's users of public services expect them to meet their individual needs, offer choice and provide means for seeking redress. Customer charters improve accessibility as a key element of service quality, through reference to opening hours, response times, standards of courtesy and measures catering to special needs (e.g. those with disabilities). By introducing service charters and providing redress mechanisms, governments have provided citizens and businesses with a means of assessing their experience of public services as users against declared standards of service.

Cutting through "red" tape: Reducing the transaction costs of dealing with government through administrative simplification is a key concern for governments and businesses alike. Policy measures to reduce administrative burdens can also contribute to improving access through one-stop shops (both physical and electronic), providing assistance and advice in complying with regulations (e.g. to small and medium-sized enterprises) and Internet-based portals and electronic forms. In 2000, out of 28 OECD countries surveyed, 26 stated that they had a government programme to reduce administrative burdens (OECD, 2003b, p. 16).

Reducing barriers and fostering inclusion: Barriers to access may be of distance, time or language. Application of the principle of subsidiarity and progress in devolution and decentralisation have been among the most important reforms to bring government closer to people. Greater accessibility to government also depends upon the language in which information and services are provided. Those OECD countries with more than one official language (e.g. Belgium, Canada, Denmark, Finland, New Zealand and Switzerland) go to considerable lengths to ensure that all are equally represented. Only a few national governments have made significant efforts to provide information and services in minority languages (*e.g.* Spanish in the United States; a range of "community" languages in Australia). Translation of key administrative documents and intercultural mediation may ensure greater access to government by marginalised groups, support social inclusion and foster the peaceful development of a multicultural society. Making government intelligible to native speakers is perhaps an even greater challenge. Requirements for "plain language" law drafting – removing obscure terms and complex constructions and including guides to the structure and meaning of legislation – are now in place in over half of OECD countries and may be supported by guidance manuals and training (OECD, 2002h, p. 70).

Online access to government: E-government can significantly lower barriers for citizens and businesses by reducing costs, collapsing distances (*e.g.* between remote rural areas and the capital) and providing virtually unrestricted access to government information and online services. User-focused e-government, centred on the needs of businesses and households, employs ICT to cut across multiple agencies and levels of government to provide easier access to seamless services (OECD, 2005a). E-government initiatives designed to improve access include: portals that provide a single entry point for sector-specific information and transactions (*e.g.* for small to medium-sized enterprises, SMEs), access to a number of levels of government through one portal, measures to ensure access by users with disabilities (*e.g.* screen readers for the visually impaired), and access via mobile devices (*e.g.* mobile phones) (OECD, 2003a, p. 35).

6.3. Building responsive government

Responsive government: key trends

Public consultation for law making and rule making was once rare. Today, it is increasingly accepted as a valuable means of improving the quality of public policy while strengthening its legitimacy. Further efforts to improve tools, mainstream procedures and integrate the results of public consultation in established decision-making processes will be needed if governments are to become more responsive and adaptive in the future.

Responsive rule making: Almost a decade ago, OECD member countries pledged to ensure that regulations are: "...developed in an open and transparent fashion, with appropriate procedures for effective and timely input from interested parties such as affected businesses and trade unions, other interest groups, or other levels of government" (OECD, 1995a, Annex). Regulatory impact analysis (RIA) is a regulatory tool that examines and measures the likely benefits, costs and effects of new regulation and changes to existing ones. It provides decision makers with valuable empirical data and a comprehensive framework which they can use to assess their options and alternatives. It has helped many governments to reduce regulatory costs to business, while maximising the effectiveness of government action in protecting public interests. Consultation procedures are central to this process. In 2000, just over a third of OECD countries required RIA documents to be publicly released for consultation (OECD, 2002h, p. 46). Consultation on draft regulations has proven to be an effective way of obtaining information on the nature, size and distribution of costs and benefits directly from those most likely to be affected.

Expanding use of public consultation: Governments increasingly realise that they will not be able to conduct and effectively implement policies, as good as they may be, if citizens and business do not understand and support them. Thus, governments are looking for new ways of engaging a wider range of actors throughout the policy-making process. Efforts to introduce a greater element of public consultation between elections are not intended to replace but to rather to complement traditional representative democracy and the key role of elected governments and parliaments in the policy process. While in some OECD countries (*e.g.* Canada, Iceland, the Netherlands, Norway) public consultation is a long-established practice, in most it has only recently been recognised as a key element of modern policy making. As the United Kingdom's online consultation portal states: "Consultation – involving the public in the work of government – has become an integral part of the policy-making process. It is not simply about more open government, although that too is important, it is about making policies more effective by listening to and taking onboard the views of the public and interested groups."[7]

Building consultation frameworks: While legal, policy and institutional frameworks are still under development, initial experience has shown that, to be effective, consultation must have clear goals and rules defining the limits of the exercise and government's obligation to account for its use of the input received (OECD, 2001b, p. 11). The place held by laws and regulations governing public consultations varies considerably among OECD member countries, from being a fundamental feature of the constitutional system (*e.g.* Switzerland, where obligatory and consultative referenda are held on a regular basis) to being relatively limited in scope, application and impact. Legal requirements to consult with specific interest groups (such as trade unions and professional associations) or with indigenous peoples (also known as "first nations") may hold in some countries in order to safeguard constitutionally protected or treaty rights during policy making. The relative benefits of formal institutional mechanisms for consultation must be assessed in the light of the potential risks of "lock-in" and the lack of renewal of external partners. In most OECD countries, public consultation is generally conducted by line ministries, with centres of government (*i.e.* the Prime Minister's Office, Chancellery or equivalent) providing guidance, support and quality control.[8] Canada's 2004 guidance on the New Cabinet Papers System requires ministries to provide a proposed consultation strategy and, in some cases, background discussion documents to Cabinet when seeking approval to undertake a public consultation process on a key government initiative. When submitting recommendations to Cabinet, a summary is presented of the consultations undertaken, the key stakeholders consulted, the processes used and their outcomes.

Harnessing the potential of e-consultation: The unprecedented degree of interactivity offered by new ICT has the potential to expand the scope, breadth and depth of government consultations with citizens and other key stakeholders during policy making. New tools for online consultation include: government consultation portals or Internet sites; e-mail lists; online discussion forums; and online mediation systems to support deliberation (OECD, 2003e, p. 15). Despite its promise, online consultation for policy making is new and examples of good practice are scarce. Few expect new tools to replace traditional methods in the foreseeable future. Initial experience indicates that they are most effective when integrated with "offline" tools for consultation (*e.g.* online discussion groups coupled with "face-to-face" consultations). All OECD countries are working hard to bridge the "digital divide" (which generally mirrors longstanding socio-economic divides), and to ensure that all citizens, whether online or not, continue to enjoy equal rights of participation in the public sphere.

7. Oversight for open government

Key trends in oversight

As open government standards and public expectations have risen over the past two decades, existing institutions for ensuring oversight have evolved (*e.g.* supreme audit institutions) and new ones have appeared (*e.g.* Ombudsman offices). When coupled with the growing role of CSOs and the media, public scrutiny of government has reached unprecedented levels – and shows no signs of abating in the future.

7.1. Ensuring robust external audit

Supreme audit institutions (SAIs) are of central importance in exercising oversight of the executive branch and ensuring accountability for the use of public funds (OECD, 2005b). All OECD countries have an SAI, and in most cases it is an independent authority whose head is appointed by the legislature and which reports directly to it. SAIs undertake independent review of public accounts provided by the executive, as well as of the execution of government programmes and projects (OECD, 2002i, p. 11). They ensure that standards of openness are applied by monitoring government activities, by making their own reports public and by contributing to the role of legislatures in exercising parliamentary oversight.[9] While SAIs in most OECD countries date back to the 19th century or earlier, their functions, tools and scope of action have evolved considerably to meet the oversight challenges posed by modern government. This modernisation trend is discussed in more detail in Chapter 3.

7.2. Establishing Ombudsman offices

Ombudsman offices are a far more recent innovation in most OECD countries (see Figure 1.2). Only three had such institutions in 1960 (i.e. Denmark, Finland and Sweden); today 90% of countries have one. Ombudsman offices are generally appointed by legislatures and offer an important point of contact for citizens' complaints, appeals, and claims for redress in their dealings with the public administration. Ombudsman offices examine complaints brought against administrative authorities, indicate shortcomings in existing legislation and make recommendations for improvements. While their recommendations are rarely binding, they have proven to be a powerful source of pressure on governments to take remedial action. Some countries have dedicated Ombudsman offices for specific groups (e.g. for children in Iceland, for minorities in Finland and Hungary) or policy areas (e.g. health services in the United Kingdom). Ombudsman reports submitted directly to parliament provide a valuable "barometer" of public satisfaction with government performance and openness.

7.3. Strengthening parliamentary scrutiny

The separation of powers is designed to ensure that the executive is held to account for its actions and that government business is conducted in the open. This is reinforced in some OECD member countries by ministers' obligation to respond to questions by members of parliament, either orally or in writing. Many legislatures have established special organs of control to track budget execution (e.g. budget and/or audit committees) and the actions of the public administration (e.g. dedicated committees in Greece, Sweden, the United Kingdom). Legislatures in the majority of OECD countries have the power to launch parliamentary inquiries, although the extent to which they make use of their powers of investigation varies. A parliamentary committee of inquiry may have all or some of the following powers: to summon witnesses to testify under oath, demand or seize documents and order on-site inspections. Hearings and testimony to parliamentary committees of inquiry

Figure 1.2. **OECD countries with Ombudsman institutions (date of establishment)**

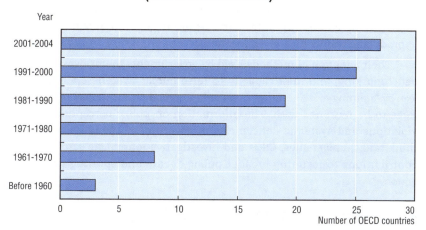

are generally public and their results published. In a growing number of countries, analytical bodies, like the United States Congressional Budget Office, are being established to help parliament with understanding the budget. The effectiveness of parliamentary oversight depends upon the legislature's formal powers, its willingness to act independently of the executive and – as the ultimate sanction – to exercise its power to dismiss the government (OECD, 2000a).

Over two-thirds of OECD countries have also established parliamentary commissioners for data protection and privacy. Parliamentary commissioners for oversight in the field of access to information are also common. Some countries have special commissions or parliamentary committees to exercise control over the secret services (*e.g.* Belgium, Germany, the Netherlands, Norway and Portugal) and other agencies where they have the power to intrude on the rights of citizens. All report directly to parliament, which contributes to effective oversight of these highly sensitive areas.

7.4. Role of public watchdogs

The number of CSOs with a sectoral (*e.g.* environmental) or specific interest in ensuring government openness (*e.g.* anticorruption, good governance) has risen significantly in the past decade. Their capacity for monitoring government action is enhanced by:

- participation in global networks which can mobilise diverse sources of expertise; and

- innovative use of new e-tools to collect, share, analyse and disseminate publicly available information (*e.g.* on budgetary or human resources) in more practical, relevant and user-friendly formats (*e.g.* via a single Internet site, or by combining data from different government databases and producing results for a given location).

Their adoption of methods used by governments themselves (*e.g.* audits, benchmarking) and their capacity to raise public awareness via the media (*e.g.* by "naming and shaming" or awards for good performance) make them a force to be reckoned with. The information on public perceptions, specific violations and systemic deficiencies in government openness collected by think tanks, universities, CSOs and investigative journalists can be valuable contributions to fostering broader public debate and spurring government action.

8. Open government in context

8.1. Evolution of open government

Today, there is substantial convergence between OECD countries in terms of their formal institutional arrangements for open government. As in many areas of public governance, however, context matters. When it comes to the implementation of open government measures, the differences between OECD countries remain greater than their similarities. Each has sought to achieve greater openness in government from different starting points, with different administrative cultures, political priorities and policy tools. The underlying informal institutions (*e.g.* norms, values) present in each OECD country have a substantial impact on how formal institutional measures for open government will work in practice.

8.2. Implementing open government: Lessons from diversity

Achieving open government is a long-term endeavour and is context dependent. Fostering openness in practice may require greater attention to:

- ensuring a whole-of-government perspective in order to deal with systemic impacts of single measures;
- identifying and managing unexpected consequences;
- establishing a solid legal basis for open government efforts, clearly setting out rights and responsibilities;
- applying a mix of legal provisions, policy measures, institutional reforms and new tools;
- accepting incremental change and ensuring sustained efforts over time; and
- sustaining momentum by harnessing external pressure for change.

Of the 30 OECD countries, 29 have at least four of the following pieces of legislation and institutions: Freedom of Information Act; Privacy and Data Protection Act; Administrative Procedure Act; Ombudsman/parliamentary commissioner; and supreme audit institution. For more details on specific countries, see Annex D.

9. Future challenges: Understanding the limits of open government

Openness is not an absolute good, nor should it automatically override other all other public values. This section briefly reviews some of the limits and unintended consequences of open government provisions as well as their challenges.

A difficult balancing act: Openness is one of many cherished public values citizens would like to see promoted by government. They also expect equity, efficiency, responsibility and due respect for individual privacy in the use of public power and resources. A key challenge for all OECD countries, and other democracies the world over, is to preserve government openness while ensuring national security and effective law enforcement. Since the events of 11 September 2001, several OECD countries have issued new guidelines or legislation setting limits to existing statutory provisions for access to information.[10] In many countries, the lack of a precise definition of "national security" together with a greater degree of discretion for public officials when deciding whether to withhold information or not has meant that secrecy, rather than disclosure, is now the default position.[11] At the same time any attempt to dilute or reverse previously declared standards will be perceived as a step backwards by sectors of public opinion – even if it may support other important policy goals (*e.g.* protection of the community against terrorists). Parliamentary oversight, judicial review, independent scrutiny and vigorous public debate remain the most effective means for reconciling these conflicting goals while preserving established standards of open government.

Managing the public-private interface: In the course of the past two decades, OECD countries have undertaken a wide range of reforms that have shifted the boundaries between the public and private sectors especially through privatisation and the use of market-type mechanisms such as contracting out and public-private partnerships (see Chapter 5). There has also been the introduction of elements of private sector approaches – such as managerial autonomy and competition – into the public sector (*e.g.* arm's-length agencies, performance contracts). Today, the public-private interface is a "grey zone" where the boundaries between the two sectors are not always clear and the rules to be applied can easily be confused. Yet citizens and businesses expect continuity in the rules, allowing them to trust their interlocutors regardless of whether they are ministries, independent public agencies or private sector subcontractors. Citizens and businesses demand full information on the use of public funds collected through charges and taxes no matter who is spending them (Pope, 2002, p. 20). Clear guidelines are needed – and strong oversight – for the application of statutory provisions for access to information, data protection and privacy by private enterprises and agents that provide publicly-funded services, handle sensitive personal data, and build key public infrastructures (e.g. IT providers). Without such guidelines and oversight, there will be ample scope for intentional abuse and innocent mistakes to undermine efforts to build openness and trust.

Governing in a fish bowl: Greater public scrutiny, stronger accountability mechanisms and better tools for measuring government performance may have impacts on programme design, human behaviour and working practices which, in the long run, have significant implications for governance. The majority of these are positive, such as the creation of a culture of openness in government, but some may have unintended consequences:

- Performance measurement may have perverse side-effects if organisations focus on what is measurable rather than what is important. For example, if the number of FOI requests processed per month is taken as a measure of performance, civil servants may devote most of their attention to straightforward and easily processed requests for information rather than ensuring equitable treatment of all applications.

- The quality of advice to policy makers may be undermined if all policy deliberations are always held in the public realm. This entails striking a balance between openness to public scrutiny (e.g. rules for access to information applied to civil servants' e-mails containing informal discussion of policy options) and the ability to give "free, frank and fearless" advice to ministers.

- Civil servants may adopt strategies that leave an incomplete paper or audit trail (e.g. where telephone conversations replace e-mail traffic) and in which key information is no longer preserved as a public record, amenable to future parliamentary scrutiny.

Reconciling equity and openness: Greater openness introduces a wider "market" for government information, but not all actors have the same capacity to make use of such measures. Limited public awareness of information rights, daunting procedures and high fees deter many. In most cases, the principal users of FOI provisions are businesses seeking information on forthcoming government contracts or regulations, rather than the media, civil society organisations or individual citizens.[12] Businesses are prepared to pay large sums to specialised intermediaries who gather "regulatory intelligence" through the judicious use of FOI provisions (MacDonell, 2003).

Whether such strategies work in favour of the public interest or facilitate "state capture" remains an open question.

Greater public awareness of the rights and responsibilities entailed by open government provisions may create a more level playing field. Public advertising campaigns (e.g. radio, TV, print media) coupled with improved interfaces (e.g. call centres, public Internet access points) and capacity building for key public stakeholders (e.g. targeted training) are among the measures to be considered. While most people will not want to know all there is to know about government all of the time, they will generally feel more comfortable in the knowledge that they could obtain all relevant information on government decisions, actions and officials should they choose to, and that others will shoulder the burden of monitoring government's power on their behalf (e.g. the media, professional associations). A necessary counterpart to open government is therefore a vibrant and dynamic civil society in which businesses, professionals, CSOs and individual citizens have the capacity to effectively monitor and interact constructively with government.

Political accountability and openness: The extent to which greater openness, accountability and public involvement in decision making impacts on representative institutions must also be considered. Ministers, members of legislatures and senior officials may have to invest more time and energy in explaining their proposals, seeking citizens' views and providing reasons for their decisions. However, this does not mean that elected and appointed officials should relinquish their responsibility for taking final decisions (OECD, 2001b). To do otherwise would undermine the established ministerial accountability mechanisms of representative government – a key governance pillar. Participatory democracy in the form of consensual decision making and "direct democracy" has its uses – and in a very few countries, binding referenda and continuous polling are an important component of public governance. Whether they do undermine or strengthen the institutions of representative democracy depends on context and circumstance.

More openness, less public trust? Most open government reforms are undertaken with the aim, either explicitly or implicitly, of strengthening public trust. However, trust may also be undermined by openness (O'Neill, 2002). In government, ensuring the basis for public trust in terms of responsible decision making may require a degree of confidentiality. Without it, hard truths are not told, mistakes are covered up, frank advice is replaced by self-censorship and the collective decision making and responsibility which is characteristic of cabinet government in most liberal democracies cannot function. Outside government, conducting public affairs in full view may contribute to public disaffection and cynicism – prompting governments to invest in even more public communication as a means of filling their credibility gap. The end result may be a downward spiral of trust as members of the public perceive, rightly or wrongly, all government communication as manipulative "spin".

It must also be recognised that opposition parties, the media – particularly its tabloid component – and CSOs are not always responsible and constructive critics of government. In the competition for votes or funds or circulation they may conduct vigorous and less than altruistic campaigns against particular government decisions, presenting an incomplete view of the issues and processes, implying (or explicitly claiming) incompetence or worse. However, it would be a council of despair to suggest that openness should be wound back because the information put in the public domain may be misused or distorted by other players in the political process. It is more important than ever in the era of global terrorism to distinguish those areas of government where confidentiality is genuinely in the public interest from those where confidentiality merely serves the interest of the government of the day.

While the causal link between government openness and public trust remains to be proven, it is likely that the response to the crisis of confidence lies in greater efforts to meet rising public expectations and to assess the effectiveness of government measures for openness.

9.1. Ensuring public trust is strengthened, not undermined

How can governments ensure that public trust is strengthened and not undermined by their efforts to build open government? Among the many challenging issues yet to be addressed, the following appear to merit further attention and, above all, open debate:

- Assessing the relative merits of openness: public officials need clear criteria for deciding the merits for or against openness in concrete cases. Who will provide this guidance? Can wider public debate on the merits and limits of open government foster political commitment and better public understanding?

- Openness vs. equity: does government openness empower previously marginalised groups, or does it simply increase the risk of capture by special interests? How can public awareness of openness provisions and its capacity to use them be enhanced?

- Private partners and public scrutiny: can independent media, businesses, think tanks, professional associations and civil society organisations play a greater role in fostering open government (e.g. as information mediators actively disseminating government information) and monitoring its performance?

The examples discussed in this section illustrate how efforts to enhance openness may, in some circumstances, undermine other key governance principles such as accountability and equity. Prior analysis of the systemic impacts of openness measures may help to mitigate any negative externalities. How open governments are now may well be the product of history and context. How open they are in the future will be the result of key policy choices being made today. Better tools for self-assessment, as well as comparative benchmarking based on key indicators of government openness, may contribute to clarifying the opportunities and risks of building open government.

10. Findings and conclusion

An open government is now recognised to be an essential ingredient for democratic governance, social stability and economic development. This chapter examined how OECD countries have responded to growing demands for greater openness and identified future challenges.

What is "open" government? While there are multiple meanings of the term, three dimensions appear to be most relevant, namely a government which is **transparent, accessible,** and **responsive**. As used here, "openness" both encompasses and goes beyond the more commonly used term of "transparency". It introduces two further aspects, namely "accessibility" and "responsiveness", in order to capture other qualities of the interface between government and the wider community it serves. While these three dimensions are closely interlinked, they remain distinct and may be present to differing degrees in practice.

Different contexts, different priorities: While all OECD countries have invested in greater government openness over the past three decades, their policy choices reflect different national priorities. Some countries privilege instruments that make government more open to public scrutiny (*i.e.* exposed) in the interest of fighting corruption (*e.g.* Korea, Mexico). Others focus on making government more user-friendly (*i.e.* accessible) in order to improve service delivery (*e.g.* Denmark) while yet others seek to enhance government interaction with external stakeholders (*i.e.* responsive) in order to foster better quality and more inclusive policy making (*e.g.* Canada, Finland).

The demand for open government: In response to rising shareholder and public expectations, the standards of openness to which both private and public sector organisations are held have become far more demanding over the past 30 years – and this trend may be expected to continue in the future. Calls for greater government transparency and accountability have grown, as public and media scrutiny of government actions increases and standards in public life are codified and raised.

The key trends and challenges in building open government are:

● **Transparency:** The scope, quantity and quality of government information provided to the public has increased significantly in the past 20 years and the provision of information is now an objective shared by all OECD member countries. The adoption of freedom of information (FOI) laws has gathered pace in the past two decades, and such laws are present today in 90% of OECD countries. A challenge for the future will be to maintain quality standards for government information (i.e. which is relevant, timely, complete and objective) given the ever-increasing quantity available online.

● **Accessibility:** Governments are more accessible and user-friendly today than they have ever been. Reducing physical, organisational and linguistic barriers, cutting through "red tape" and expanding online service delivery have all helped. The challenge will be to meet ever higher expectations from citizens and businesses for streamlined transactions, tailored services and ubiquitous access.

● **Responsiveness:** Public consultation for law making and rule making was once rare. Today, it is increasingly accepted as a valuable means of improving the quality of public policy while strengthening its legitimacy (e.g. through RIA, e-consultation). Further efforts to improve tools, mainstream procedures and integrate the results of public consultation in established decision-making processes will be needed if governments are to become more responsive and adaptive in the future.

Openness is just one of many cherished public values citizens would like to see from government. They also expect equity, efficiency, responsibility and due respect for individual privacy in the use of public power and resources. OECD countries face multiple challenges as they seek to: preserve government openness while ensuring national security and effective law enforcement; reconcile equity and openness; and ensure that standards for government openness are applied across the public-private interface.

Notes

1. A proxy indicator is offered by the number of NGOs having consultative status with the UN Economic and Social Council which more than tripled between 1994 (784 registered NGOs) and 2004 (2 531 registered NGOs). See *www.un.org/esa/coordination/ngo/*.

2. See Finland Government (2004), "Civil Participation Policy Programme", *www.valtioneuvosto.fi/vn/liston/base.lsp?r=40242&k=en*.

3. Also see Islam (2003), p. 23.

4. International covenants and treaties are another source of access to information provisions that are binding on signatories. Article 19 of the Universal Declaration on Human Rights (1948) guarantees the right to freedom of expression and

includes in this the right to "seek, receive and impart information". More recently, Article III on Transparency of the General Agreement on Trade in Services (GATS), which entered into force in January 1995, requires each member to publish, or make publicly available, all relevant measures affecting operation of the Agreement. All OECD member countries have signed the GATS while a third of them are also signatories to the 1998 Convention on Access to Information, Public Participation in Decision-making and Access to Justice in Environmental Matters (known as the Aarhus Convention).

5. See United States Office of Management and Budget, *Program Assessment Rating Tool (PART)*, *www.whitehouse.gov/omb/part*.

6. See Australian Government Information Management Office, *Australia's Online Information Service Obligations*, *www.agimo.gov.au/information/oiso*.

7. See: *www.consultations.gov.uk*.

8. For example, the United Kingdom Cabinet Office issued a new "Code of Practice on Written Consultation" in January 2004. See: *www.cabinet-office.gov.uk/regulation/consultation*.

9. Judicial review by the courts is, of course, another important non-parliamentary source of control and a means for holding governments accountable for their actions.

10. For example, the US Patriot Act and Canada's Terrorism Act both of which were passed in late 2001.

11. Measures contributing to the "normalisation of secrecy" have been criticised for undermining the accountability of government without effectively enhancing national security. See Campbell Public Affairs Institute (2003) and Lawyers Committee for Human Rights (2003).

12. In Canada, in the period 2002-03, requests under the Access to Information Act were filed by: business (45.0%); the public (29.6%); organisations (13.4%); the media (11.1%); and academics (0.9%) [Source: Canadian Government (2003), see *www.infosource.gc.ca*].

ISBN 92-64-01049-1
Modernising Government: The Way Forward
© OECD 2005

Chapter 2

Enhancing Public Sector Performance

1. Introduction

Over the past two decades, enhancing public sector performance has taken on a new urgency in OECD member countries as governments face mounting demands on public expenditure, calls for higher quality services and, in some countries, a public increasingly unwilling to pay higher taxes.

To address these challenges, various OECD countries have sought to enhance their public sector performance by adopting a range of new levers and approaches to management, budgeting, personnel and institutional structures. Within government, these have included the introduction of performance measures into budgeting and management, the relaxation of input controls, the delegation of responsibility to line ministries/agencies, and changes in public employment typified by the adoption of contracts for public servants and the introduction of performance-related pay. Examples of institutional change include the creation of executive agencies and the privatisation or outsourcing of the provision of public services. These developments are discussed in more detail in later chapters.

This chapter concentrates on attempts by OECD countries to introduce performance or results-based budgeting and performance management. This lever of reform seeks to move the focus of budgeting, management and accountability away from inputs towards results. Managers and/or organisations are given flexibility in order to improve performance and are then held accountable for results measured in the form of outputs and outcomes. The provision of performance information is not an end in itself; rather, its overall objective is to support better decision making by politicians and public servants leading to improved performance and/or accountability and, ultimately, enhanced outcomes for society.

The quantity of performance information available to decision makers has substantially increased; however, countries continue to struggle with issues of quality and ensuring that information is used in decision making. It takes time to develop performance measures and indicators, and even longer to change the behaviour of key actors in the system (politicians and bureaucrats) so that they use this information and develop a performance culture adapted to their particular country. The performance movement is here to stay. The benefits of being clearer inside and outside government about purposes and results are undeniable. But to gain these benefits governments need a long-term approach, realistic expectations, and persistence. This chapter looks at the development of performance-based budgeting, management and reporting in OECD countries and identifies the trends, the strengths and the limitations of current approaches and future challenges. First it discusses the wider perspective of government performance.

2. What does performance mean for government?

"Performance" is a term that encompasses many different concepts. Performance means the yield or results of activities carried out in relation to the purposes being pursued. Its objective is to strengthen the degree to which governments achieve their purposes.

The desire to improve government performance is not new. Governments have always wanted results from their spending and regulation. What is new is that, increasingly, governments are facing overall spending constraints. With no new money to spend, more attention must be given to achieving better results from existing funds. At the same time new ideas have emerged about how to re-organise and better motivate public servants to achieve results.

In the traditional public sector bureaucracy, performance was driven by ensuring compliance with set rules and regulations, controlling inputs, and adhering to the public sector ethos. This system generally worked well when governments had less complex and more standardised tasks to perform – and when complying with the rules was considered more important than efficiency or effectiveness. The system has been criticised, however, because employees tended to become more focused on process than on results, and there were weak incentives to use funds efficiently to achieve objectives. Modern public administrators not only have to serve collective interests of fairness and probity, but also have to meet individual needs and address complex social problems. Traditional public administrative systems were not designed to be flexible and adaptive in a modern society with customised services, the need for constant adaptation, pressure for efficiency, and the increased use of private agents. There is a call for sharper performance incentives than are provided by a traditional bureaucracy. Furthermore, governments have taken on more challenging and complex tasks, which do not lend themselves to the traditional approach.

Performance information is important for governments in assessing and improving policies:

- in managerial analysis, direction and control of public services;
- in budgetary analysis;
- in parliamentary oversight of the executive;
- for public accountability – the general duty on governments to disclose and take responsibility for their decisions.

Governments have adopted a number of different approaches to improving the efficiency and effectiveness of the public sector. These include: strategic management; business planning; performance budgeting and management; devolved and delegated decision making; structural change such as the creation of executive agencies; the use of contracts; and the introduction of competition and market-type mechanisms in service provision.

This variety of approaches towards improving public sector performance is rich but confusing. Each approach has different strengths and weaknesses and the best choice of approach depends on the purpose to be served.

Some of these approaches to improving performance are examined in subsequent chapters. Chapter 4 explores the changes in government structures and the introduction of agencies; Chapter 5 examines the introduction of market-type mechanisms in the provision of public services. Chapter 6 discusses changes in the nature of public employment, such as the introduction of contracts, performance-related pay, and the delegation of decision making in human resources management.

This chapter explores the introduction of performance measures into budgeting and management and their use in decision making.

3. Performance budgeting and performance management

OECD countries use a variety of mechanisms to assess the efficiency and effectiveness of programmes and agencies. These include performance measures, benchmarking and evaluations. Evaluations can incorporate programme reviews, cost effectiveness evaluation, *ad hoc* sectoral reviews and spending review.

The term "performance information" includes both evaluations and performance measures. While this chapter concentrates on examining the latter, it is important to acknowledge that evaluations have a valuable role to play in assessing the performance of programmes.[1]

Currently, the strongest trend in performance across OECD member countries is the introduction of performance-oriented budgeting and performance management. Many governments have sought to adopt an approach to both management and budgeting which seeks to shift the emphasis of budgeting, management and accountability away from controlling inputs towards achieving results. In theory, input controls are relaxed and managers and/or organisations are given flexibility to improve performance. In return they are held accountable for results measured in the form of outputs and/or outcomes.

Moves to formalise targets and measurement in government management and budgeting systems have a long history. In fact, performance budgeting has existed in one form or other since the first Hoover Commission in the United States recommended it in 1949. Performance budgeting and performance management are used to describe a range of rather diverse interpretations and approaches (see Box 2.1). For example, they can simply refer to the presentation of performance information as part of the budget documentation or to a budget classification in which appropriations are divided by groups of outputs or outcomes. A more narrow definition of performance budgeting is a form of budgeting that relates funds allocated to results measured in the form of outputs and/or outcomes. Performance management also has diverse definitions: it can refer to corporate management

---

Box 2.1. **Performance management and performance budgeting**

Broadly, performance management covers corporate management, performance information, evaluation, performance monitoring, assessment and performance reporting. In the context of the new performance trend, however, a stricter definition is a management cycle under which programme performance objectives and targets are determined, managers have flexibility to achieve them, actual performance is measured and reported, and this information feeds into decisions about programme funding, design, operations and rewards or penalties (OECD, 1995b).

Results/performance-based budgeting too is subject to diverse interpretation. It can be broadly defined as any budget that presents information on what agencies have done or expect to do with the money provided (Schick, 2003). In this case it can simply refer to performance information presented as part of the budget documentation or to a budget classification in which appropriations are divided by groups of outputs or outcomes. A strict definition of performance-based budgeting, however, is a form of budgeting that relates funds allocated to measurable results. These results are measured in the form of outputs and/or outcomes. Resources can be related to results either in a direct or indirect manner.

Indirect linkage means targets being actively used to inform budget decisions, along with other information. Performance information is very important in the decision-making process but it does not necessarily determine the amount of resources allocated.

Direct linkage involves the allocation of resources directly and explicitly linked to units of performance. Appropriations can thus be based on a formula/contract with specific performance or activity indicators. This form of performance budgeting is used only rarely and in specific areas in OECD member countries.

---

or systems for evaluating and assessing individual or group performance. A more holistic definition, which is applied in this chapter, is a management cycle under which programme performance objectives and targets are determined, managers have flexibility to achieve them, actual performance is measured and reported, and this information feeds into decisions about programme funding, design, operations and rewards or penalties.

Although various interpretations of performance budgeting and management exist, the common trend is that governments have sought to adopt a results-based approach to both management and budgeting which shifts budgeting, management and accountability away from inputs towards a focus on measurable results.

4. Country approaches to implementing performance budgeting and performance management

Many OECD member countries have introduced performance measures into their management and budget systems. However, countries are at different phases of introduction and have varied objectives and approaches to implementing these reforms.

4.1. Different phases

New Zealand was among the first to begin the present round of performance management and/or budgeting in the late 1980s, followed in the early to mid-1990s by Canada, Denmark, Finland, the Netherlands, Sweden, the United Kingdom, and the United States. A further phase began in the late 1990s to early 2000s (Austria, Germany and Switzerland). Turkey has recently begun a pilot phase of performance budgeting and management.

Country approaches to performance management are constantly evolving. For example, New Zealand began by concentrating on outputs and is now moving to an outcomes approach. Denmark is changing its accounting and budgeting systems to focus on outcomes. France recently passed a law which requires the production of outputs and outcomes in budget documentation for the majority of programmes.

4.2. Various objectives

It is possible to discern four broad objectives for which countries have adopted the formalisation of targets and measures in the government management process:

- Managing the efficiency and effectiveness of agencies and ministries and/or the internal control and accountability within individual ministries.
- Improving decision making in the budget process, and/or in the allocation of resources and accountability of ministries to the Ministry of Finance.

- Improving external transparency and accountability to parliament and the public and clarifying the roles and responsibilities of politicians and civil servants.

- Achieving savings.

Some countries have given attention to one or two of these objectives only. Other countries (Australia, Denmark, the Netherlands, New Zealand, the United Kingdom, and the United States) have embraced all four objectives, seeking to introduce performance-based management and budgeting across central government and to improve both performance and internal and external accountability to the legislature and the public.

4.3. Various approaches

In some countries (the United States is a good example) ministries have developed strategic and performance plans which include performance targets. Other countries have adopted performance agreements either between a minister/ministry and a subordinate agency, or between a minister and a department. Such agreements can also be between the Ministry of Finance and a ministry or agency.

In New Zealand there are purchase agreements between the minister and the relevant department which set out the agencies' agreed outputs. There are also formal performance agreements between ministers and chief executives of the departments. In the United Kingdom, ministries approve agencies' annual business plans, which establish performance goals and targets for the coming year. There are also performance agreements between departments and H.M. Treasury stating agreed objectives and targets. In Australia there are resource agreements between the Department of Finance and Administration and the relevant departments and agencies. In Denmark, there are performance contracts between ministries and agencies and between chief executives and ministries; these include links to performance-related pay.

4.4. Implementation

Some countries have adopted an incremental approach. For example, the United States had a four-year pilot phase before the government-wide implementation of the Government Performance and Results Act. Other countries have chosen an incremental approach which allows agencies to participate voluntarily in these reforms without moving towards total implementation across government. Germany and Ireland both use pilot schemes.

Australia, the Netherlands, New Zealand, and the United Kingdom have taken a top-down and total system approach to implementation. Others (Finland in particular) have taken a more bottom-up and *ad hoc* approach where agencies have been given freedom to develop their own method with less enforcement from the top.

Box 2.2. **New Zealand experience of performance budgeting and performance management**

The reform of New Zealand's public sector management was part of a broad reform agenda which began in 1984 with a new government and a financial crisis. The government initially focused on a programme of liberalisation of the economy, moved on to restructure the government's commercial activities (through both privatisation and corporatisation), and then undertook to reform public sector management and the labour market. The public sector management reforms are distinctive for their conceptual coherence, comprehensive nature and consistent application over the last 20 years. The reforms have been broadly supported by politicians and officials.

The reform and its journey

The State Sector Act 1988 made heads of government departments chief executives and made them responsible for running their departments. Chief executives were given the freedom to make all input decisions – pay, appointments, organisational structure, and systems for delivery of services. The Public Finance Act 1989 introduced accrual-based accounting and budgeting. The distinctions between inputs, outputs and outcomes were made more transparent, and ministers were responsible for outcomes with chief executives accountable for the delivery of outputs. There was a reliance on formal contractual devices (purchase agreements) as the basis for agreeing and recording the outputs to be supplied.

To aid fiscal management, the Fiscal Responsibility Act 1994 detailed increased reporting requirements for the government including the Budget Policy Statement and the Fiscal Strategy Report which related to the long-term intentions of government, while the remainder were designed generally to disclose and verify as much information as possible about the state of the economy and the progress of the government's strategies.

Subsequent developments have sought to address specific concerns arising from the initial reforms without challenging their fundamental structure. These developments have principally been attempts to deal with the rigidities and limitations of the contractual focus and have included: the adoption of key result areas (KRAs) and strategic result areas (SRAs) in the mid-1990s; and subsequently statements of intent, which are part of ongoing attempts to address the relationship between outputs and outcomes, and to encourage a greater focus by managers on outcomes. Also, attempts have been made to strengthen the role of the government's central agencies so as to increase integration, build capability and increase focus on evaluation of the achievement of outcomes.

Box 2.2. **New Zealand experience of performance budgeting and performance management** (cont.)

Positive results from the reforms:

- increased focus on the medium to longer term in fiscal management;

- strengthened fiscal discipline resulting, for example, from the introduction of measures such as accrual accounting, capital charging, and the requirements for the disclosure of fiscal risk;

- operational efficiencies resulting from the delegation of operational responsibility to chief executives; allowing managers to manage.

Recognised criticisms are that the reforms:

- encouraged a focus on the delivery of annual outputs at the expense of a focus on longer-term outcomes (doing what has been contracted for rather than what is right);

- provided clarity and encouraged a focus on what can be readily specified in contracts, but struggled to cope with the informal relationships and the complexity of many of government's functions;

- arguably inhibited debate on allocation issues. Although ministers are responsible for outcomes, much of the debate appears to revolve around their role as purchasers of outputs. Any debate on allocation appears in practice to focus on spending at the margin: new initiatives. Major areas of core spending are not subjected to the same scrutiny;

- encouraged a focus on "box-checking" compliance with contracts over a concern for the whole-of-government and collaborative action;

- resulted in the development of a costly (and distributed) infrastructure for negotiating, reporting on, monitoring, and auditing compliance with contracts.

The delegation of responsibility for management to chief executives, together with the rigid contractualism of the New Zealand system, has led to the need for a focus on how best to maintain or strengthen the collective values of the public sector and the commitment to the collective good across the public sector, and the development of public sector capability and leadership. It remains to be seen whether the developments to the New Zealand reforms will be successful or whether more fundamental reform of the New Zealand model, challenging the conceptual underpinnings of the model, will be required.

Source: Pallot (2001 and 2002), Schick (1996 and 2001).

5. What is the current state of play?

Despite the differences in approach, a common trend in OECD member countries is to introduce a focus on measurable results in management and budget processes. This section examines the current trend in performance management and budgeting in OECD member countries using data obtained from the OECD/World Bank Budget Practices and Procedures Database Survey.[2]

5.1. Performance information and targets in budget documentation and the budget process

Among OECD member countries there is a strong trend of routinely including non-financial performance information in budget documentation:

- 72% of countries include non-financial performance data in their budget documentation.

- In 44% of countries, these data are available for more than three-quarters of programmes.

- In 71% of countries, performance data include performance targets although there is a wide variation in terms of programme coverage.

- In 65% of countries, these results are included in the main budget documents and/or the annual financial documents.

While the introduction of performance information into budget documentation is becoming common, it has not been embraced by all OECD member countries. Over a quarter of countries that responded to the survey do not include any non-financial performance data in their budget documentation. Iceland includes performance data but not performance targets.

The most common way of including performance targets in the budget process is a combination of outputs and outcomes. Only 27% of countries include mostly outcomes and no country has mostly outputs. Countries appear to have recognised the difficulty in following an approach that concentrates solely on either outcomes or outputs. Only concentrating on outputs can give rise to goal displacement as agencies lose sight of the intended impact of their programmes on wider society and concentrate solely on quantifiable measures at the expense of activities that are less measurable. It can also result in less attention being paid to cross-cutting issues. While outcomes incorporate a wider focus on the impact of programmes on society and have greater appeal to politicians and the public, they are very difficult to measure. As will be discussed later in this chapter, in many cases a mix of outputs, outcomes and inputs is desirable.

5.2. The current trends in performance budgeting

Some OECD countries have actively attempted to integrate performance targets into the overall budget process, but very few can be said to be carrying out "real" performance budgeting. This means including performance information in budget documentation and linking expenditure to outcome/output targets, reporting performance against these targets and using the information to make decisions on future resource allocation. Using this strict definition, performance budgeting is very rare. The OECD surveyed the degree to which countries apply performance budgeting in this strict sense.

While 72% of OECD member countries routinely display targets in budget documentation given to the Ministry of Finance, the linking of expenditure to output and outcome targets is not common among OECD member countries:

- 46% of countries either do not link expenditure to targets or only do so for a few programmes.

- 35% of countries reported that they link expenditure to some targets.

- Only 18% of countries reported that they specifically link expenditure to all or most of their output or outcome targets.

A mixed picture emerges with regard to the use of performance results in determining budget allocations, with over 31% of countries stating that performance results are not used for this purpose. It is not common for politicians to use performance results in allocating resources between programmes or in any sort of decision making. Forty-one percent of OECD member countries reported that it was not common for politicians in the executive or the legislature to use performance measures in any decision making. This includes countries that have long experience of this area, such as the United States.

It is apparent that very few countries engage in any form of direct performance budgeting, since many countries do not even link expenditure to output and outcome targets, let alone make the appropriation of funds an explicit function of performance. This form of budgeting is only applied to a limited number of functional areas and only in a few countries. It is most commonly found in health and education, especially higher education. In Denmark, Finland, Norway, and Sweden, for example, it is the main form of budgeting used to fund higher education.

As Figure 2.1 highlights, very few countries appear to have formal mechanisms in place that relate the success or failure in achieving a target to the reward or punishment of individuals or agencies:

- In 46% of OECD member countries no rewards or sanctions are applied if a target is met or not met.

- In 20% of countries rewards/sanctions are reflected in the size of the budget for the government organisation.

Figure 2.1. **Are rewards and/or sanctions applied if performance targets are met or are not met?**

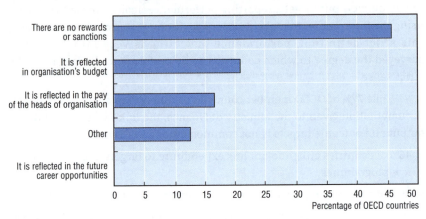

Source: OECD/World Bank Budget Practices and Procedures Database 2003.

- In 16% of countries pay is sometimes linked to performance. In all these cases performance is linked to the pay of a civil servant or a number of civil servants. For example, in the United Kingdom, performance against organisation targets is linked to the pay of the agency's chief executive.

5.3. *Current trends in performance management*

Greater progress has been made in implementing performance management reforms than performance budgeting. This section examines if OECD member countries have a system of performance management which incorporates the setting and reporting of targets and their subsequent use in the internal decision-making process of ministries and agencies:

- In 67% of countries, the relevant minister or the head of department is formally responsible for setting performance targets.

- In 56% of countries, performance against targets is continuously monitored internally in the relevant ministry.

- In 63% of countries, performance against targets is reported in a systematic annual report for some or most programmes.

Performance results that feed into decision-making processes appear in a number of countries. In nearly 50% of countries, performance results are used internally within agencies/ministries to set programme priorities, to allocate resources within programmes, and to change work processes. Performance results are used by the parent ministry in approximately half of countries to set programme priorities and in over a third in adopting new programme approaches. This information is used least in setting individual staff performance plans.

While this information is used in the decision-making process, it is not clear what other types of information are used (if any) and how much weight is given to performance results compared to these other types of information.

Approximately 50% of countries reported having a system of performance management. However, within a given country, there is variation in the number of programmes and agencies to which performance management is applied. Australia, the Netherlands, New Zealand, Norway, and the United States have taken a comprehensive approach and it is applied to nearly all ministries and agencies. In Belgium, Canada and Germany it is only applied in approximately a quarter of programmes.

The introduction of output and/or outcome targets as a system of management control calls for relaxed input controls in order to give managers the freedom to use resources to achieve results and improve performance. To what extent has this trade-off between performance and controls been achieved in practice? In terms of the whole-of-government control processes, the information gathered from the OECD/World Bank Budget Practices and Procedures Database does not provide much evidence that this trade-off has occurred.

Among countries with a long experience of introducing performance indicators into budget and management systems, there is a large variation in terms of the degree of relaxation of input controls. Australia and the Netherlands appear to have extensively relaxed central controls. Others (such as Denmark, New Zealand, and Norway) have also made substantial moves in that direction. However, in some countries (for example the United States), the introduction of performance indicators in management and budgeting does not appear to have been accompanied by a relaxation of central input controls.

Countries like Finland and Sweden register a high degree of management autonomy. This is to be expected given their long tradition of agencies. Equally, given that performance budgeting is a centrally driven device, they have only a moderate level of formalisation of performance indicators in their budget system. It is of interest that Australia, the country which shows the strongest trend of substituting input controls for performance controls, is, according to recent advice from the Department of Finance and Administration, finding the current reporting from departments insufficient for whole-of-government purposes.

6. Accountability to the public

As Figure 2.2 indicates, in OECD member countries the provision of information to the public on government performance is widespread.

Figure 2.2. **Are performance results made available to the public?**

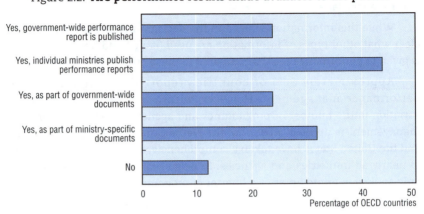

Source: OECD/World Bank Budget Practices and Procedures Database 2003.

In the survey, 24 OECD member countries claimed to report to the public on performance results. This is strong evidence that transparency has improved. In presenting this information to the public, the aim is to improve trust in government by showing what government does and most importantly how well it does it. As improving public sector performance becomes more important to citizens, in electoral terms it becomes increasingly necessary for governments to demonstrate that they are achieving these improvements.

The problem for governments is that improvements in performance take time to achieve but the electoral pressures are such that they need to show improvements in the short term. Some governments believe that the public will be more convinced that services have improved by the presentation of numerical performance information. However, even with numerical information there are questions about quality and accuracy. While governments present performance results as objective evaluations, this information, depending on the nature of the political system, can become part of the political dogfight between the government and the opposition. This is more a problem in political contexts where the norm is adversarial rather than consensual politics. In this context, the opposition can use the very same results to discredit the government's performance and to raise questions about their objectivity. The media also has a large role to play: if the information is presented as pure party political propaganda and government spin, this could do more to increase public scepticism than to create trust. This point was discussed in more detail in Chapter 1.

A related issue is whether the public and interest groups are willing to accept the government's presentation of performance results. Performance results are generally aggregated outcomes for the whole country, a region or a single large institution. Even if accurate the general conclusion may be at odds with some individual experience. Thus it is almost inevitable that performance results will be challenged on the basis of that experience. Thus the views of the public are more likely to reflect personal experiences or views presented in the media rather than the government's performance reporting.

6.1. External performance auditing

Having externally audited performance information would help to assure the public of the quality and accuracy of the information presented in government reports. One might have expected that, with the great increase in the number of countries with performance information in their formal reporting systems, there would be a commensurate rise in the routine auditing of performance reports by supreme audit institutions. There is indeed some trend in this direction, but it lags behind the introduction of performance reporting.

Assuring the credibility and quality of performance data is a key issue for OECD countries; taking performance information at face value can give a distorted picture. Threats to quality can come from poor practices in gathering and analysing data and from political pressure to look good (Schwartz and Mayne, 2005). The independent audit of performance data helps to reduce these problems.

Auditing performance information is costly and it is also different from auditing financial information. Therefore, auditors must have the necessary expertise and training to conduct these audits. In addition, there is a danger

Figure 2.3. **Is the performance data externally audited?**

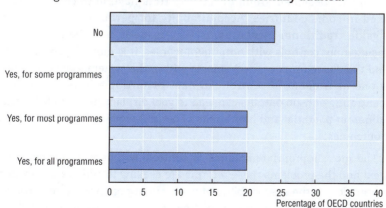

Source: OECD/World Bank Budget Practices and Procedures Database 2003.

that performance becomes compliance – that is, too much emphasis on compliance with rules and regulations can reduce emphasis on flexibility and innovation needed to improve performance.

6.2. Summary of trends

Across OECD countries, there is a strong trend of introducing performance indicators into management and budgeting. There is also a strong common trend of introducing a systematic approach to performance management. While many countries have reached the stage of introducing performance targets into their budget documentation, fewer countries have integrated this information into their budgetary decision-making process and even less have used it in the allocation of resources. There is also a strong trend of reporting this information to the public and the legislature, although the tendency is for legislatures not to make much use of this information. In general, the performance budgeting movement seems at the moment to be stronger on process than on results.

7. Why context matters

The successful use of the formalisation of performance in the budgeting and management processes depends on other factors in the political and administrative environment of the country concerned. Reformers do not begin with a blank sheet; performance indicators and targets are introduced into existing and established systems of accountability and control, which have both informal and formal components.

Performance is only one dimension of accountability. Other aspects include assuring that correct administrative procedures have been followed and that funds have been spent as allocated. Traditional accountability mechanisms designed around input controls have not been extensively relaxed in some countries. Accountability for performance will co-exist alongside traditional mechanisms. The issue is not about completely replacing input controls with outputs/outcomes, it is more a question of how to find the desired mix of mechanisms within the system. Concentration on only one instrument of control can have distorting effects. For example, concentrating only on outputs can lead to goal displacement. Table 2.1 shows the different potential and limitations of control regimes for inputs, outputs, and outcomes.

The most appropriate balance of controls will depend on the country context and the problems these reforms are seeking to address. For example, if the problem is the susceptibility of a system or organisation to corruption, then placing the stress on input controls is a more suitable approach than stressing outcomes. For other systems and organisations where the problem

Table 2.1. **Potential and limitations of different management control regimes**

	Potential	Limitations	Suitable contexts
Input	Easy and affordable Strengthens compliance	Does not support efficiency Can be inflexible	Low confidence and variable competence
Output	Facilitates efficiency Facilitates control of aggregate expenditure Accountability for results	Can distort focus Measurement problems Information overload	Confidence, sound accounting and professionalism
Outcome	Supports policy formulation and co-ordination Long term	Measurement problems Accountability problems Costs Information overload	The above plus dedicated politicians and the ability to set clear objectives

is inflexibility and lack of adaptation, a combination of outputs and outcomes could be a more suitable approach. Within each system it is necessary to find the desired combination of controls between outputs and inputs. Furthermore, it can be desirable to have some flexibility to allow for a different mix of controls for different organisations.

Chapter 3 considers the implications of these reforms for accountability and control systems and the broad changes underway. The challenges resulting from those changes are also examined.

7.1. Whole-of-government approach: Changing the behaviour of key actors

Whatever the balance or mix of controls in a given country, when outputs and outcomes are introduced they have to be accommodated within the existing control system and this requires a realignment of relationships. In introducing these reforms it is important that governments take a whole-of-government approach – as the integration of performance measures into budgeting and management systems is not just about changing processes but is also about transforming the behaviour of both public servants and politicians throughout the political system. This is especially the case if governments have taken a comprehensive approach and seek to apply this reform across government to the majority of programmes. The key actors in this case can include public servants and managers in ministries/agencies and in the Ministry of Finance, and politicians in the legislature and the executive. The challenges in changing the behaviour of public servants in ministries/agencies and in the Ministry of Finance have been discussed elsewhere.[3] This section will briefly examine the challenges in changing the behaviour of politicians.

Performance-oriented budgeting and management as a reform lever has wider governance implications: it has the capacity to help elected leaders to steer the public sector towards their policy objectives. It provides a mechanism for politicians to clearly articulate their goals and objectives for the government as a whole or for the relevant ministry and the means to monitor progress towards achieving these goals.

In theory, this model should help to clarify the respective roles and responsibilities of ministers and public servants. Politicians set the objectives; these cascade down to the relevant ministry and/or organisation and are translated into performance measures and/or targets. The results against these targets are used to hold agencies to account and to provide better information to be used in decision making on policy, budget and management issues. For this model to succeed it is important that politicians use this information in decision making.

7.2. Motivating politicians to use performance information

Do politicians use performance information? The answer, it appears, according to Figure 2.4 is "not much", with the exception of ministers responsible for the department delivering a target.

In 72% of OECD member countries, targets are routinely displayed in budget documentation presented to the legislature. However, in only 19% of countries do politicians in the legislature use performance measures in decision making. The percentage is even lower for politicians in the legislative budget committee, with only 8% using this information.

For countries that have introduced these reforms, clearly a major challenge is to change the behaviour of politicians and to create the right mix

Figure 2.4. **Is it common that politicians use performance measures in decision making?**

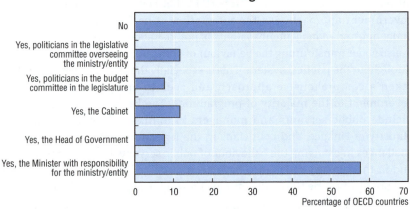

Source: OECD/World Bank Budget Practices and Procedures Database 2003.

of incentives to motivate them to use this information. Table 2.2 summarises the necessary but not sufficient behavioural changes that are needed from politicians in the executive and the legislature if these reforms are to achieve their aims. The table lists some of the possible incentives that could motivate these actors to change their behaviour and also the negative factors that discourage them from adopting this approach and using the performance information provided. This list of behavioural changes and incentives is not meant to be exhaustive.

The impact of these incentives will vary with the political and institutional contexts and to some extent with the individual minister. In Westminster systems, accountability is focused on individual ministerial responsibility, and there can be a strong emphasis on faultfinding and blame. In these systems, there is a danger that despite the formal system of accountability, which concentrates on performance, politicians may be more concerned with avoiding errors and managing public perceptions and will use the various accountability mechanisms selectively to that end. Systems in which responsibility is more collective and the political system less adversarial may offer more room for the constructive use of performance information.

Despite these issues, according to the OECD survey, ministers with responsibility for a relevant ministry/entity have paid more attention to performance indicators than other politicians. There is a particular problem, however, with getting politicians in the legislature interested in using performance results. The factors which can discourage them are listed in Table 2.2. They include questions about quality, readability and relevance of information.

In a system of separation of powers with a strong legislature that has a say over the setting of objectives like, for example, in the United States, there needs to be a high degree of institutional co-operation between the two branches of government. This need for strong co-operation is less of an issue in a country like the United Kingdom with a very powerful executive branch. Again, the behavioural changes required and the influence of incentives will vary to some extent with the political and institutional structures.

However, if performance management and budgeting is to have any impact in any political system it is important that the key actors in decision-making processes are provided with motivations and incentives to change. Without these provisions, performance information becomes a mere paper exercise. The combined experiences of OECD countries highlight the importance of taking a long-term approach. It takes time to change behaviour and to see the benefits of this approach emerge.

Table 2.2. **Incentives influencing whether politicians in the executive and the legislature change behaviour and use performance information in decision making**

Key actors	Behavioural changes needed	Positive incentives and factors encouraging change	Negative incentives and factors discouraging change
Ministers and politicians in the executive	Provide leadership support for reforms	Process to set objectives and monitor progress in achieving them	Concerns about quality of information
	Set clear objectives and targets	Good quality information	Information not relevant for real political issue and day-to-day concerns
	Use performance results to hold agencies to account	Information relevant to political needs	Cost of being informed and monitoring
	Use performance results in decision-making processes on policies/programmes or budgeting	Provide information to voters on achievement of political goals	Lack of time to use information
	Respect managerial freedom granted – by non interference in delegated areas	Compatible with existing informal and formal mechanisms of oversight	Little or no influence on career advancement
Politicians in the legislature	If applicable, set objectives	Help to oversee government progress in achieving outcome goals	Poor quality of information
	Use performance results for oversight purposes	Good quality information	Information less relevant to political needs
	Use information in decision making on programmes and/or policy and/or budgeting	Relevant to political needs	Cost of learning about new lever, continuing costs
	Respect managerial freedom	Presented in easy readable manner	Lack of time to use this information in decision making
		Compatible with existing informal and formal mechanisms of oversight	Information presented in an unreadable manner
		Provide benefits over and above traditional approach	Receiving less detailed information
			Concerns about having less control

8. Limitations and tensions

This section considers some of the limitations and tensions which need to be considered when introducing performance budgeting and management.

8.1. Performance measures: Only one source of information on performance

Performance indicators and targets provide a snapshot of performance in time. They do not provide a guide to future performance nor do they explain why a target has been achieved. Therefore, when making decisions about the performance of an agency or a programme, it is important to consider different types of performance information. To obtain an encompassing picture of organisational and programme performance, evaluations and performance indicators can be considered with other formal and informal sources of information and feedback. Unlike targets, evaluations can explain the results of a policy or programme and what changes will improve its performance.

8.2. Not everything can be measured

Unlike financial information, with performance information it is difficult to apply a "one size fits all" approach across government. Governments carry out a large variety of diverse functions, from building roads to providing advice on foreign travel. The experience of OECD countries indicates that performance indicators and measures are more easily applied to certain types of functional and programme areas than others. Three types of programme can be distinguished: tangible and non-tangible individually tailored services, and non-tangible ideal services (OECD, 2001c). Performance indicators are more easily applied in programmes which involve the delivery of a tangible good or service with observable outputs such as issuing passports or driving licenses or collecting taxes. It is easier to create reliable unit cost measures for this type of activity. It is possible, although more difficult, to design performance measures for complex services to individuals such as education and health care. Performance indicators are very difficult to apply to activities such as policy advice where the service is non-tangible and outcomes are not visible. In these areas where process is readily observable, a more obvious approach is to assess and control organisations on the basis of compliance with procedures.[4] In some activities and organisations where neither outputs nor outcomes are observable, performance indicators are not a suitable option.

Given the different functions performed by government, consideration should be given to adopting an approach to performance management that is flexible enough to allow for the diversity of programmes and also for the fact that for certain functional areas other methods of assessing accountability and evaluating performance are potentially more effective.

8.3. Limitations of costs, capacity and time

Public sector performance information is, potentially, limitless, complex and expensive to collect. Any formal system of gathering such information must of necessity be highly selective. Complex areas of government are primarily managed in the context of a well-developed professional culture. Performance targets and information are of value only insofar as they strengthen the performance orientation of that culture. Good management seeks to maximise the internal motivation of staff and to minimise the need for formal management controls. These controls are expensive to operate, and at a certain point formal management systems reduce internal motivation.

There are limits to how much information decision makers can use; people have "bounded rationality" and so do organisations. Decisions are taken by busy, often distracted ministers and senior managers who operate under complex incentives. Providing them with more information does not necessarily help their decision making and may actively hinder it.

9. Future challenges

A great deal of rhetoric has surrounded the introduction of performance management and budgeting. Supporters claim that it has the capacity to transform governments. However, it is important that this reform should not be seen as a panacea and that governments have realistic expectations about what it can achieve and the time needed to reach these objectives.

9.1. Measurement

Even countries that have been using this approach for over 15 years continue to struggle with issues of measurement; this is especially the case for outcomes. A key challenge for all countries is obtaining good quality information which is valid, reliable, and timely. Numerous challenges can be encountered including setting clear objectives, finding accurate measures of performance and having good systems of data collection.

Setting objectives: For some agencies or programmes, even setting clear objectives can be a problem when there is no agreement on what the mission is, or there are diverse missions, overlapping and fragmented programmes, and stakeholders with different interests.

Finding accurate measures of performance: The design of measures is made difficult by finding measures for specific activities, and relating what an agency or programme actually contributes towards achieving specific outcomes. Output and outcome measures each present a different set of challenges (OECD, 2002d). Outcomes are technically more difficult to measure; they are complex and involve the interaction of many factors, planned and unplanned. Also, there are problems with time lag issues and in some cases the results are not within the control of the government. Outcomes, however, have a strong appeal for the public and politicians. Most countries appear to have adopted a combination of outputs and outcomes.

Establishing and maintaining systems of data collection: To ensure quality there needs to be a process by which the data collected are verified and validated. However, setting up and maintaining these systems can be both complex and costly. As discussed in Section 6, the auditing of performance information can help to improve standards and provide some legitimacy for the reported results. It is especially challenging to assure the quality of the data when agencies are dependent on third parties to provide the information. This is particularly a problem in federalist systems (Curristine, 2002).

9.2. Setting and using performance targets

Performance targets help to clarify performance expectations for an organisation for a given time period. Countries, however, continue to struggle with the issues of target level and numbers. There are problems with setting targets too low and/or too high. Setting targets too low means that agencies are not challenged to improve performance. Setting them too high, while it can motivate organisations, also creates unrealistic expectations and situations in which agencies will fail (Perrin, 2002). It takes time to get the right level and to get the comparative data to realise that targets are set at too high or too low a level.

Too many targets: There is also an issue about how many targets to have. Too many targets create information overload and make it difficult to select priorities; too few targets create distortion effects. Again it takes time to get a realistic balance. Several countries have started out with a large number of targets and subsequently reduced them. For example, in the United Kingdom when performance agreements for departments were first introduced as part of the comprehensive spending review in 1998, there were in total 600 targets across government. By the time of the revised spending review in 2002, that number had been reduced to 130 targets (H.M. Treasury, 2004).

Avoiding distorting behaviour: This is a challenge for all governments. Possible perverse effects include goal distortion – that is, organisations and managers focusing on a few specific indicators and targets, usually the most achievable or "saleable", at the expense of the overall objectives or pro-gramme. In extreme cases of goal distortion, agencies or staff, under pressure to meet targets, may deliberately present misleading information.

9.3. Challenges with using the budget process to improve performance

In many OECD countries, the objective of introducing performance into the budget process is to improve budgetary decision making and to act as an incentive for agencies to improve performance. Most countries, however, continue to struggle with this approach. As discussed above, one of the key issues is obtaining good quality and reliable performance data. Briefly, other challenges include establishing some link between financial information and performance information. This is particularly challenging for outcome measures. In many countries there are also problems with the structure of the budget and accounting issues. Budgets tend to be structured in accordance with institutional and functional boundaries and not according to results categories. Also if there is no system of cost recording, it is difficult to relate true costs to results.

Getting the right mix of incentives: This is particularly important when countries use performance information in resource allocation. A fundamental question is whether financial rewards should be given for good performance and bad performance should be punished and, if so, how. Punishing failure by removing resources creates a clear signal to other agencies that performance is considered important. However, it does not help address the underlying causes of poor performance. Indeed in some cases failure to meet targets can be the result of lack of funding or other resources. While rewarding good performance is intuitively appealing, it does not take into account cost issues and government priorities. In a climate of budgetary saving, a question is whether to give additional funding to an agency, especially one that is not a government priority. In either case, there is always the danger that linking results to financial resources can create incentives to distort and cheat in presenting information.

9.4. Changing the behaviour and culture

One of the most difficult challenges is to create a results-based culture within organisations and throughout government. To achieve change in behaviour and culture across government requires a whole-of-government approach and the creation of the right mix of incentives that takes account of how the actions of key actors influence each other. Most countries continue to struggle with achieving change in the behaviour of public servants and politicians; this is a long-term process.

Obtaining and maintaining the support of managers and employees within government organisations is crucial. This reform has the potential to improve the focus on organisational goals, to provide managers with better information for decision making on programmes, budgets and policies, and to improve internal reporting and controls. Gaining these benefits is challenging because it requires technical as well as cultural change. In technical terms it can be difficult to measure what an agency does and to link organisational objectives to individual goals. It is important to obtain the buy- in of front line employees; this can be facilitated by the right mix of formal and informal incentives and controls (discussed in Chapter 6). Obtaining the strong support of the organisational leadership and managers can be facilitated by giving them the necessary flexibility to achieve goals. Without this flexibility, managers will have the responsibility for achieving targets without the ability to deliver, and no one wants to be held accountable for targets that are not within his/her control.

Within the context of a government-wide approach, if and how the performance information is used by politicians and the Ministry of Finance can create incentives which impact on how managers behave. If performance information is required but not used by leaders or managers in decision making, there is a danger of it becoming a burden on organisations in terms of cost of information systems and staff time. The provision of this information, in addition to the requirements of the traditional control mechanisms, can interfere with getting the job done. If this happens, then performance management and budgeting can become a distraction, a distortion or an expensive paper exercise rather than a means to transform organisations and an essential part of good management.

Obtaining and maintaining the support of politicians: As discussed in Section 7, this is a key challenge facing reformers. The support of politicians in the legislature and the executive helps to reinforce the need for change and to push reform, although it is particularly difficult to obtain the support of politicians in the legislature.

Issues of horizontal and vertical co-ordination: Many goals and outcomes cut across government organisations and involve the work of many agencies. While some OECD countries have established cross-governmental horizontal goals and targets, it is proving difficult to achieve co-ordination across departments and to hold them accountable for results. At a vertical level there is an issue with different actors wanting the same information for diverse purposes; their informational needs are not the same.

Managing expectations: Realistic expectations are needed both about what can be achieved by this reform and how long it will take. A long-term approach and persistence are needed: it takes time to overcome the technical issues and to change the behaviour of public servants and politicians.

10. Findings and conclusion

The performance of government can be improved through a focus on results in policy advice, central and departmental management processes, and parliamentary and public accountability. It is important to first identify the relative priority of these areas in a particular country. What a government should do is different in each case.

The majority of OECD countries are implementing performance management and performance budgeting, although the extent and the approaches vary widely across countries. The introduction of performance management and budgeting appears to be an important and enduring innovation in public management. It is clearly a strong device for horizontal priority setting, policy alignment and cost analysis. These reforms have improved transparency through the provision of more information on government performance to the public. However, some initial hopes have been too ambitious.

Most countries continue to struggle with changing the behaviour of public servants and politicians. This is a long-term process. To achieve change in behaviour and culture across government requires a whole-of-government approach and the creation of the right mix of incentives and controls (formal and informal) and an understanding of the systems and how the actions of key actors influence each other.

There is no clear pattern of input controls being lightened as performance indicators are strengthened. This raises issues about balancing accountability and flexibility. Whatever the accountability systems in place, they need to be balanced against the freedom required by managers to do their jobs. Critics of the traditional system of accountability argue that rules had become ends in themselves, that accountability stressed compliance, and that hierarchical structures hindered efficiency and performance. Thus, the critics emphasised the needs to relax input controls.

There are obvious dangers in relaxing input controls too soon after the introduction of output and outcome measures. However, there are also dangers in failing to relax these controls sufficiently, with the possible effect that output and outcome measures become an expensive paper exercise, with little impact on managers' ability to improve performance. If the system has too many restrictions and managers do not have enough freedom to improve performance, then failure to relax input controls can result in inefficiency.

The common assumption that the performance information that is useful for the executive would also serve the legislature remains unproven. With a few exceptions, performance reporting has been neither welcomed nor used by OECD member country legislatures in their oversight and decision making. Performance measures and targets are only once source of information about performance, and they are no substitute for the independent, in-depth qualitative examination of the impact of policies that evaluations can provide.

The combined experiences of OECD countries highlight the importance of taking a long-term approach and having realistic expectations about the capacity of performance management and budgeting to improve performance and accountability. A long-term approach and persistence are needed to achieve the necessary technical and behavioural changes that this lever requires.

Finally, from a wider perspective, the design of cross-government performance interventions needs careful analysis and consideration of options. Broadly, these interventions are: leadership; strategic planning; performance management; the inclusion of targets and measures in the formal budgeting, management and oversight processes; and policy evaluation. Each has different strengths and limitations. There is a danger of governments becoming fixated on a particular formal solution to the problem of improving performance.

The performance orientation of public management is here to stay. It is essential for successful government. Societies are now too complex to be managed only by rules for input and process and a public-spirited culture. The performance movement has increased formalised planning, reporting and control across many governments. This has improved the information available to managers and policy makers. But experience shows that this can risk leading to a new form of bureaucratic sclerosis. More attention needs to be given to keeping performance transactions costs in check, and to making optimal use of social and internalised motivators and controls.

Notes

1. See OECD (2005c) for more details on evaluations in the budget process.

2. These data were originally collected in 2003. Twenty-seven out of the 30 OECD countries responded to this survey. All answers are self-reported.

3. See articles in OECD (2002c).

4. Although outputs can be observed in limited cases. See Wilson (1989).

ISBN 92-64-01049-1
Modernising Government: The Way Forward
© OECD 2005

Chapter 3

Modernising Accountability and Control

1. Introduction

How governments keep control over large and complex operations and how they are held to account has changed over the past 15 years because of technological innovations, changes in the size and structure of government, and the introduction of performance budgeting and management. This chapter examines this modernisation trend and looks at the challenges and changes under way to control systems in OECD member countries.

While the term seemingly translates easily among languages, there are wide variations in what is meant by the word "control". For the purposes of this chapter, control means ensuring that an organisation is operating as intended. Systems of control provide internal and/or external assurance that the management systems are operating well. Traditionally, they focus on ensuring that funds are properly accounted for and regulations complied with. In modern management, control systems can extend to the quality of performance information, and internal control can cover the processes for strategic and performance management.

The main story of control in OECD member countries is the move from *ex ante* to *ex post* control, and the development of stronger processes of internal control. Simply put, the *ex ante* to *ex post* trend is from a system where transactions (payments) were approved prior to commitment from a controller outside the spending ministry, to one where internal management makes many financial and non-financial resource allocation decisions which are externally checked after the event. This move puts a new burden on managers to implement processes to achieve effectiveness, reliability and compliance. In practice it means trading the inefficient but relative certainty of checking the regularity and legality of individual transactions for the more efficient but relative uncertainty of verifying the proper operation of systems.

The trends to *ex post* controls and managerial flexibility do not mean there is less control – in fact there are more and more varied controls. Up to 50% of the work of external auditors is now performance audits. Many more financial and non-financial reports are produced. *Ex ante* internal controls are being replaced with *ex post* internal audits. New and more complicated auditing and accounting regimes are being put in place, for example accrual accounting.

There is no one event that prompted this move, nor one reform that brought countries to this stage. Rather it was the steady accumulation of many influences and the gradual evolution of systems. The changes include the growth in size and complexity of government; technological advances; a focus on performance; increased delegation of decision making; and the use of service delivery entities outside direct government influence.

Despite the many changes in control systems, there are challenges ahead. For example, governments are delegating more service delivery functions to entities outside direct ministerial control. With third-party providers, the responsibility for the programme is further from those who are held to account for the funds. Many countries are trying to give managers more flexibility to achieve performance goals, but political systems deal poorly with mismanagement of funds and have a low tolerance for risk.

What are the implications of control changes for accountability? As control becomes *ex post*, accountability becomes more important. If decisions are audited after the fact but the audit is not made available to the public and/ or if there is no body obliged to ensure that corrective action is taken for non-compliance or malfeasance, then the control purpose is not being served. If there are more controls, it means that there is more information generated. The formalisation of performance, and of controls of information generated, runs the risk of creating too much information and obscuring the most important controls of public service behaviour, which are those values that public servants have internalised.

Many reformers expected that with new public management approaches, formal controls would be reduced and managers would be freer. This has not happened as envisaged. What has resulted is both more managerial freedom and more formal control – but the nature of control is changing because of the complexity and ambition of the contemporary public management agenda. There is in fact a gap between those ambitions and what control has so far been found feasible. Consequently, control systems are in transition. This gives rise to questions such as: Who takes control of ensuring that the public service is spending its money on the tasks assigned to it and carrying out the job efficiently? How do governments exercise that control over large and complex operations?

This chapter covers the key elements of control systems in OECD member countries,[1] the broad changes under way and the challenges resulting from those changes. It is part of a broader study looking at how control systems have changed and what the effects are on wider systems of accountability. In modern societies governments are accountable for the use they make of public resources. This accountability in OECD member countries is based on a democratic mandate, spanning government's promises to the public, its management behaviour and the expected outcomes. While there are suggestions of what helps promote accountability, the chapter focuses principally on control systems.

2. What is accountability and control?

The terms accountability and control at first glance seem straightforward. Linguistically, they are words and concepts that seemingly are easy to translate. For example, the word control in English translates easily to *contrôle* in French and *kontrol* in German and is used universally as a term in budget execution systems. However, the English meaning evokes an active authority to manage, whereas the French meaning implies a more passive oversight and other terms in French like *direction* and *responsable* fill out the meaning of the English word control. As a concept, given the country, control can run the gamut from an *ex ante* to an *ex post* system, from one that focuses purely on financial transaction to a wider set of procedures that is often described as management control. Accountability, too, is a difficult term across languages. For many languages, the translated equivalent of accountability is limited to a strict meaning of the accounting system or is thought of as a reporting obligation. Other cultures use accountability to mean how those entrusted with the powers of State are held responsible for their actions. These differences in meaning, concept and practice must be acknowledged for an international dialogue to occur.

For the purposes of the work undertaken by the OECD, the terms accountability and control will be wider, more encompassing terms. Accountability is the obligation to present an account of and answer for the execution of responsibilities through the political and constitutional structure. Control[2] is broadly defined as a process designed to provide reasonable assurance regarding the effectiveness and efficiency of operations, reliability of reporting and compliance with applicable laws and regulations.

Accountability and control are complementary, but not symmetrical. Control can be either *ex ante* or *ex post*. Accountability can only be *ex post* – officials cannot be held accountable for a responsibility until they have had the opportunity to discharge it. The two ideas intersect because control is necessary to lend credibility to the account given by a public body. Without good control systems, accountability is impaired as claims to compliance and performance are unsubstantiated for outside observers who lack the knowledge to judge the character, veracity and reliability of the actors involved.

For the purposes of this chapter, a distinction is made between external control and internal control, and between *ex ante* and *ex post* control. External control means the audit process performed by a central and often independent audit agency.[3] Internal controls are the management processes, regulations and structures that provide senior management assurance of the legality, regularity, efficiency, effectiveness and economy of actions. *Ex ante* controls refer to those requirements, for example an expenditure or employment decision, which must be approved or pre-specified by a supervisory body before implementation. *Ex post* controls refer to checks after implementation that an action was according to policy and within the rules. Internal or – more broadly – management controls refer to systems of control within an organisation, and they can be of an *ex ante* or *ex post* nature. Control systems have formal components (special rules, dedicated people or organisations) but the informal and cultural environment can also have a strong impact on whether control is achieved.

3. What are the trends in control?

The move to *ex post* control puts a new burden on managers to implement processes to achieve effectiveness, reliability and compliance. In practice it means trading the inefficient but relative certainty of checking the regularity and legality of individual transactions for the more efficient but relative uncertainty of verifying the proper operation of systems. The rise of internal control has freed up external auditors and controllers to adapt their processes to focus on government performance. Rather than internal control coming at the expense of external control, this change has tended to provide more work for both external and internal auditors. *Ex ante* controls have been generally reduced but they remain important because of the move to performance goal setting and for sensitive spending and large spending projects (*e.g.* large IT systems).

The tendency to more internally controlled management applies to all OECD member countries, but countries are at different points on a spectrum. At one end are the heavily *ex ante*, externally controlled systems in classic continental European systems such as in France, Italy and Spain where delegated treasury controllers and quasi legal "courts" of auditors approve and oversee spending. At the other end are the Westminster and Nordic countries that are externally controlled but on an *ex post* basis. Each country seems to have moved relative to its starting position. Some countries have abandoned external delegated financial controllers in favour of internal auditors but have been slower to relax input controls, while others have delegated and decentralised more decision-making authority and are confronting challenges in employing risk management and more complex management controls.

There is no one event that prompted this move, nor one reform that brought countries to this stage. Rather it was the steady accumulation of many influences and the gradual evolution of systems. These influences and changes include:

- the growth in the size of government, including the sheer magnitude of transactions;
- the growth in the complexity of government (*e.g.* government trying to correct social problems);
- the emergence of technology to improve the efficiency and oversight of the transactions;
- the growing focus on the performance of government rather than simple conformance with law (see Chapter 2 for more details);
- the increasing delegation of decision-making power to government units closer to clients;
- the use of entities outside of direct government control to deliver services, including agencies, lower levels of government and other third parties (*e.g.* banks).

These changes have been set against a backdrop of maturing economies and the need to limit aggregate government spending. It is worth noting that many of the changes in budget rules have been accompanied by or resulted in changes to accounting regimes, structural changes, managerial freedom and the like. Each change has posed challenges to accountability and control systems.

4. How have countries confronted the changes?

Generally there have been more, and more varied, changes to the internal control process than to external controls. For example, internal audit and other internal management processes have replaced *ex ante* control while management information has changed to better reflect organisational objectives.

External control units have seen relatively fewer reforms and are more homogenous because of the constitutional and statutory basis of their work and the existence of international norms for auditing. As most OECD member countries have incorporated performance into their budget and management systems, value-for-money and performance audits by external auditors have become virtually universal. This move to value-for-money auditing has been partly in response to strengthened internal control. As internal control has dealt more with financial reliability and compliance, audit offices have played a much larger role in promoting government accountability – notably by strengthening their links with legislatures.

Table 3.1 shows some reforms made in a selection of countries in the last 10 years. The chapter continues with a closer look at changes in internal and external control systems.

Table 3.1. **Control reforms over the last decade**

Country	Reforms in internal control	Reforms in external control	Reforms in reporting requirements	Other reforms
Denmark	Chief executive contracts (1995). Controller units (1996).			Pilot project for accrual accounting and budgeting.
Germany	Replacement of pre-audit offices by internal control.			Budget pilot project (output-oriented).
Ireland	Accounting officer's statement on internal financial controls. Review of internal control systems. Creation of audit committees.		Management information framework.	Risk management to be introduced. Expenditure review initiative.
Italy	The traditional financial control by the Ministry of Finance is moving from a sanction type to a "collaborative" kind of *ex ante* control. Efficiency and effectiveness controls have been introduced since 1993 (management and strategic control). Management controls are performed at the departmental level of each ministry, while strategic control is at the ministerial level.	*Ex ante* external control by the SAI has been reduced to a few issues (regulatory acts, contracts above EU levels, budget reallocations). *Ex post* performance-based control has been introduced.	Performance reporting (efficiency, effectiveness and economy) is made by internal control bodies to the ministers. The SAI is experimenting with an *ex post* aggregation of financial data based on broad policy goals. The Ministry of Finance reaggregates traditional financial information by centres of responsibility.	
Japan	Evaluation of ministry/agency policies (necessity, efficiency, effectiveness).	Enforcement since 1998 of 3E audits (economy, effectiveness, efficiency).	Information disclosure law (2001).	Information disclosure system (citizens' enhanced access to information). Programme budgeting.
Slovak Republic	Adoption of the Act on Financial Control and Internal Audit.			
Spain	Co-ordination of internal audit offices under a central organisation. Verifying of attainment of objectives extended to the whole general State budget (from 2005).	Extended to aggregate accounts of the State public sector.	Compliance with objectives.	Objectives-based budget.
Sweden	Results-based control in central government. Internal audit function in main government agencies.	New supreme audit institution merging the parliamentary auditors and the audit office that previously belonged to the executive branch.	Objectives and results dialogue between the responsible minister and the agency's director general.	Creation of a commission to assess improving internal audit by creating a central body.
United Kingdom	Accounting officer's statement on internal control. Risk management embedded in management of government bodies. Treasury's programme of work to enhance government's handling of risk.	Statutory right to access recipients of grants, bodies delivering public services, some non-departmental public bodies (not limited companies) and contractors working for bodies audited by the SAI.		Resource-based financial management system. Public service agreements.
United States	Chief financial officers to oversee all financial management activities.	Increased focus on review of major federal programmes and anticipating long-term issues.	Reporting on compliance with federal financial and accounting standards. Performance and accountability report.	Government Performance and Results Act.

Source: Case studies and expert meeting discussion, November 2003, OECD, Paris.

4.1. Changes in internal control systems

Wide international acceptance of the goals for internal control is articulated in a model proposed by the Committee of Sponsoring Organizations of the Treadway Commission (COSO) which states that internal control is "a process, effected by an entity's board of directors, management and other personnel, designed to provide reasonable assurance regarding the achievement of objectives in the following categories: effectiveness and efficiency of operations; reliability of financial reporting; and compliance with applicable laws and regulations."[4]

While the goals of internal control are broad, most countries focus on the latter two goals of regularity and legality of spending. Indeed internal control is mostly a financial process while only a few countries are now branching out into management control, performance audits and risk management techniques.

4.2. Internal control is primarily financial control

As shown in Table 3.2, control on transactions – commitment and payment procedures, accounting procedures and financial statements – continues to constitute the core of the executive's activity. All OECD member countries have internal control units but most have moved away from *ex ante* transaction controls to *ex post* audit. For the most part internal audit exists and is mandatory. The OECD/World Bank Budget Practices and Procedures Survey shows that of 28 countries queried, only three OECD member countries – Iceland, Sweden and Turkey – currently do not use internal auditors, and in three other countries – the Czech Republic, Germany and Greece – the use of internal audit is not widespread.[5]

4.3. Moving beyond financial control

For those countries that have moved beyond financial control, more sophisticated management controls are used as complementary add-ons rather than substitutes for the financial processes. There are meaningful differences, though, in the extent to which countries use effectiveness and efficiency audits as well as risk management techniques. Moreover, to whom the control bodies report and the degree of decentralisation of the internal control units varies markedly from country to country.

There is a steady increase in the volume of performance information. However, the quality and use of performance information is not necessarily monitored by the internal control entities. While in most countries performance information is incorporated into the formal budget formulation process, it is not always taken into account when taking decisions about budget allocations. When internal control incorporates non-financial aspects,

Table 3.2. **A snapshot of internal control systems**

Country	Unit responsible for execution	Level of control co-ordination	Reporting destination	Typology
Denmark	Spending ministry	No	Managers; external control	Financial audit
Germany	Spending ministry	Department	Head of department	Ex ante budget; financial audit
Ireland	Spending ministry	Department	Management; accounting officer; audit committee	Ex ante control; financial audit; risk management to be applied
Italy	Ministry of Finance; spending ministry	Ministry of Finance; spending ministry	Ministry of Finance; ministers and managers; technical committee at the Presidency of the Council of Ministers	Ex ante control; financial and compliance audit; management and strategic control
Japan	Spending ministry	Ministry	Head of department; rarely minister	Financial audit
Slovak Republic	Ministry of Finance; spending ministry	Ministry of Finance	Ministers; cabinet	Ex ante control; financial audit
Spain	Ministry of Finance	Central unit in Ministry of Finance	Managers; ministers; Ministry of Finance; cabinet	Ex ante control; financial audit; evaluation of programmes (a few)
Sweden	Agencies	Management unit	Agencies' management	Value for money; Compliance
United Kingdom	Spending ministry	Department	Accounting officer	Management control; internal audit; risk management
United States	Spending ministry	Department/agency	Head of department/ agency; chief accounting officer	Management control; financial audit

Source: Case studies and expert meeting discussion, November 2003, OECD, Paris.

one finds a performance-oriented audit closer to financial performance or value-for-money (economy, effectiveness and efficiency) than results auditing. Thus, countries moving away from financial control to wider management control regimes tend to focus on programme effectiveness rather than whether the performance data are accurate.

Recently, a few countries (Australia and the United Kingdom) have formalised risk management techniques into their management control structures and other countries have become actively interested in this development (Ireland and Japan). These countries had more elaborate internal controls as a starting point and have gone the furthest in relaxing input controls and managing by performance and contract. However, most countries follow a more classical approach of external audit risk assessment, since individual managers lack a global view of risks, both financial and non-financial.

4.4. Co-ordination of internal control

One issue encountered by countries is how to relate internal and external control. Because internal control is responsible to management, its independence, impartiality or objectivity can be called into question. According to Figure 3.1, half of OECD member countries have created central co-ordination, policy and/or monitoring units to oversee the departmental internal control systems. Half of these units are located in the finance ministry. These range from units that actively audit internal auditors, to small units that set standards and co-ordinate specific overlapping issues. Some countries have explicit links between the external audit institutions and internal control units. The supreme audit institutions (SAIs, see Section 4.7) evaluate internal control systems in deciding on the extent and depth of their own auditing work.

4.5. Ex ante *remains important*

Ex ante control still exists in important ways. Top-down budgeting requires stronger *ex ante* control, with input rationing, rules, control systems and incentives to ensure that departments, and government as a whole, receive and spend no more than they were allocated. Performance-oriented

Figure 3.1. **Is there a central office for controlling and monitoring audits?**

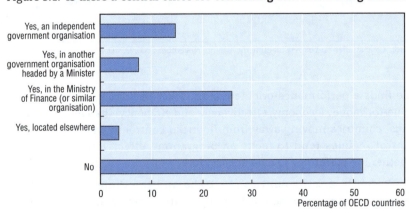

Source: Question 4.1.I. OECD/WB Survey 2003.

budgeting and management requires a limited return to centralised planning of performance (*ex ante* specification of intended outputs and impacts) but also more *ex post* performance reporting, audit and evaluation.

4.6. Internal control reporting

In OECD member countries, most internal control reports are issued and used at levels below the ministerial level. Only a few countries, including Italy and the Slovak Republic, report beyond the senior management level. Internal control units are generally independent of line management. Senior management, ministers and the cabinet tend to receive summary reports on financial and management activity on an annual or semi-annual basis.

For example, in the United Kingdom the head of internal audit of any department reports to the accounting officer with the necessary information to issue the annual statement on internal control, providing the accounting officer with an opinion on the body's arrangements for risk management, control and governance. In Spain, internal auditors report to top managers and to the central unit in the Ministry of Finance. Special reports can be addressed to ministers and the cabinet. The central unit provides the cabinet with an annual report with the most relevant features, findings and recommendations on the financial activity.

4.7. The external control system audit

While there has not been the same range of changes to external control bodies, they have almost universally added performance and/or value-for-money audits to their workload. External audit ensures that planning, budgeting and use of public resources conform to a country's laws, pursue the objectives defined by parliament and government, and are linked to the real world of programme operation. In most countries, the main body responsible for this is the national audit office often known as the supreme audit institution (SAI). The role of the SAI has evolved from the traditional task of verifying legality and regularity of financial management and of accounting.[6] The modern SAI audit objectives cover both the traditional focus of legality, regularity and economy, and reviews of efficiency and effectiveness of financial and programme management.[7] The United States Government Accountability Office, given the constitutional framework of the United States, stands alone in pushing beyond these objectives to provide policy advice and make management recommendations. Budget offices and finance ministries in general also perform what some people term external controls: both *ex ante* and *ex post* reviews of spending, process, performance and value-for-money evaluations. However for the purposes of this chapter, the reviews by the finance ministry are considered as internal control mechanisms.

4.8. Independent, but how independent?

The most significant changes in external control have been to secure the independence of auditors and to reinforce the links between the audit office and the legislature. Either at the constitutional or the statutory level, most SAIs are now independent of the executive. In Nordic and other OECD member countries, the audit offices have been made independent offices of parliament.

In most countries, the audit office determines its own workload with some countries allowing audit subjects to come from parliament (40% of OECD member countries) or even the executive itself (25% of OECD member countries – see Figure 3.2). This means that despite moves to make the office more independent, there are still some countries with audit offices that cannot fully determine their workload.

4.9. Differences in the scope of audit

Some differences appear in the scope of institutions overseen by the SAIs, including, for example, control over regional or local governments and State enterprises in Italy and Japan. Also, in many continental countries SAIs continue to have a jurisdictional role for enquiries and for sanctions of an individual's use of public resources. The most important reasons for changes in scope have been decentralisation and changes resulting from privatisation.

4.10. SAIs do performance audits

As internal control and the rise of automation has made financial auditing easier and less burdensome, external auditors have addressed

Figure 3.2. **How are audit subjects determined?**

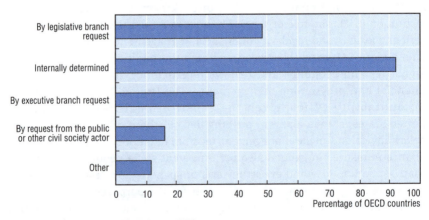

Source: Question 4.5.n. OECD/WB Survey 2003.

programme effectiveness or value-for-money audits (Table 3.3). However, financial audits still comprise the majority of the SAI workload. Because internal control focuses on financial audits as well, most SAIs either co-ordinate or use the reports from the internal auditors if they are confident of their credibility.

Only in a few countries such as the United Kingdom and the United States do value-for-money (VFM) and effectiveness audits account for more than half of the work performed by the SAI. As the United States moves beyond traditional financial, performance and risk audits, the linkages within the executive branch must necessarily be stronger, and the Government Accountability Office is attempting to maintain its objectivity while being intimately involved in management operations.

5. Future challenges

This section examines the modernisation challenges potentially facing governments resulting from the reforms to accountability and control.

The complexity of government: The complexity of government requires more varied and performance-related internal controls. As government diversifies its services, external auditors must also adapt and expand their oversight in equally diversified ways.

The formalisation of performance: Reforms to accountability and control systems have paralleled efforts to introduce performance budget and management reforms aimed at giving service delivery organisations more managerial freedom to comply with programme objectives. Tight *ex ante* control is inefficient and incompatible with the needs of a performance-oriented system.

The limitations of setting performance goals and then measuring and auditing them are well documented. In current practice in OECD member country governments, for the most part, performance data are accepted at face value. Parliaments have been interested in the programme evaluations conducted by auditors, but they have so far lacked significant interest in performance measures. Since the linkages between available resources and performance are weak, internal control systems still focus primarily on financial measures. While international bodies are working on creating standards for auditors and, to a limited degree, internal control for performance audits and performance information, countries have been slow to adopt them in their systems.

Decentralisation and delegation: As countries fund service delivery and even policy making at lower levels of government, overseeing and accounting for those funds is difficult. Other levels of government sometimes have their own control and audit procedures that can be at odds with national systems.

Table 3.3. **A snapshot of external control systems**

Country	Scope of audit	SAI's status[1]	Audit typology	Reporting
Denmark	Government; Institutions funded by government; local government areas funded with national funds.	Parliamentary office.	Financial (including regularity) audit; performance audit (VFM).	Parliament (Public Accounts Committee).
Germany	Federation; federal public corporations; social security; federation shareholders' interests.	Independent office; provides assistance to parliament and the executive.	Regularity; VFM; effectiveness for large-scale programmes.	Annual (both houses); special reports; impact report on recommendations' remedial actions.
Ireland	Whole government (but not the State debt policy); agencies; universities; etc.	Independent office.	Financial audit; certification of accounts; VFM.	Committee of Public Accounts (parliament).
Italy	Whole government; State enterprises; autonomous bodies; main local authorities.	Independent office (president and magistrates appointed by the President of the Republic).	Regularity; financial audit; performance audit (objectives).	Two Chambers and Treasury.
Japan	Whole national government; bodies receiving government financing or grants (agencies, prefectures, municipalities).	Independent office.	Regularity; financial audit; certification of government accounts; VFM.	Annual (Diet).
Slovak Republic	Whole government; public entities; territorial units.	Independent office (president appointed by parliament).	Regularity; performance audit (VFM).	Parliament.
Spain	Whole public sector; (co-ordination with regional courts of accounts).	Dependent on parliament (not hierarchical subordination).	Regularity; financial audit; economy and efficiency audit.	Mixed Congress-Senate commission; government.
Sweden	State; agencies and government-owned companies; government grants and benefits conceded by government; Bank of Sweden; social insurance fund.	Parliamentary office (as of 2003).	Financial audit; performance (effectiveness) audit.	Annual financial audit report to government; annual agency reports to parliament.
United Kingdom	National government (local and health authorities controlled by the Audit Commission).	Office of the House of Commons (through the Comptroller and Auditor General).	Financial (including regularity) audit; certification of accounts; VFM audit.	Parliament (Committee of Public Accounts).
United States	Federal government.	Congressional entity.	Financial audit; reviews of major federal programmes.	Congress.

1 Refers to the legal relationship with the legislature.

Source: Case studies and expert meeting discussion, November 2003, OECD, Paris.

Figure 3.3. **Does the supreme audit body co-ordinate with or use the reports of internal auditors?**

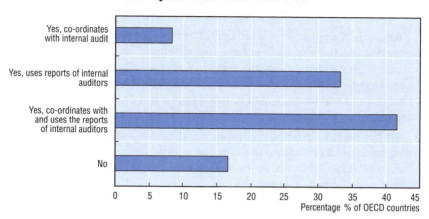

Source: Question 4.5.s. OECD/WB Survey, 2003.

The potential for political interference may also increase as a result of competition (or collusion) between elected politicians at different levels. Monitoring and holding officials of other levels of government to account is more difficult than in direct line ministries. As systems become decentralised or deconcentrated, there is a need for better co-ordination of internal controls and more robust external oversight.

Partnering and third-party delivery: In the drive to make government more efficient and responsive, governments have turned to agencies and other arm's-length bodies to deliver services. Moreover, as discussed in Chapter 5, governments are partnering with private companies and non-governmental organisations. These are subject to private sector audit standards, can withhold non-public portions of their records from governments, and are subject to contractual arrangements. Programme managers must rely on external, *ex post* control, which means that they have few tools at their disposal to correct problems mid-stream. Most countries still place ultimate accountability on ministers and senior civil servants. With third-party providers, the responsibility for the programme is placed further from those who are held to account for the funds.

Automation and technology: The introduction of automation and other technology, combined with conceptual advances in accounting and auditing, has been the true success story in control. In general terms, the information provided is better and more reliable, as a consequence of improvements in terms of performance information, the introduction in the accounting systems of some accruals information, and the use of information and

Box 3.1. **Management accountability and control trends in Canada**

Reform in the public service of Canada is an ongoing process. Inevitably or intentionally, these initiatives have had an impact on the management accountability and control regime in place. Since the early 1990s, a number of trends can be observed in the external and internal control regimes for both financial and non-financial (performance) information, as well as the overall accountability regime.

With respect to external control by the supreme audit institution (the Auditor General of Canada) there has been little change in the level and nature of financial attest audits which examine the public accounts of Canada. Government departments and agencies are now starting to produce their own financial statements but, with a few exceptions, these are not yet being audited by the SAI. In terms of performance, there has been some increase in the numbers of performance audits (until recently called value-for-money audits), although that trend is now reversing somewhat. What is new is the tabling since 1997 of performance audits by the Commissioner of the Environment and Sustainable Development – green audits – now a part of the SAI. Audits by other independent parliamentary officers such as the Language, Access to Information and Privacy Commissioners continue to be tabled in Parliament.

Internal control continues to be exercised by both the central agencies (Treasury Board Secretariat and the Department of Finance) and each departmental organisation. In terms of central financial and administrative regulations, the trend has been towards streamlining and simplifying controls and the adoption of accrual accounting, but not yet accrual budgeting. Budget allotment controls have for some time moved to the organisational level from earlier programme and sub-programme levels. Administrative policies are being recast in terms of general good management principles and away from detailed directives, and reduced in number. Risk management is receiving increasing attention.

However, the trend to increased flexibility was abruptly reversed as the result of several major mismanagement scandals. In the last several years, there has been an increase in requirements for public disclosure of expenditures such as hospitality and international travel for senior executives and contracts. And the Office of the Comptroller General has been re-established to strengthen financial management and internal audit. On the performance side, there has been an increase in dialogue with the centre on setting the objectives and performance targets sought by departments, and an increase in policies and guidelines on reporting, management and accountability frameworks from a results perspective.

Box 3.1. **Management accountability and control trends in Canada** (*cont.*)

Internal control within departments has seen first a decline and more recently an increase in internal audit. This pendulum swing is also apparent in the degree of flexibility given to managers. Major efforts in the mid-1990s to "cut the red tape", streamlining and reducing administrative regulations, have given way in the last few years to a need for stronger oversight of the management of public funds. The increasing attention being paid to performance and results has led to departments developing their own policies and guidelines for measuring results. Evaluation efforts have also ebbed and flowed during the period. After growth in the 1980s, evaluation was linked with internal audit by the mid-1990s, only to be separated again in the early 2000s. Evaluation resources, reduced in the mid-1990s as part of overall spending reductions, have only started to return.

There have been significant trends in the accountability regime also. Most importantly, since the late 1990s, each department and agency has tabled in Parliament an annual report on its plans for the upcoming years and a performance report on what has been accomplished, all as part of the expenditure budget process. Unfortunately, parliamentary review of these reports has been limited to date. Most of these reports are not audited, although in the case of four specific service agencies, the information – including their financial statements – is audited by the SAI and an auditor's report appears in each performance report. There are continuing initiatives to improve reporting to Parliament. The other major trend in the accountability regime has been a move by the government away from the traditional structure of reporting through ministers to Parliament. A range of new organisational forms have been created, including a number of foundations with considerable less oversight by ministers and Parliament. The SAI and some parliamentarians have expressed concern that, in these cases, accountability of public funds to Parliament is being lost as a result. A final trend in accountability has been increasing discussions in Parliament on strengthening its oversight. Some steps have been taken, but the debate on how best to proceed continues.

communication technology, both for reporting and for controlling. Also, the use of the Internet allows more possibilities for open government, with feedback from citizens. Through technology, internal and external controllers have been able to enlarge their scope and types of audit without abandoning their traditional functions of preventing mistakes and fraud and conducting financial analyses. Of course, there are risks from technology. The design of computerised control systems can be difficult and expensive.

Innovation, flexibility and risk: The fundamental challenge to control is the move from expecting conformity with tightly defined rules to a flexible system where managers are given the scope to achieve wider goals. This means that the model for control is moving from a fundamental distrust of management to a model that values management taking calculated risks and making decisions based on performance rather than rules. Political systems deal poorly with mismanagement of funds and have lower tolerance for risk, and lack the private sector discipline of the market-place. A handful of countries have attempted to incorporate risk management into their accountability and control systems, but at this point experience is limited and lessons are few.

6. Findings and conclusion

This chapter examined control systems in transition. In the past two decades, new technologies, privatisation and new forms of management have changed the way governments operate, but have also created a need for new ways of making governments accountable for what they do.

The new performance focus of most governments has led to or created differentiated organisational structures, new reporting regimes and data, new service delivery arrangements and new management techniques, including performance-oriented budgeting and management. This complexity of government intervention requires a generally *ex post* orientation with new internal and management control regimes, and more external attention to value-for-money and performance audits.

Modernisation has meant more control. Enhanced internal control is needed for delegated management systems, which internalise performance and compliance incentives. More external control is needed for more diversified structures (*e.g.* executive agencies) and non-governmental providers, and explicit performance contracts with separate organisations require external verification of reporting. There is a strong trend of external control bodies adding performance and/or value-for-money audits to their workload.

Customising management and formalising performance create formidable problems of control – both internal and external. Delegated and deregulated management requires a deep change in how management happens. In the OECD member countries with highly delegated systems, managers have heavy responsibilities for strategy, reputation, the deployment of human and financial resources, internal control and accountability. Theory justifies such delegation on the basis that organisations are likely to perform better if those who know the business best can tailor it to suit its function.

For the manager in such an environment, there are additional management systems over and above the traditional control concerns about accounts and regulations. This requires systems of "management control" with much wider scope than conventional internal financial control. This widening of scope itself creates such a plethora of potential things to check, that departments need a risk assessment and management process, so that control resources are deployed where they matter most.

Delegated and deregulated management relieves central agencies of the need to micro-manage, and control agencies of the need to micro-check. But what happens in one part of government can affect the whole. Government is left exposed to risk, which relatively free agents are meant to manage. Formal controls may not be able to manage this risk. The more appropriate tools may be performance management, a strengthened sense of collective responsibility amongst senior public servants, and strengthened accountability. A handful of countries also encourage or require departments to have in place formal risk management techniques.

In accountability and control, as in all other dimensions of management, the informal systems – the individuals' motivation, values and attitudes – are as important as formal systems. Strategies to strengthen control and accountability must take account of this or fail. Performance-oriented management can allow a lightening up of input and process controls. But this is not because formal performance planning and reporting become the control system, but rather because formal controls can be partly replaced by social controls as staff internalise organisational goals. The cost of this is that senior officers must give much more attention to management than was the case in a traditional bureaucracy.

The desirable off-set therefore, between performance orientation and input and process controls, applies largely to management **within** an organisation. Where organisations are at arm's length from each other, social controls are more difficult to apply. With the fragmentation of the public sector discussed in Chapter 4, the control burden, including for performance, is likely to get heavier.

In the early stages of the period under review, there was an expectation that formal controls would be reduced – and managers would be more free. This has not happened as envisaged. What has resulted is both more managerial freedom and more formal control – but the nature of control is changing because of the complexity and ambition of the contemporary public management agenda. There is in fact a gap between those ambitions and what control has so far been found feasible. Consequently, control systems are in transition.

In summary, whereas traditional public management featured purely financial *ex ante* external controls, modern systems rely on internal controls backed up by strong *ex post* audits by SAIs. In OECD member countries, control is still generally financial in nature – although less and less exclusively so. There is much more financial reporting because of improvements in technology, freedom of information laws, parliamentary needs and new accounting regimes (*e.g.* the introduction of accruals). *Ex ante* control still exists, since reforms such as top-down budgeting require stronger *ex ante* control with input rationing, rules, control systems and incentives to ensure that departments, and government as a whole, receive and spend no more than they were allocated.

Table 3.4. The modern control framework

	External control		Internal and management control					
			Central control			Organisational control		
	Ex ante Indirect	Ex post	Ex ante Direct	Ex ante Indirect	Ex post	Ex ante Direct	Ex ante Indirect	Ex post
Financial	SAI observations and recommendations	SAI attest audits	Budget controls, such as spending controls	Accounting and financial management policies and guidelines	Spending reports	Financial management controls, such as signing authorities	Entity financial management policies	Spending reports, internal financial audits
Trend	–	Expansion for some SAIs of coverage to individual entities ↑↑	Budget controls now at entity or large programme level →	Modernising of policies occurring –	Much more financial reporting ↑↑	More flexibility given to managers →	Modernising of policies occurring –	New auditing and accounting regimes (e.g accruals) both require and allow more reports ↑↑
Performance	SAI recommendations, guides and best practices	SAI performance audits; audits and reports from other legislative officers	Dialogue on setting objectives and results	Performance-related policies and guidelines	Central evaluations and audits	Entity dialogue on objectives and results	Entity performance-related policies and guidelines	Entity evaluations, internal audits
Trend	Increasing issuance of guidelines etc. by some SAIs ←	Increasing coverage of performance audits and audits/studies by other independent agents ↑↑	Occurring at least in some countries, such as Sweden, United Kingdom and United States ←~	Now occurring in most countries ←	Some increase here, especially audits; others have backed off ←~	Occurring as a result of the results focus (?) ←	Occurring as a result of the results focus (?) ←	Increasing internal audit in most places with some increase in evaluations (?) ←

Notes

1. There are two primary sources for this chapter. The first is a set of case studies developed by OECD member countries participating in an expert meeting held in November 2003. These countries appear in the series of tables on changes in control systems. The other source is the OECD/World Bank Survey on Budget Practices and Procedures that was completed in 2003 and includes 28 OECD member countries as well as a number of non-member countries. The data from this survey are the basis of the figures. See *www.oecd.org/gov/budget*.

2. This definition is generally taken from the Committee of Sponsoring Organizations of the Treadway Commission (COSO) model, *www.coso.org*. COSO is an international, voluntary professional organisation dedicated to the improvement of financial reporting through ethics, effective internal control and corporate governance. While originally a private sector group, the COSO definitions and procedures are generally relevant to public sector organisations.

3. Classically, external control included central executive branch entities which provided, for example, *ex ante* transaction level spending authority. This is no longer an accepted concept, and typically not employed in OECD member countries.

4. The Committee of Sponsoring Organizations of the Treadway Commission, "Internal Control – Integrated Framework. Executive Summary", *www.coso.org/ publications/executive_summary_integrated_framework.htm*, accessed 16 June 2005.

5. Question 4.1.g. of the OECD/World Bank Survey on Budget Practices and Procedures, *www.oecd.org/gov/budget*.

6. See International Organization of Supreme Audit Institutions (INTOSAI) (1977), *Lima Declaration of Guidelines on Auditing Precepts, www.intosai.org/Level2/ 2_LIMADe.html*.

7. *Ibid.*, Section 4.3.

ISBN 92-64-01049-1
Modernising Government: The Way Forward
© OECD 2005

Chapter 4

Reallocation and Restructuring: The Heavy Machinery of Reform

1. Introduction

In the period under review, it has become clear that the public sector cannot be static; it must respond to change not just at the policy level but in the way it carries out its responsibilities. Faced with fiscal stringency but increasing demands, government departments have sought to develop more efficient administrative structures to enable them to "do more with less". Similarly, the demands for greater choice in the types of services provided and the way in which they are provided have forced the public sector to adopt a range of structures tailored to the specific requirements or particular policy areas.

Change in one area also tends to drive change throughout a system. Arm's-length agencies may be a response to a particular management demand but their adoption will be accompanied by new regulatory and reporting methods, different budgetary requirements and innovative staffing arrangements. Conversely, demands for more responsive management or the potential of information technology to enhance fiscal supervision may facilitate the creation of arm's-length agencies.

This chapter looks at the ways in which the structure of public sector organisations has adapted to the changing demands both from within the public sector and from the community at large. It also examines the role of the budget as a tool of central agencies in driving structural change and resource reallocation.

2. What are the different ways of restructuring?

During the period under review, there was an unprecedented level of organisational change undertaken for a wide variety of reasons:

- In a number of countries, including France, Italy, Japan, Korea, Spain, Turkey and the United Kingdom, there was a significant devolution of authority and functions from central to local government.
- Across OECD member countries generally there was re-organisation of functions driven by the globalisation of public concerns such as trade, environment and anti-terrorism, and the demands of membership of regional groupings.
- In all countries to different degrees, governments have been withdrawing from/selling off their interest in activities that could be conducted by

private entities without direct involvement by the State, under contract to the State or under a bespoke public regulatory regime. This meant the shutting down or radical restructuring of major government departments dealing with enterprises such as railways, energy, post office, telecommunications, and public works.

- In moving from being a direct provider of services to creating market structures in new areas (*e.g.* telecommunication services), government's regulatory role grew. This required the setting up of new regulatory bodies – often with a degree of statutory independence from government – to help, among other things, to establish a level playing field. With the increasing importance of regulating markets, governments also had to move beyond traditional sector-focused and subsidy-based trade and industry concerns, to make a new investment in policies and capacity for whole-of-government interests such as competition, pollution control and regulatory harmonisation.

- In a few countries, (the Netherlands, New Zealand and the United Kingdom provide the clearest examples), governments undertook whole-of-government re-organisation of core public service departments as a lever of reform. More recently Japan and Korea have taken moves in the same direction.

- Devolution, privatisation, the move from direct service delivery to regulation, and contracting out have produced by far the most significant changes to the machinery of government across OECD countries. However, this chapter mainly focuses on changing organisational structures of those areas that remain within government.

3. Why do governments change their organisational structures?

Government re-organisations respond to immediate concerns, both internal and external. Internal reasons can be political – rewarding a politician with a larger ministry, increasing the size of the cabinet – or aimed at improving general management processes and culture by splitting or merging ministries or separating policy making from policy implementation.

External pressures can come from the emergence of a new policy priority, as was the case, most dramatically, following the 11 September 2001 attack on the United States. That event led to proposals for a new national Department of Homeland Security and a new organisation to take charge of airport security. This illustrates a wider tendency in governments: when confronted by a threat to security, they tend to re-centralise authority. The response to the longer-term pressures referred to earlier is more typical of the way external forces drive administrative restructuring.

Organisational change can also be used to signal political intent to address a problem, without guaranteeing that anything else will be done. In some cases re-organisation is used as a substitute for making hard choices about management and priorities. Creating an agency and labelling its work a priority does not automatically mean it will be treated as such.

A number of underlying trends influence governments to review and reorganise the way they work. These include:

Incentives: There is a new tendency to apply to government organisations the thinking derived from economics on the way incentives of different kinds influence people's behaviour. This has meant that attempts to change the public service culture increasingly include organisational change.

Confidence building: Modern governments need to ensure that the public has confidence in the decisions they make. As communication becomes increasingly important, announcing a new organisational structure has strong symbolic value. Governments can also use new structures to "tie their own hands" by setting up an organisation in such a way that it will be difficult for governments to change it. This creates confidence in the durability of the policies represented by the structure. Credibility has also become a crucial resource for policy makers at the national level, and increasingly it comes from persuasion rather than coercion.

Accountability: The tendency for governments to move from controlling processes to controlling performance is increasingly seen as possible only if an individual can be held responsible and accountable for such performance and his or her incentives modified accordingly. This trend away from the "faceless bureaucrat" and towards more personal accountability appears to create a preference for organisational structures that facilitate such accountability.

Diversification: The move towards measuring and controlling output, rather than input and processes, increases the tendency towards organisational diversity. Some governments have taken the view that as long as outputs can be controlled, it matters less what kind of organisation does the production.

Specialisation: There is an increasing need for specialised skills as society and government become more complex, and as governments are required to provide more individualised services to citizens.

4. Changing the number, size and functions of ministries

4.1. Changing the functional mix of ministries

The number of government ministries and their structures change constantly. Most newly-elected governments shake up the cabinet structure and the number of ministries. In general, core ministries in charge of sovereign functions of government such as defence, finance, and foreign affairs are less likely to be re-organised, along with core departments indispensable to the functioning of government such as cabinet offices and budget offices. The costs and dangers of such re-organisations for the overall functioning of government are too important for them to be undertaken lightly.

As for the creation of new ministries, or State secretariats within a ministry, this is often a way of signalling a new policy priority, as has been the case in recent years with implementing equal rights policies for women and protecting the environment. These new structures allow the creation of capacity in a new government policy area and provide an opportunity to bring new people into government, but the risk is that such structures may remain marginalised within government, headed by relatively junior ministers and having a weak bargaining position.

Not all new policy priorities involve the creation of new ministries. In some cases, those responsible for a new issue are given some kind of autonomous or independent status, and many new issues also cut across all sectors of government. This has been the case, for example, for sustainable development or regional development. Such priorities, which require co-ordination among existing ministries, do not lend themselves to being dealt with by a separate functional body. Few OECD countries have set up specific ministries for these issues, preferring what are essentially co-ordination processes although of many different types.

4.2. Changing the number and size of ministries

The overall size of ministries in OECD countries has fluctuated in most countries for the other functions of central government. While the size of a ministry should depend on the nature of the functions, the wider institutional setting, and the culture of the organisation, it should also depend on the management goals one is trying to achieve. In general, smaller organisations offer tighter focus and clearer accountability, but make collectivity harder. Larger organisations can offer economies of scale and can merge ill-functioning units into well-functioning ones, but may take decisions internally which should be addressed politically.

With regard to the size of cabinets or councils of ministers, however, there are some converging trends across OECD countries. Cabinets tended to grow rapidly from 1950, then stabilised in the mid-1980s and have since even decreased in some sectors of the economy. Today, most OECD countries have a cabinet or council of ministers of between 15 and 20 ministers, with support in some areas by junior ministers or secretaries of State.[1]

This stabilisation of the number of cabinet ministers is not surprising, as any extreme reform in cabinet size will necessarily open up some new governance weaknesses. While a small cabinet may be more manageable and efficient, it may also risk poor representation and capture. A larger group may offer broad representation of a full range of interests, but may be unable to take clear decisions.

In general, a well-functioning large cabinet will require a strong political and administrative centre, a well-developed sub-committee system, and standardised bureaucratic processes and structures across ministries, while a smaller cabinet will require well-functioning competitive mechanisms for budgeting and funding.

5. Creating arm's-length bodies: A lever for reform

In the past two decades, the most important organisational change that has taken place within central government has been the creation of arm's-length bodies or the devolution of significant autonomy to existing bodies that are separate from traditional vertically integrated ministries.

Traditionally, in most OECD countries, core government is defined as the ministries and departments of the executive, under the direct hierarchical control of a minister or of the head of state in presidential systems. These direct accountability lines provide a simple and stable governance model in which policy making and the delivery of services fall under the responsibility of a government clearly accountable to parliament and ultimately to the people. The same set of financial and management laws and reporting mechanisms generally applies to all of these bodies.

This picture has been significantly altered by distributing government responsibilities to bodies at arm's length from the control of politicians, with different hierarchical structures from traditionally functioning ministries and in some cases management autonomy or independence from political influence.

The reasons for creating these bodies or giving greater autonomy to long standing ones have been to make the system more efficient and effective or, depending on the type of body, to legitimise decision making by providing some independence from direct political intervention. The main theoretical ingredients that led to the changes varied, and included:

● The view of traditional centralised government bureaucracies as a bad thing *per se*. Structural separation and accountability were seen as a better form of organisation. Sometimes this was allied with the view that structures *per se* were of less importance than performance. In other cases, countries put a lot of emphasis on separation and contractual arrangements between core ministries and "agencies" (for example, the Netherlands, the United Kingdom).

- From New Institutional Economics literature came a preference for organisations with simple and clear purposes to make it easier to align the incentives of officials with public purposes and to reduce scope for "opportunistic" behaviour. This approach, which was applied in its purest form in New Zealand, recommended separate organisations for policy, delivery, and regulation.

- In general management thinking, and this was particularly influential in the creation of the Next Steps agencies in the United Kingdom, there was a strong disposition to "let managers manage" – to free operational managers from the constraints of the policy-oriented Whitehall. There had also been a trend in management away from vertical company structures covering a wide range of businesses towards companies which concentrated on their own task.

- The interest in private sector practices also led to attempts to replicate the board structure of publicly-listed companies in arm's-length, non-commercial public functions. These boards differed from traditional advisory boards of public entities in that they, rather than ministers or bureaucrats, were to have decision-making rights over the entity.

- There is the long-standing example of Sweden, and to some extent other Scandinavian countries, of government services being provided by "agencies" with high managerial autonomy, and the overall direction and co-ordination of government being handled by very small policy ministries (small by international standards).

6. The major trends in the distribution of power within core central government

Two major trends affected the distribution of power within core central government: increased managerial autonomy for some government bodies and the arrival of new agencies.

i) Many countries have had central government bodies that are separate from traditionally structured ministries or departments and to which different financial and human resources management rules apply. In some countries, these bodies are a separate legal entity; in others they are just institutionally separate. Most of these long-standing bodies have been created over time, some for political reasons and others for more managerial purposes. Some function mostly under public law. Examples include the "*établissements publics administratifs*" in France, "indirect public administration" in Germany, many Crown entities in New Zealand, the long-standing "agencies" in Sweden and some of the "non-departmental public bodies" in the United Kingdom. Others function mostly under private law (public enterprises, quasi public enterprises). In recent years, however, these bodies have been given additional managerial autonomy through contractual arrangements with their parent ministries, output/outcome oriented management and multi-year budgeting.

ii) A number of governments have also recently created what may be called "agencies". These are bodies that remain ministerial bodies in most cases, and are thus not separate entities. They are managed under clear contractual arrangements within the reporting hierarchy and benefit from a high degree of relaxation of their input controls. They have been used specifically for delivering services as governments, under pressure to focus increasingly on performance, have felt the need to better focus the individual accountability of staff and the organisations themselves. The scope of these reforms varies significantly. The United Kingdom has created 131 departmental agencies since 1988, employing more than three-quarters of the civil service. Other more limited reforms, such as the *centres de responsabilité* in France or the performance-based organisation programme in the United States, have concerned a more limited number of organisations. Important reforms were also carried out for example in Korea, where 23 departmental agencies have been created since 1999 and now employ more than 5 000 staff and account for 7% of the government budget.

6.1. *Independent regulators*

A third separate but related trend is the establishment of independent regulators. The number of independent regulators, with delegated powers to

---

Box 4.1. **The Dutch agencies**

In the 1980s, a number of services were named independent administrative bodies ("ZBOs"). These are not parts of ministries but are definitely parts of the public sector. Their most important characteristic is that ministers cannot be held responsible for all aspects of their operations. Their financial and management rules are tailor made. Some are legally parts of the State, while others have their own legal personality. Some are governed by public law, while others are governed by civil law. Their funding mechanisms vary as well: some are entirely funded from a ministry budget, while others collect fees or national insurance contributions.

At the beginning of the 1990s, the Netherlands Chamber of Audit severely criticised ZBOs as an organisational form. Their main criticisms included those of unjustified limitation to ministerial responsibility, inadequate rules for monitoring their activities, and neglect of management. In a number of cases, ZBOs were used to avoid management rules of ministries which were considered too burdensome.

Box 4.1. **The Dutch agencies** (cont.)

The Dutch agency model was introduced in 1994 partly as an alternative to ZBOs. The goal was to create bodies which could avoid applying some of the management rules of ministries, without limiting ministerial responsibility.

In the Dutch agency model, agencies have a results-oriented operating system that is supported by accrual accounting. The model was introduced under the flag of differentiation in rules of control as a means to achieve greater efficiency:

- **Managerial differentiation.** Agencies have been given their own separate identity. This differentiation has taken shape by distinguishing a number of roles: the contractor (the agency), the principal (chiefly, the policy department), and the owner (chiefly, the [deputy] secretary-general). The relationship between the agency and the principal is characterised by making agreements in advance about the products and services that will be supplied and giving account of their realisation. Management is in terms of achievements and cost prices. An internal market has been created. Some agencies have several clients, others only one. Most agencies function more or less as a monopoly.

- **Administrative differentiation**. Agencies are the only services that make use of accrual accounting. This involves, among other things, creating reserves, drawing up a balance, a cash-flow review and a profit-and-loss account, and the creation and maintenance of internal capital. Accrual accounting provides better opportunities for determining cost prices than the commitment-cash accounting system.

In January 2003, 65% of civil servants were working in agencies, and expectations were that the number would rise to 80% in January 2005. Most agencies implement services and inspectorates and it is expected that what will remain within the ministries – in the long term – is a nucleus involving policy that does not seem suited to the agency model.

The conditions for establishing an agency have tightened considerably following their first nationwide evaluation in 2002. There are now 12 establishment conditions that apply, that regard mostly having an environmental analysis, a good identification of measurable services, a description of the operating processes, a cost price model, a model of evaluation, an external results-oriented planning and control cycle, the identification of risks, and a number of conditions that apply to agencies that will be using accrual accounting.

Source: Drawn from Van Oosteroom (2002a and 2002b).

Figure 4.1. **Trends in independent regulatory authorities in OECD countries**

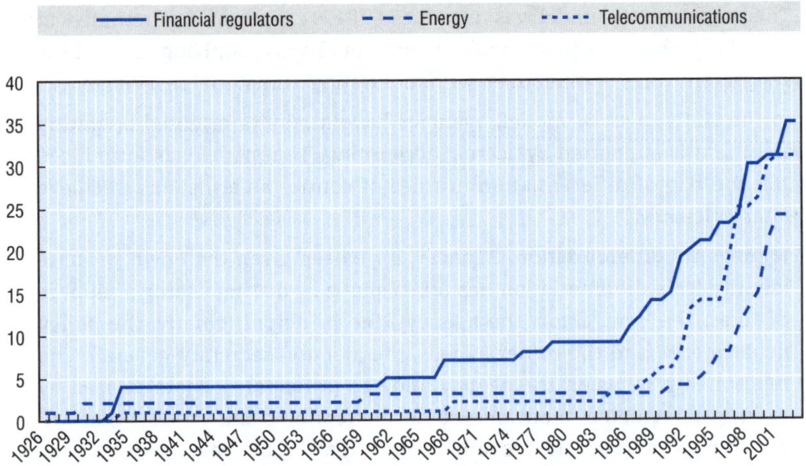

Source: OECD (2004e).

implement specific policies, has increased significantly across OECD countries. This trend has accompanied the deregulation and privatisation process experienced in OECD countries since the early 1970s. Many countries have set up or are establishing new market-oriented regulatory arrangements for utilities such as electricity and water and for telecommunications, financial services, or the social and environmental area.[2] The independent regulators play an important role in balancing the public interest in access to utilities at a reasonable cost with the commercial imperatives of the supplier while keeping the whole system at arm's length from political interference.

7. An organisational zoo?[3]

Partial data show that in some OECD countries these arm's-length bodies in central government now account for more than 50% of public expenditure and public employment.

However, there is no universally accepted classification of arm's-length bodies. They differ widely in terms of organisation, legal status, and degree of management autonomy or political independence. Basically governments have used three main methods to distance these bodies from core ministries:[4]

1. A top governance structure:

- A different hierarchy from traditionally functioning vertically integrated ministries, reporting directly to the minister, the chief executive of the

> **Box 4.2. Examples of arm's-length government in some OECD countries**
>
> - In the United Kingdom today, there are 131 executive agencies employing over three-quarters of the civil service. All executive agencies have been established within the past 15 years. In addition, as of March 2000, there were 1 035 non-departmental public bodies, employing over 115 000 staff and spending approximately £24 billion per year.
>
> - In Spain, more than 51% of the budget is spent by government-related entities (including entities that provide goods and services for commercial transaction but that are not State-owned enterprises); most of this, however, is allocated to the administration of social security.
>
> - In Sweden, there are approximately 300 central agencies today and only a small percentage of civil servants are employed by ministries and not by agencies.
>
> - In France, there are approximately 1 300 "public establishments" created by the national government and an estimated 50 000 created by local authorities.
>
> - In New Zealand, there are 79 Crown entities – excluding schools, tertiary education facilities, fish and game councils and reserve boards – employing approximately 80% of State sector employees and representing 58% of the Crown's expenses.
>
> - In Germany today, only about 6% of federal public employees work directly within federal ministries, while 22% work in federal agencies and 40% are civilians working in the military.
>
> - In the Netherlands, the Dutch agencies alone represent approximately 30% of the civil service, and it is estimated that by 2004 this percentage will increase to 80%. In addition, there are 339 independent administrative bodies ("ZBOs").
>
> Source: Drawn from OECD (2002a).

ministry, and in a few cases to the head of government or the whole of Cabinet. The chief executive is usually nominated through procedures that differ from those which apply in the traditional civil service. The chief executive can be nominated by the line minister (sometimes requiring the approval of the full Cabinet or the legislature), or by governing boards where they exist.

- Different responsibilities at the top of the hierarchy. The chief executive is generally responsible for the overall organisation, management and staffing of the entity, and for its financial and other procedures, including conduct and discipline. Programme design is a shared responsibility between the line minister/ministry, the governing boards (where they exist), and the chief executive. Depending on the nature of the entity, the minister may inform the entity of the government's expectations and policies, direct the board, take part in decisions about capital injections, monitor performance, and decide on the nature of regulations.

- Governing boards. In some cases, these bodies are directed by a governing board, which usually includes high-level civil servants designated by central government but also other representatives from the private sector and civil society. Governing boards have extensive strategic decision-making power that can extend to developing policies and strategies, providing information about objectives and their achievement, and ensuring commitment to core values and compliance with legal and financial requirements. They might even choose the chief executive. Usually, ministers remain responsible for appointing board members and, more often than not, have a role to play in the appointment of the chief executive.

- Management boards. In other cases, bodies are directed by a management board, which includes officials from the agency and officials from the reporting ministry and the Ministry of Finance and even, in some cases, external members. Managing boards generally lack the policy and strategic decision-making capacity of governing boards.

- Advisory boards. Finally, the governing of agencies and authorities may be shared between the line ministry/minister and the chief executive, but with advice from an advisory board with no decision-making power.

2. A different control environment:

- Personnel rules. Depending on the type of body, personnel may be employed under general civil service rules with flexibility in fixing grades, pay, bonus schemes and recruitment and promotion systems. In other cases, staff may not be considered part of the civil service and may be employed under general employment laws.

- Budgeting, accounting and finance rules. Depending on the type of body, these bodies may be fully funded by taxes, or partially or completely funded by user fees or private revenue. They may be authorised to borrow, lend and carry forward their surpluses.

3. Some management autonomy:[5]

- Management autonomy refers to senior management's ability to make decisions concerning the overall organisation and financial and personnel management of the entity without the constant involvement or need for approval by the line minister or ministry. While this has not been the case in many countries, an increasing proportion of these bodies now seem to have acquired significant management autonomy.

- Contract management. Many of these bodies have a quasi or fully contractual relationship with their line ministry/minister. Targets are set jointly by the line ministry and the chief executive and boards (where they exist), and chief executives report on, and are accountable for, the achievement of these targets.

- Output/outcome-oriented budgeting and management. In many cases, contract management increasingly goes hand-in-hand with output/ outcome-oriented budgeting and management. Controls on inputs are being increasingly relaxed.

- Multi-year budgeting. Increasingly, governments are trying to establish multi-year budget allocations for these bodies in exchange for a commitment to a range of services and results.

8. How successful are arm's-length bodies?

In the case of bodies functioning with some managerial autonomy, various internal government studies point to improved efficiency and effectiveness or to major cultural change. A United Kingdom report says the government has achieved "revolutionary changes in the culture, process and accountability of services directly delivered by central government" (H.M. Treasury and the Prime Minister's Office of Public Services Reform, 2002, p. 5), as well as "genuine improvements in customer service and an increased focus on results and business planning." In 2002, a Dutch government evaluation of its new agency model concluded that the agency form does contribute to improving efficiency (Van Oosteroom, 2002b).

It is also significant that, over the past 50 years, only a few autonomous bodies have been brought back under the core traditional hierarchy. Many countries are trying different organisational forms to find the best institutional features to fit their own needs, but the idea that some important parts of core government should be at arm's length is not called into question. What is now at the core of the debate is what institutional features give the best balance between autonomy and control.

8.1. What are the new governance challenges?

There is mounting evidence that OECD countries that have delegated a lot of responsibility to arm's-length bodies are rethinking the challenges this creates. So far they have reported the following main problems which have arisen as a result of distributed governance:

- The large number of new organisational forms and governance structures, management regimes and reporting mechanisms has resulted in a blurred picture of how the system is functioning. Ministries are having to adapt their steering and control mechanisms to too many different types of bodies. This weakens overall control by parliament and may damage citizens' confidence and trust in the system because it is too complicated to understand. A few OECD countries have addressed this problem with umbrella legislation that defines the options for different organisational structures within the public sector and creates standard for their governance.

- Delegating responsibilities to arm's-length bodies has led to difficulties in co-ordinating government work. Government coherence suffers from a lack of co-ordination in the definition of objectives, but also in the way government functions to perform these objectives. The lack of co-ordination may also eventually result in overlaps and duplication of work. This will be all the more damaging as arm's-length organisations are more difficult to restructure than classic units within ministries.

- Perhaps more importantly, distributed governance has inherent risks for democratic control and accountability. When bodies are removed from immediate supervision and have a more complex governance structure involving other stakeholders than their parent ministries, political control of these bodies may suffer. Without adequate steering, arm's-length bodies may follow policies that favour their own interests and are not responsive to policy needs. In addition, output/outcome budget and management rules require that reporting bodies have very strong capacities in these fields, for which they remain unprepared in a large number of cases. In addition to the risks of undiagnosed non-performance, this may also eventually result in increased corruption.

Not all of these risks, however, apply to all types of arm's-length organisations. They vary significantly with different institutional features.

It is possible to draw conclusions from OECD countries' experience as to the basic conditions for a successful and sustainable distributed governance system for most of them. These conditions include a sound legal and institutional framework that would limit the number of types of arm's-length bodies, give them a clear legal basis and justify any exceptions to the stated rules. A well thought through structure for individual institutions is

Table 4.1. **Matching the organisational features of agencies, authorities and other government bodies with the reasons for their creation**

| | Organisational features | | |
Reasons for their creation	Differentiated governance structure	Differentiated control environment	Management autonomy
Specialisation and focus on clients' needs	Possible	Possible	Required
Managerialism and focus on outputs/outcomes	Possible	Possible	Required
Lighter administrative and financial rules	Possible	Required	Not required
Policy independence	Required	Not required	Possible
Policy continuity	Required	Possible	Possible
Civil society participation	Required	Possible	Possible
Collaborative partnerships	Required	Possible	Possible

Source: OECD (2002a).

also important, as is a phased process for the introduction of new organisational types. Not all bodies will be ready at the same time to accept a high degree of autonomy, not least because governments need to make sure they have enough managers available to work at arm's length in an outcome-based environment. This is especially an issue in relatively small countries.

One problem is that the ministries responsible for monitoring the arm's-length bodies may be slower to adapt to performance-based management than the newly-created organisations, and dealing with this is a key challenge in establishing a well-functioning distributed governance system.

In any case, building capacity takes time. It takes months, and often years, to transform part of a traditional ministry hierarchy into an arm's-length body that functions well, and for the supervisory ministry to be able to steer it well. The process of getting things right cannot be entirely driven by the top but depends on co-operation and learning from both parties.

9. Balancing benefits and risks of organisational change

To conclude, structural change can be a powerful lever for reform but it can also be risky. The political benefits of signalling change through re-organisation tend to come at the beginning, and the real costs later. This is particularly the case where re-organisation is used to distinguish a government from its predecessor or to give the impression of activity while avoiding hard decisions. Re-organisations can distract staff attention, increase staff insecurity, and distract management attention from immediate challenges. If major staff changes occur, there can be significant costs due to the time necessary to make new appointments, and there are also risks associated with the loss of institutional memory, networks, and values.

The consequences of structural change sometimes go beyond their original intent and may influence not only the decision-making process and management culture of the organisation concerned, but also the whole government decision-making process. So governments must be aware of the direct and indirect costs when adapting the machinery of government to changing national circumstances, and of the alternatives to re-organisation. It is thus important to ensure that the threshold for creating new organisations is high, that the requirements for different kinds of organisational form are spelled out in legislation in many cases, and that other alternatives for solving the problem are fully considered. Alternatives to structural changes include improving decision-making processes, performance management, accountability and control, programme design, administrative and financial processes, level of resources, and leadership.

The politically-driven trends of merging and separating public sector functions as ministerial portfolios are changed by policy and political considerations seem likely to intensify because they have become part of government's armoury of public persuasion. If the civil service is to be able to adjust to these changes without unnecessary loss of capacity to serve the government and the public, it is important that senior public servants are able to move to different functions within the organisation and that there is a whole-of-government culture that transcends the diversification in individual ministries and departments.

It is also important to remember that changes to organisational structures do not, of themselves, ensure management changes. For example, separating ministries into different entities cannot in itself create more focus or more management if other incentives are not established. Achieving the purposes of changes to structures requires good leaders driving a determined process of aligning policies, procedures and ultimately the hearts and minds of staff with the wider government purpose.

The wholesale creation of agencies within the public sector has been used in recent times with success in three OECD countries – the Netherlands, New Zealand and the United Kingdom. It has a much longer history in Scandinavia, particularly in Sweden. There are two very important points to note. First there are very big differences in how these countries have set up and managed these more independent bodies. Second, their success has been highly dependent on the nature of the wider political and administrative culture in which they are embedded. The same organisational structures in a different institutional setting will produce different results.

10. Using the budget process for strategic reallocation and re-engineering

After decades of annually increasing public expenditure relative to the economy, beginning from the 1970s OECD member countries began to run into serious fiscal difficulties and had to cap public expenditure, including the cost of public debt, at a sustainable level. This situation forced governments to make more aggressive and strategic use of the budget process. It was to render these policies effective that some governments began to budget over a longer time period – another important trend. Budget limits for a one-year period tended not to be effective as officials were tempted to fiddle with the timing of expenditure rather than take hard decisions.

The most important change was the move to "top-down" budgeting. Instead of deciding what public services were needed in detail, and then budgeting the necessary total resources, governments took a single decision on the total expenditure limit for government (sometimes broken down into major sectors) for the period, and then allocated funds to specific activities only up to these limits. This took the budget from being a financing device to a tool for strategic management. And this gave many budget offices a new role as the secretariat for the whole-of-government strategic management. The trend to top-down budgeting was further strengthened when the European Union set upper limits to its members' budget deficits and debt.

The transitions governments made during the 1980s and early 1990s were typically not smooth. In that period fiscal stress was usually caused by increased demand for services and by their increased costs, especially in the spheres of health, social security and education, and stagnating revenue due to sluggish macroeconomic performance. When it became apparent that the some of the upward pressures on expenditure were not cyclical, and the deficit continued to grow, governments were forced into strong action to reduce debt and public expenditure to a sustainable level. These episodes, of which there have been several amongst OECD member countries, can be described as "Big Bang" reforms (OECD, 2005d). In many cases, the government announces its intention to reduce or reallocate public expenditure as a national priority and then supports a group of central agency officials in a top-down expenditure cutting process which continues until the target is met – or political support expires. Typically these adjustments are painful both for politicians and public servants but they seem to be unavoidable.

This type of across-the-board reduction, coupled with the realisation that it was not a temporary budgetary expedient, put pressure on governments to find ways of making real long-term savings and finding efficiency gains so that they could continue to meet their responsibilities with a lower level of funding. Thus it tended to encourage structural and procedural changes and innovative thinking about public sector management.

In the 1990s, patterns of reallocation typically changed. In this period reallocation was caused not so much by fiscal stress, but by fiscal abundance. Many countries experienced strong economic growth and reallocations tended to be caused by the reorientation of political priorities or overspending on specific programmes, often in the sphere of social security or subsidies to the private sector, which turned out to be ill-designed. Fiscal abundance, in contrast to fiscal stress, generally gives rise to the adjustment of programmes (extensions in this case) in specific areas, rather than adjustments across the board. Although programme extensions during the 1990s went in different directions in OECD countries, there was a general tendency towards increased expenditures on infrastructure, education and health.

At the end of the 1990s, the fiscal situation started to tighten again and this time reactions were different. Many countries strengthened their fiscal rules or rules of budgetary discipline and tried in this way to avoid the painful experiences of the 1980s. Some introduced or reinforced procedures aimed at a more systematic and regular review of existing programmes in order to avoid the Big Bang retrenchment operations of the past. The most notable examples of such review procedures are the spending review process in the United Kingdom and the process of interdepartmental policy review in the Netherlands (see Box 4.3 for details).

Box 4.3. **Designing successful programme review mechanisms**

Relevant cases:

- United Kingdom: Spending Reviews 1998
- Netherlands: Interdepartmental policy reviews

Of the numerous efforts to establish ongoing programme review exercises that facilitate targeted expenditure reallocation, only those of the Netherlands and the United Kingdom appear to have been successful. Attempts have been made in Canada and New Zealand to establish a similar system but neither of these processes was sustainable, although both countries continue to move toward this objective. In addition, the Program Assessment Rating Tool (PART) system introduced in the United States may prove successful, although it is still too early to judge. Given the interest in establishing programme review mechanisms, the processes of spending review and interdepartmental policy reviews are described below.

Box 4.3. **Designing successful programme review mechanisms** (*cont.*)

Spending review process

The government of the United Kingdom introduced a new biannual Spending Review process to set departmental spending plans for the three years following, as part of broader budget reforms in 1998. The reforms were intended to address criticism of the previous control regime – that is, that it did not distinguish between capital and current spending, that it was focused on cash inputs instead of outcomes, and that the annual spending round was too short a planning horizon. The Spending Reviews cover discretionary spending (with the exceptions of transport and health) and set new spending and performance plans (public service agreements, PSAs) for two additional years beyond the existing plans. Non-discretionary, so-called annually managed expenditure (AME) is also excluded from the process.

While the review process has been adapted each year since implementation, the basic steps remain unchanged. The process lasts about one year and includes the following key milestones (based on the 2002 Spending Review):

● The chief secretary (budget minister) writes to departments setting out the framework for the review.

● The Cabinet Committee on Public Services and Public Expenditure (PSX) (chaired by the chancellor) meets with secretaries of State of spending departments to discuss progress against targets and objectives, and considers papers from each department setting out key strategic challenges.

● Departments submit an analysis of resources and a draft public service agreement to the treasury. The latter sets out what the department proposes to achieve with its resources over the Spending Review period.

● The budget in March forecasts revenues over the period covered by the Spending Review, and an envelope for total public spending for the period is derived from that forecast, split into current and capital spending.

● Analysis of resources and draft PSAs are scrutinised by treasury spending teams and treasury ministers; negotiations take place at official and ministerial level between the treasury and spending departments.

● Departmental spending plans and PSAs are discussed and agreed between the chancellor, the prime minister and the relevant departmental minister. The outcome of the review is published; spending plans decided on in the Spending Review are fixed and not subsequently reopened.

Box 4.3. **Designing successful programme review mechanisms** (cont.)

Interdepartmental policy review

The Reconsideration procedure introduced in the Netherlands in 1981 forms the basis of the current system of programme review. Under this system, policy reviews are conducted with the purpose of developing alternatives that would yield savings preferably based on efficiency measures but, if necessary, based on reduction of service levels. Only alternatives costing the same or less can be considered. Each review has to produce at least one alternative that would lead to a 20% reduction of expenditure after four years compared to the current estimate of the last out-year. In the 1990s, the Reconsideration procedure was gradually adapted to changing economic circumstances. The mandatory 20% savings alternative has been abolished and reviews have become focused on institutional changes.

Nonetheless, the procedural and organisational aspects have remained unaltered since 1981, and include the following stages:

● Policy areas are proposed for review by the minister of finance, and the cabinet approves approximately ten reviews each year.

● The reviews are conducted by small working parties in which the spending ministry, the ministry of finance and the ministry of general affairs (the prime minister) are represented (often there are interdepartmental subjects so that more spending ministries are represented). The ministry of finance provides the secretariat for all reviews.

● External experts can also be invited to participate and at present the working parties conducting the review are mostly chaired by independent persons (university professors, officials who do not bear responsibility for the policy to be reviewed). In the working parties there is no right to veto against proposals for policy alternatives or against inclusion of factual information in the report.

● The whole procedure is supervised by a small interdepartmental committee of senior officials chaired by the director-general of the budget and a ministerial committee consisting of a few ministers chaired by the prime minister.

● All reports are made public and submitted to parliament. Reviews have to be finished in the spring so that their results can be used by the spending minister as well as by the minister of finance during budget preparation. The spending minister can use them, for instance, to comply with compensation requirements under rules of budgetary discipline. The minister of finance can use them in negotiations with spending ministers or while preparing general retrenchment operations. Apart from use in the budgetary process, the spending minister has to produce a cabinet statement on each review which, after approval in the cabinet, is submitted to parliament. A summary report of all reviews is submitted to parliament as part of the annual budget memorandum.

Box 4.3. **Designing successful programme review mechanisms** (*cont.*)

In summary, both processes are intended to provide budget decision makers with advice on resource allocation and possible reallocations; however, differences in budgetary procedures and political systems have produced quite different models of programme review. The United Kingdom system is biennial and incorporated into the broader system of resource allocation and performance management. The reviews cover all areas of departmental programme spending, and are undertaken by line agencies (albeit in consultation with the treasury). While the final report is published, the alternative recommendations constitute advice to the minister and the cabinet. In contrast, the process in the Netherlands focuses on relatively few policies (approximately ten) every year and is designed to focus exclusively on undertaking those reviews and developing recommendations. Reviews are conducted by cross-departmental working groups that include and are often chaired by external participants. The recommendations developed in the reviews are made public and can be used by line or central agencies, the cabinet, or opposition parties.

Finally, recent experience in the Netherlands highlights the fact that in both countries, reviews undertaken by the bureaucracy constitute advice to politicians and it is they who must then decide whether and how to implement those recommendations. During 2000 and 2001, active labour market policies were reviewed in an effort to make them more cost-effective, less complex, and more aligned with the shift toward private sector delivery agents. Completed during the summer of 2001, the review recommended a range of policy redesign measures that would enable substantial budgetary reductions. The political sensitivity of these reforms made implementation difficult and it was not until a right-wing coalition government was elected in May 2002 that any changes were implemented.

Source: OECD (2005d).

The budget process was the main instrument for signalling and enforcing fiscal restraint. Because the budget and reporting processes set the main rules for the public management system generally, it is also used by governments as the platform for public management reforms covering such policies as greater public transparency, emphasis on accountability for outputs or outcomes, better accounting information, conditions for grants, or changes in delegation to and autonomy of arm's-length bodies.

11. Findings and future challenges

Governments need to keep adjusting structures and reallocating. The pace at which societies are changing means that governments must keep adjusting their structures and reallocating resources if they are to discharge their responsibilities effectively. The long-standing tendency in many governments to accept structural arrangements as a "given" will be difficult to sustain in the future. Equally unsustainable is the deeply engrained disposition towards incremental budgeting.

The ability to look at public sector organisations in total and to make timely adjustments to them in response to the whole range of pressures operating on the public sector is essential for a modern government.

Restructuring should not be undertaken lightly. At the same time there are good reasons for conservatism in structural policy. In any complex area of activity, individuals are more effective if they work as part of an organisation, not only because of the advantages of division of labour and specialisation, but because organisations "contain" the professional culture which provides the values, capacity, knowledge and memory necessary for effective public policy. These attributes take many years to build up. Also, public sector organisations are not just a managerial device – they carry part of the burden of maintaining trust and confidence in the governmental process. Citizens expect continuity and "readability" in the organisation of government, and are disconcerted by change – though it is sometimes inevitable.

Furthermore, organisations need the reputation and professional relationships that allow them to work effectively with other organisations and individuals inside and outside government. Such relationships do not just happen – they are earned over time. Until this fabric of reputation and relationships is in place, any new public sector organisation is bureaucratically and politically very vulnerable, which explains the debilitating experience of reforms on top of reforms in some OECD member countries. Finally, if it is too easy for either politicians or bureaucrats to change organisational structures, there is a real risk that organisations will simply be changed, with all the attendant costs and collateral damage, instead of having their internal problems solved.

There should be a whole-of-government approach to restructuring. Whether governments are active or conservative relative to their organisation, there is a very strong case for a whole-of-government perspective on how structure relates to government's overall purposes and interests, and for whole-of-government rules and processes for the oversight and democratic accountability of such bodies.

The development of modern accounting and information technology has made arm's-length management of public agencies more possible. However, such bodies should still operate within the main body of administrative law, and cannot exist at the expense of the capacity for whole-of-government policy making and accountability. Countries wanting to transform some core ministerial bodies into more arm's-length agencies find the need to invest in strengthening their co-ordination mechanisms and core government steering capacities.

More autonomy is given to spending departments. The move to top-down budgeting and giving individual ministries an aggregate budget has meant a big change in where decisions are made within government. Spending departments now have much more autonomy and greater incentive to prioritise their own spending. This freedom has had a major impact on the dynamics of public management in those governments that have gone down this route. In some countries a little of this freedom has subsequently been clawed back by the formalisation of performance objectives and reports. However, it remains one of the most significant public management developments of the period under review.

The strategic use of the budget process emerged as the most powerful management innovation of the period under review both for resource reallocation and as a platform for management changes. Important too was the decentralisation of management responsibility which accompanied bulk funding.

Notes

1. As well as an increasing similarity in cabinet size, OECD countries have also converged in the overall governance structure of their cabinets. With the exception of New Zealand, for example, individual ministries have only one representative in the cabinet, and generally there are strong similarities in decision-making processes.

2. For further analysis and information on independent regulators, refer to the outcome of the meeting on regulatory authorities held in London in January 2005 (GOV/PGC/REG(2005)5 "Regulatory Authorities: Summary and Conclusions of the Expert Meeting"). The full proceedings will be made available on the Internet at *www.oecd.org/regref*. For a comparative overview of regulatory authorities, refer to OECD (2004e).

3. The following sections do not refer to independent regulatory agencies.

4. Drawn from OECD (2002a).

5. In many cases, a differentiated control environment is a key aspect of management autonomy. However, this is certainly not always the case. For example, central civil service rules on recruitment and remuneration conditions might be relaxed for some bodies (allowing employment of staff under general employment laws), but with a remaining strong control of central reporting

ministries on hiring levels, remuneration, etc. Conversely, entities might have considerable management autonomy (with flexibilities on overall inputs) while having to abide by budget financial and personnel rules that apply to all central ministries. For example, general civil service rules on hiring and remunerations might apply to an entity which still would have a lot of flexibility on hiring levels.

ISBN 92-64-01049-1
Modernising Government: The Way Forward
© OECD 2005

Chapter 5

The Use of Market-type Mechanisms to Provide Government Services[1]

1. Introduction

Market-type mechanisms are a broad concept. In the early 1990s, the OECD adopted the very comprehensive definition of "encompassing all arrangements where at least one significant characteristic of markets is present." In the area of service provision, the prime instruments include outsourcing (contracting out), public-private partnerships (PPPs) and vouchers. Other examples of market-type mechanisms include user charges and the use of transferable permits for allocating and managing limited-supply "public" goods (greenhouse gas emission, for example).

The use of market-type mechanisms is increasing in OECD member countries, although there are marked country differences in this respect. The driving force behind this phenomenon is the need for governments to secure increased value for money in their operations. Some market-type mechanisms, most notably vouchers, move beyond this and have as their primary goal to increase the choices offered to the users of services.

The evidence that market-type mechanisms can secure such efficiency gains, either through lower costs or improved service levels, is substantial. However, the decision to use market-type mechanisms needs to be made on a case-by-case basis and the specific design of these instruments is critical to their successful application.

There are significant management challenges for governments in moving to a market-type mechanism model, especially in separating the roles of government as purchaser and provider of services. Traditionally, governments performed these roles concurrently. Governments will have to invest in capacity for specifying services and contract management skills that they have not typically possessed in the past. It concerns both new technical skills and an overall culture change in the public service. By definition, it will not happen overnight.

Concerns have also been raised about the governance implications of the use of market-type mechanisms. At present, their use is secondary and operates at the margin of an overall dominant traditional role for government provision. The governance concerns will therefore likely increase as the use of market-type mechanisms expands. This is especially relevant for accountability, transparency, regularity and the access to redress mechanisms for citizens.

This chapter covers the main market-type mechanisms used for public service provision with a section each on outsourcing (contracting out), public-private partnerships (PPPs) and vouchers. Each section describes the instrument, surveys its use in OECD member countries, analyses the key issues involved – both in terms of design and governance factors – and offers an overall assessment. A box at the end of the chapter highlights the other principal market-type instruments. The chapter concludes by drawing together the main messages emerging from the discussion.

2. What are market-type mechanisms?

A broad definition of market-type mechanisms is that they encompass all arrangements where at least one significant characteristic of markets is present. Examples of specific kinds of market-type mechanisms are defined below.

Outsourcing is the practice whereby governments contract with private sector providers for the provision of services to government ministries and agencies, or directly to citizens on behalf of the government. Different terminology is used in different countries for outsourcing, including competitive tendering, contracting, and contracting out. The range of services outsourced in OECD member countries is very wide. They include blue collar support services (building cleaning, catering), professional services that are considered ancillary to the core mission of the ministry or agency (information technology), and core government functions (prisons).

Public-private partnerships (PPPs) refer to arrangements whereby the private sector finances, designs, builds, maintains, and operates infrastructure assets traditionally provided by the public sector. PPPs can also involve the private sector purchasing already existing infrastructure assets and redeveloping them. Public-private partnerships bring a single private sector entity to undertake to provide public infrastructure assets for their "whole of life", generally 20-30 years. (The asset usually reverts to the government at the end of this period.) The private sector partner then charges an annual fee for the use of the infrastructure assets. This can either be paid by the government or through user charges, or a combination of the two. PPPs are also known as private finance initiatives (PFI), projects for public services, and private projects. PPPs have been most extensively used in the provision of transportation infrastructure, but other examples include schools, hospitals, office buildings, and water and sewage treatment facilities.

Vouchers separate the provision of public services from its financing. The funding remains with the government in the form of a voucher that is issued to individuals and which entitles them to exchange the vouchers for services at a range of suppliers. The individual voucher-holder chooses among the different suppliers and pays with the voucher. Vouchers have been used for the provision of low-income (social) housing assistance, primary and secondary education, child care services, and care for the elderly.

Each of these mechanisms will be examined in turn.

3. Outsourcing

The primary objective of outsourcing is to increase efficiency by introducing a competitive environment for the provision of the services. The specific "business cases" for outsourcing generally cite one or more of the following points:

● to reduce costs;

● to access expertise not available in-house to meet one-off needs;

● to access expertise on a long-term basis in order to be able to vary its quantity and mix over time;

● to replace current government operations in extreme cases where their provision is unsatisfactory. This is rare and limited to cases where there is a long history of poor performance.

The use of outsourcing is clearly increasing in OECD countries although it is difficult to quantify precisely since governments do not maintain standardised or comparable data over time on their use. It should also be emphasised that outsourcing *per se* is not new in OECD member countries. For example, the use of private contractors for the construction of various infrastructure projects has been the norm in most countries for an extended time. Conceptually, this was viewed as an acquisition (procurement) rather than as outsourcing.

Figure 5.1, using data from Government Finance Statistics (GFS; see International Monetary Fund, 2001) as a proxy, quantifies the use of outsourcing in selected OECD member countries. The figure looks at the share of government's purchase of all goods and services from outside vendors as a proportion of total expenditures, excluding transfers and interest payments. As such, the figure includes purchases of items that would generally not be classified as outsourcing and the aggregate numbers should be deflated appropriately – most likely equivalent to about 15-20 percentage points of reported total outsourcing. The figure also applies only to central (national/federal) governments. As a result, country differences may in some cases reflect the different assignment of functions among different levels of government. Nonetheless, the strong variations between individual countries are striking.

Based on these calculations, the United Kingdom has the highest level of outsourcing activity among the selected countries. Its level of outsourcing is

Figure 5.1. **Outsourcing of government services**
Purchase of goods and services *vs.* in-house provision

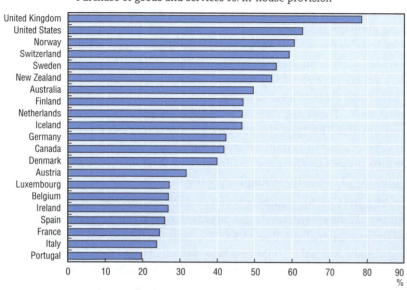

Source: OECD Secretariat calculations based on GFS data.

nearly four times that of the country with the lowest calculated level of outsourcing. In general, outsourcing is applied to a greater extent in the English-speaking countries and the Nordic countries, and much less so in the continental European countries. Among the first group of countries, outsourcing has also been increasing significantly in recent years. For example, outsourcing is estimated to have increased by 33% over the past 10 years in the United States (Eggers and Goldsmith, 2003).

Aside from different views of the appropriate role of the State, the strong country differences in the use of outsourcing also reflect the nature of the public sector labour market in individual countries. Continental European countries tend to have a less flexible public service which can make it prohibitively expensive to retrench public servants and outsource their activities. (See Chapter 6 for a more detailed discussion on delegation in the public sector.)

3.1. Outsourced activities

The range of services outsourced in OECD member countries is very wide. These can be divided into three distinct groups. The first consists of various blue collar support services. These are generally the first activities that governments outsource and are common to all countries. In some, the outsourcing of such services is essentially complete, with the government having withdrawn completely as a direct service provider. The second group consists of various activities that are considered ancillary to the core mission of the ministry or agency. This moves beyond the blue collar support services to include various high-value professional services – often "back-office" activities. This is an area where the greatest growth has occurred in recent years but country variations are more pronounced. The third group includes the outsourcing of mainline functions previously conducted by the government. These are core activities that many would view as inherently governmental. This type of outsourcing is rare across OECD member countries but is prominent in certain sectors in individual countries. The three groups are also progressively more challenging in implementation, including the availability of competitive supplier markets.

The first group includes services such as the cleaning of buildings, facilities management, waste management, operations of food service outlets and the provision of guard services. The common thread is that these services are generally low-value, relatively labour-intensive and not considered critical to the mission of the agency. However, these can take place under extreme circumstances – catering for combat soldiers in hostile environments or the protection of high-risk facilities such as nuclear sites.

The leading example of the second group is the outsourcing of information technology functions. This has been a major trend over the past years with private providers taking on ever larger parts of the information technology infrastructure in government ministries and agencies. This often entails the outsourcing of related back-office operations. Other common examples include the outsourcing of legal, human resource management, banking and financial services. These are generally high-value services that are ancillary to the core mission of an agency but are nonetheless critical to its operations. Another characteristic of this group is that the functions outsourced are often complex in nature and involve rapid change in their operating environment.

The extreme example of outsourced services that many would view as inherently governmental is the outsourcing of prisons (Australia, Canada, United Kingdom, United States). Other core functions that have been outsourced include emergency rescue and fire services (Denmark), enforcement activities such as food inspection (Iceland), and the services of the audit office (New Zealand).

The use of outsourcing in health, education and welfare services has made important inroads in certain countries. This includes employment (job placement) services, diagnostic services, specialised hospital care, care centres for children, education, child welfare services, and long-term care institutions for the elderly and for the handicapped. Outsourcing in this field has in some cases been motivated primarily by the poor performance of the previous government providers. In some cases, contracts are awarded based on a standard competitive tendering process. In others, contracts are made with a set of suppliers allowing users a choice of supplier as with a voucher scheme (see subsequent section on vouchers).

The outsourcing of research and development functions whereby private institutions compete for project-based funding has increased significantly and is an area where government withdrawal from a core area has been most pronounced across OECD member countries. Similarly common is the outsourcing of technical assistance in foreign aid programmes of OECD countries. The use of outsourcing for the operation of various infrastructure assets – transportation, water supply, sewerage – is also increasing in individual countries.

The evidence that outsourcing increases efficiency is substantial, with extensive studies having been conducted on the impact of outsourcing on service quality and costs. A survey of 66 large cities in the United States found that 82% of the cities reported they were satisfied or very satisfied with the resulting performance, and the remaining 18% were neutral. None were dissatisfied. The report found a 25% improvement in service on average. The shift to a competitive environment also resulted in savings of up to 60% (Dilger et al., 1997). A study of over 2 000 outsourcing initiatives in the United States federal government found an average cost savings of 33% with same or higher levels of service (Clark et al., 2001). In other countries, average cost savings have been estimated at 15-20% in Australia, 5-30% in Denmark, 20-25% in Iceland and 20% in the United Kingdom.

3.2. Key issues

A number of governance-related issues arise from outsourcing, many of which are applicable to the use of market-type mechanisms more generally.

There are strong obstacles to the introduction of outsourcing. This can be due to public concern about private sector involvement in traditional government activities. The variety of services outsourced in different countries shows that there are very few services that technically cannot be outsourced. Where outsourcing involves a direct challenge to existing government service provision there may be strong resistance from affected government employees, unions and their political allies.

Some OECD member countries have introduced mandatory policies to require market-testing (competitive sourcing) where existing employees compete with private providers for the provision of the services. This may be appropriate in the introductory phases of a new outsourcing policy but it creates a very adversarial relationship. More sustainable is to mainstream outsourcing policy and for it to become an established feature of everyday management decisions. Tight budgetary restrictions are a key impetus for achieving this as they promote the use of best value-for-money solutions for the provision of government services. Such an approach also makes outsourcing a more dynamic opportunity for re-engineering government services rather than being a mechanistic consideration of outsourcing existing services.

Outsourcing can generate governance concerns in terms of the accountability for the services being provided by a private contractor. This is especially relevant when that service is being provided directly to citizens on behalf of the government.

In the traditional provision of public services, accountability was essentially an in-house affair based on hierarchical controls focusing on inputs and processes. Outsourcing introduces a separation between the purchaser and provider and requires the specification of the services to be delivered together with appropriate performance measures. This should serve to significantly enhance accountability. Performance is now monitored against explicit standards, and the potential conflict of interest of having the same organisation (or even the same official) responsible both for assessing performance and acting as the service provider is avoided.

Accountability can however become blurred in this environment simply because of the introduction of a new actor. In the traditional model, accountability was clear in the sense that it was one organisation responsible for the whole process. With outsourcing, the government entity is still accountable for the service provided, including actions carried out on its behalf by the contractor, but day-to-day responsibility for specific actions will lie either with the government entity or the contractor. It may be difficult for the users of services to determine who is responsible for the delivery of the service, especially if this division of responsibility is not clear as can be the case.

In this context, the inherent political nature of the public sector needs to be recognised as well, and the role it can play in superseding a purely commercial framework. The public and the media will always hold a minister accountable overall and responsible for the specific actions of contractors. Similarly, public and media pressures focused on specific outsourcing activities can serve to override specific commercial terms in a contract, generally resulting in a renegotiation of the contract at higher cost. Such risks need to be taken into account.

The capacity of governments to outsource effectively needs to be established and sustained over time. This involves both retaining the technical expertise of the function being outsourced and developing the commercial skills for managing the outsourcing process. Based on countries' experiences, there is a risk that the technical capacity to assess future outsourcing options will be lost over time as the government is no longer directly providing the service. This may lead to a dependency on the incumbent contractor when the activity is re-tendered and/or may preclude the government from taking the activity back in-house. The commercial skills inherent with outsourcing are typically new to governments and need to be built up. It is important that these skills become an established and ongoing function rather than being seen as a one-off exercise each time. This has important implications for human resource management and internal structures of organisations.

The implications are well demonstrated in a report by a committee of the Australian Parliament reviewing the use of outsourcing for support services by the Australian Defence Forces (ADF):

> Frequently, the successful tenderer for the support contract relies on recruiting the trained Defence personnel who have been made redundant in the ADF because of the function's transfer to the commercial sector. Through employing these already-trained personnel, the successful civilian tenderer is able to provide a commercially attractive initial price for a support capability because there is no need to factor in staff training costs in the contract. This process becomes disadvantageous to Defence where the successful tenderer becomes the monopoly supplier of the support service, and Defence must subsequently renegotiate that contract from a position of weakness, having eliminated its own in-house capability to perform the particular function.

Joint Standing Committee on Foreign Affairs,
Defence and Trade (1998), p. 35.

Concerns have been raised about the nature of contract specificity in the public sector. Government contracts have a tendency to be prescriptive and process oriented, whereas private sector contracts tend to be more output (or outcome) oriented. There are several reasons for this. First, government agencies are rightly concerned with the accountability implications of outsourcing as noted above and are often more comfortable with these traditional means. Second, this may be a manifestation of resistance to outsourcing in agencies and designed to undermine its success. Third, it may be difficult to specify outputs (or outcomes) in concrete terms in some instances – in which case the decision to outsource in the first place should be questioned. The more prescriptive or input oriented the contract is, the more difficult it is for the contractors to be flexible and innovative in order to secure efficiency gains, which is the raison d'être for outsourcing.

The studies cited above on gains from outsourcing generally show the lower range of savings coming from input or process oriented contracts whereas the higher range of savings came from output (or outcome) oriented contracts. An innovative solution is for governments to engage in a two-stage bidding process. First, the government formally issues a tender offer but specifies its needs only in general terms. Contractors are invited to be creative in responding to those needs. Based on the information gathered in this first round, the government puts out a more detailed tender offer in the second phase (Healy and Linder, 2003). This strives to achieve a balance between efficiency (flexibility) and specificity.

In general, the flexibility (discretion) of a contractor needs to be weighed against the notion of regularity (equal treatment) which is a hallmark of the public sector. Contractors' discretion can become an issue when a service provider is accorded "the power of the State" in determining eligibility or levels of eligibility for certain services (for example, case management in social services). Similarly, contractors could offer services to different client groups in different manners. For example, an outsourced job placement provider may decide to provide an individual client with a bicycle in order to commute to a new job. As a result, the service provider secures a payment from the government for having successfully placed the individual in a job. However, there may have been another individual in a largely similar situation that was not provided with a bicycle. *Prima facie* this could be interpreted as violating the regularity principle of the public service. As part of their contracting functions, governments will need to be clear in establishing the boundaries for appropriate flexibility (discretion) in such cases.

Competitive supplier markets are a prerequisite for successful outsourcing. The government has a clear role to play in developing and sustaining such markets. Depending on the service that the government is outsourcing – commodity-like services *vs.* highly specialised services – such markets may not be in place when the government embarks on outsourcing. The government may in effect have to create such markets through its volume buying. As a result, the full efficiency gains achieved by outsourcing may materialise over time. The government also needs to ensure that its outsourcing policies promote sustainable competitive markets by avoiding over-reliance on a single supplier. Similarly, the length and size of individual contracts can impact the number of potential suppliers. In short, the government needs to focus on the impact on the supplier market-place of individual outsourcing decisions (United Kingdom Office of Government Commerce, 2003).

Lowest cost is traditionally the main criterion that determines a winning bid. There are examples of suppliers submitting unrealistically low bids ("low-balling") and then engaging in post-contract negotiations over the lifetime of the contract to increase the price. Such practices undermine individual outsourcing projects and may lead to reliable suppliers withdrawing from the government market-place in general.

As discussed above, transparency is clearly enhanced with the specification of services to be delivered together with appropriate performance measures. As discussed in Chapter 1, there are however some aspects inherent with market-type mechanisms that can reduce transparency. This is due to the fact that information which was previously in the public domain is now in the hands of private contractors; the public's right to access that information may be impaired. The general tendency in the private sector is for contents of contracts not to be made publicly available. They are considered commercially sensitive. This may justifiably apply in some cases (for example, protection of intellectual property) but is otherwise inappropriate in the public sector context. Appropriate information needs to be publicly available in order for outsiders to be in a position to make an informed judgement about the contracting decision. More generally, contract provisions need to ensure that sufficient information is turned over from the private provider to the purchaser organisation in order for the latter to maintain up-to-date knowledge of the activity for future tendering, i.e. to maintain capacity to avoid capture by the private provider.

Finally, the public sector has over time developed elaborate redress instruments for citizens. These include laws on administrative procedure, Ombudsmen, freedom of information, whistleblower protection and the like. In general, the jurisdiction of such instruments does not extend to private sector providers. It is therefore important for contracts to incorporate appropriate redress mechanisms. These will of course vary on a case-by-case basis but are most applicable to where the contractor is exercising a degree of flexibility (discretion) as noted previously. Governments will also need to ensure that contractors employ appropriate mechanisms to protect the privacy of confidential information they acquire on individual citizens.

3.3. Conclusion

Outsourcing has grown significantly over the past 15 years. It has been shown to be applicable to a wide range of government services. Apart from transitional concerns relating to the disturbance of vested interests, or change in the familiar profile of government, the constraints relate to the degree to which the delivery of the service can be monitored at arm's length, the need to maintain government's core capacity now and for the future, and the protection of other core governance principles. The benefits of outsourcing in terms of increased efficiency can be significant and the services that have been outsourced rarely revert back to government provision. Outsourcing can be expected to increase substantially in the coming years.

Box 5.1. **Staff issues associated with outsourcing**

The manner of moving to outsourcing is important. Staff will generally resist outsourcing initiatives, and morale among staff can decline during the process. The outsourcing process can take an extended period of time with anxiety building up during this period especially if communications with employees are poor. This insecurity caused by not being kept informed has been cited by some as the main staff concern in outsourcing.

Employees are often transferred to the private provider with their working conditions guaranteed, at least for a certain time period. It is by no means a given that working conditions will deteriorate with outsourcing. For example, a staff member whose function is ancillary to the core work of an agency will likely have an improved career track in a firm that specialises in that "ancillary" function.

There is specific legislation in place for the transfer of employee rights with outsourcing in the European Union. In the United States, federal legislation is in place that stipulates that certain benefits (for example, health care) offered by private providers have to be comparable to those for government employees. In some countries, a "clean break" approach is preferred whereby the government settles any redundancy payments and there are no transfers of rights. Governments may also have policies in place whereby preference is given to staff affected by outsourcing for other positions if they do not want to leave government employment.

4. Public-private partnerships

Public-private partnerships (PPPs) refer to arrangements whereby the private sector finances, designs, builds, maintains, and operates (DBFMO) infrastructure assets traditionally provided by the public sector.[2] Private sector involvement in individual aspects of DBFMO has been the norm in most OECD member countries for an extended time. Governments contract with private sector architects for the design of assets, with private sector contractors for the construction of assets, with various private sector entities for the maintenance and operation of assets. These have, however, been discrete activities with different private sector contractors performing each different aspect. With PPPs, a single entity is responsible for the infrastructure's "whole of life." As such they can be viewed as a specialised form of outsourcing, with the very notable difference that the private partner is responsible for providing the financing for the project.

Public-private partnerships – as a distinct concept – originated in the United Kingdom in 1992. The United Kingdom is today by far the largest user of PPPs among OECD member countries. Their use has, however, expanded to virtually all other OECD countries. Table 5.1 provides an overview of PPP activity in selected countries.

PPPs have most commonly been applied for the provision of highway infrastructure. For example, Portugal's ambitious EUR 5 billion National Road Programme employs PPPs. They are also used for other transportation infrastructure – such as airports and railways. The Netherlands is using a PPP programme to introduce high-speed rail links for the Thalys trains in the Netherlands. The new Athens airport was built on a PPP basis. The light rail linking Stockholm with Arlanda Airport employed the PPP model. PPPs are increasingly being used for environmental infrastructure projects such as water systems and solid waste facilities. In terms of number of projects, the greatest use has been for the provision of buildings – including schools, hospitals, nursing homes, prisons, embassies and general office buildings. In these cases, PPPs generally cover the building only and not the specialised services operated in the respective building. For example, the clinical services of a PPP-procured hospital would not be the responsibility of the private partner.

The extent of use of PPPs should, however, not be exaggerated. In the United Kingdom, only about one-tenth of its total capital investments in public services in 2003-04 were through PPPs and this has been relatively consistent over time. In other words, about nine-tenths of investments are conducted through traditional procurement practices.

Appropriately structured PPPs have the potential to improve the efficiency of the design-build-maintain-operate phases. The largest analysis of a PPP programme was undertaken in the United Kingdom in 2003 (H.M. Treasury, 2003). Nearly 90% of all PPP projects were delivered on time by the private partner whereas only approximately 30% of non-PPP projects were delivered on time. Four-fifths of all PPP projects were delivered on budget whereas only one-fourth of non-PPP projects were delivered on budget. All PPP projects that experienced budget overruns were due to changes in requirements by the government. In terms of operational performance, 35% of projects were assessed as "expected", 16% as "surpassing", 25% as "far surpassing" expectations. One-quarter of projects, however, did not meet expectations. (This analysis can also be seen as an indictment of the traditional procurement process for such projects in the United Kingdom.)

Analysis of other national PPP programmes have not been undertaken in such a comprehensive manner but the general assessment is similarly positive with the design-build-maintain-operate phases.

Table 5.1. **Summary of PPPs by country and sector**

	Roads & bridges	Light railway	Heavy railway	Schools	Health & hospitals	Central accommodation	Airports	Housing	Ports	Prisons	Water & wastewater (including solid waste)
EU Member States	Principal sectors of PPP activity					Subsidiary sectors of PPP activity					
Austria	▲		▲	•	▲	•	•			•	•
Belgium	▲	•	•	•			▲	▲			▲
Cyprus	▲						♦		▲		▲
Czech Republic	▲	•	•	•	•		•	•			♦
Denmark	▲		▲	▲		•			▲	•	
Estonia	•			•	•						
Finland	▲	•		▲		•					•
France	★	★	▲	•	▲	▲	▲		▲	▲	★
Germany	♦	♦	♦	♦	•	▲	•			▲	■
Greece	♦					•	★				
Hungary	♦	•		♦	▲			•		▲	♦
Ireland	■	▲		♦	▲	•		▲			■
Italy	■	♦			♦	•	▲	•	▲	•	▲
Latvia	•						•				
Lithuania		•									
Luxembourg						•					
Malta					▲		•				
Netherlands	♦		♦	▲	•	•		•	•	•	♦
Poland	▲	•	•			•	•	•	▲		▲
Portugal	★	♦	•	•	▲		•	•	•	•	♦
Slovakia	•						•				•
Slovenia											♦
Spain	★	♦	•	•	▲	•	•		★		♦
Sweden	•	•	•		•						
United Kingdom	★	★		★	★	★	★	★		★	★
Other											
Bulgaria	•						•				♦
Norway	♦		•	▲	▲	•				•	
Romania	♦				▲			•			♦
Turkey	•	•	•				♦				♦

• Discussions ongoing
▲ Projects in procurement
♦ Many procured projects, some projects closed
■ Substantial number of closed projects
★ Substantial number of closed projects, majority of them in operation

Source: European Investment Bank (2004), *The EIB's role in public-private partnerships,* July.

4.1. The transfer of risk

The objective of PPPs is to achieve efficiency gains through competition by private sector providers, transferring risks from the government, and taking advantage of private sector expertise. The effective transfer of risk is paramount to the success of PPPs and a key distinguishing factor of the PPP concept. There are a great number of specific risks but they can usefully be divided into three broad categories: construction risk, availability risk and demand risk.[3]

Construction risk covers events such as late delivery, additional costs, and technical deficiency. If the government is obliged to start making regular payments to a partner without taking into account the effective state of the asset, this would be considered evidence that the government bears the majority of the construction risk.

Availability risk is when the partner does not deliver the volume that was contractually agreed or fails to meet specified safety or public certification standards relating to the provision of services to final users. It also applies where the partner does not meet the specified quality standards relating to the delivery of the services. If the government is obliged to continue making regular payments regardless of the lack of availability of the asset, it is deemed that the government bears the majority of the availability risk.

Demand risk covers the variability in demand (higher or lower than expected when the contract was signed) irrespective of the behaviour of the private partner. This risk should only cover a shift in demand not resulting from inadequate or low quality of the service provided by the partner or any action that changes the quantity/quality of services provided. Instead, it should result from other factors, such as the business cycle, new market trends, direct competition or technological obsolescence. If the government is obliged to ensure a given level of payment to the private partner independently of the effective levels of demand expressed by the final user, rendering irrelevant the fluctuations in level of demand on the private partner's profitability, the government is deemed to bear the majority of the demand risk.

The efficiency gains with PPPs derive from these transfers of risks and the whole-of-life perspective. For example, the quality of the design and building phases will have a significant impact on their subsequent maintenance and operation. The private partner has a direct financial interest in ensuring the long-term success of the project.

The objective, however, is not simply to transfer as much risk as possible to the private partner, but to assign risks to the party that is best able to manage them, whether they remain with the government or go to the private partner. In short, the entity that is best able to mitigate each risk should be responsible for it. Transferring too little risk and transferring too much risk are both equally undesirable. The government will expose itself to excessive contingent liabilities if it transfers too little risk whereas transferring too much risk can result in the private partner demanding an excessive fee for taking on the risk. There are no comprehensive rules as to what is the appropriate distribution of risk since all projects are different.

4.2. Financing

It is crucial that the private partner provide the project financing in order to have the proper incentives and assume the appropriate risks. If non-performance occurs, not only will the private partner be deprived of the annual fee paid by the government, but it will continue to be responsible for servicing the debt associated with the project. This is a powerful financial incentive for performance.

The major debate with PPPs, however, concerns the financing phase – notably how PPP financing relates to the traditional budget system and the cost of capital for the private partner.

The use of PPPs may offer governments – specific ministries – the possibility to bypass the established processes for ensuring budgetary discipline and constraining expenditure. Traditional procurements would record the investments as a "lump sum" up front and would form part of the government's bottom-line surplus or deficit in that year. It would be subject to the same scrutiny as other expenditures. In a PPP environment, the investment may not be recorded up front, with only the annual fee paid to the private partner being recorded in each year's budget for the infrastructure's "whole of life". The original investment could escape the scrutiny of the budget process, and future flexibility could be limited by the annual fees required to be paid to the private partner.

If a PPP is structured in such a way as to move the majority of the risk to the private partner, it may be appropriate to record investment and associated debt off budget. For example, the fiscal criteria for the European single currency allow governments to record transactions this way if the construction risk and either the supply risk or the demand risk are transferred to the private partner. These are however very liberal criteria. Outside the EU, not even such criteria apply. No international public sector accounting standards (IPSAS) have been developed. In fact, governments could retain all the risk and use the PPP device solely for the purpose of not recording the transaction on budget.

The private partner's cost of capital will always be higher than the government's "risk-free" cost of capital. This is regardless of whether the payments by the government for the project, as called for in the PPP contract, are used as collateral by the private partner for obtaining financing for the loan. The government's power to tax reduces default risk *vis-à-vis* other borrowers such that the private sector is willing to lend money to governments at a risk-free rate regardless of the underlying risks associated with the projects that the government may use the money for.[4]

It is, however, important to note that PPPs involve a transfer of risk from the government to the private partner, thus relieving the government of such contingent liabilities. The government's risk-free cost of borrowing does not reflect such project risks as discussed above, whereas those risks are very real. The private partner's cost of borrowing will, however, incorporate the project risks. It is inherently difficult to isolate, analyse and quantify this risk premium. It is nonetheless a fact that a private partner will have a higher cost of capital than the government, and whether the transfer of risk from the government is commensurate with that is difficult to establish (International Monetary Fund, 2004). From a public finance point of view, a PPP can only be justified if the transfer of risks and the efficiency gains outweigh the higher cost of capital. It is therefore essential that the decision to use the PPP model as opposed to traditional procurement be based on a rigorous and dynamic comparison of the benefits and costs of each approach.

4.3. Conclusion

The use of PPPs stabilised at around one-tenth of total annual capital procurement in the one country where it has been most extensively used. PPPs appear to be most appealing for large-scale projects that involve extensive maintenance and operating requirements over the project's "whole of life". This explains why highways are such prominent examples of PPPs. The size of the project is a prerequisite since the transaction costs involved in preparing the project for bid and negotiating the contracts are such that they can only be justified for large-scale projects. The bundling of projects or the use of standardised contracts may be possible for certain smaller projects. The unique efficiency gains associated with PPPs derive from the interaction of the design-build-maintain-operate phases. The greater the maintenance and operation components, the greater the potential for efficiency gains.

The appropriate allocation of risk between the government and the private partner is fundamental to the success of PPPs. Certain risks – such as changes in government regulatory or taxation policy – should not be transferred since they serve only to increase costs. A more common problem is the tendency for governments to retain the majority of the risks with PPPs. This undermines the PPP concept and may reveal that it is only being used as a vehicle to move the transaction off budget.

A comparison of the benefits and costs of PPPs versus traditional procurement needs to be rigorously and dynamically conducted, and PPPs should be subjected to at least the same scrutiny as traditional expenditures in the budget process.

In general, the governance issues identified for outsourcing apply equally to PPPs.

5. Vouchers

In a voucher environment, the provision of public services is separated from its financing. The funding remains with the government in the form of a voucher, which is issued to individuals entitling them to exchange the vouchers for services at a range of suppliers. The individual voucher-holder chooses among the different suppliers and pays with the voucher.

Four definitional issues are in order. First, the vouchers are for the use of specific services only; they are not in the form of cash. Second, the voucher can equal the total or part of the cost of the service. Third, the eligibility for the voucher may extend to the whole population or may be limited to certain groups or be means-tested. Fourth, the suppliers can be both government bodies and private bodies, or private bodies only. Regardless, the government monopoly on service provision is ended and consumers have the right to choose among them. This should lead to greater efficiency, notably in terms of quality improvements.

Vouchers can take at least three main forms. An explicit voucher is a physical coupon or smart card as described above. The supplier of the services in turn exchanges this for cash from a government body. An implicit voucher takes the form of a qualifying recipient choosing from a number of designated suppliers and, upon registering with one of them, the government pays directly to that provider of the service. The third form is for the government to reimburse the user for expenditure on qualifying services from approved suppliers. This would most often be through the tax system, but can equally take place as a traditional government expenditure programme. From the point of view of the user, these three main forms offer a choice of suppliers with the government financing the service.

5.1. Use of vouchers

The extent of use of these three forms of vouchers is significant in some sectors in OECD member countries, with their use being mainly focused on housing, education (primary and secondary), childcare (nursery education), and care for the elderly.

Housing assistance to low-income families is a particularly good example of vouchers. Instead of large housing estates that cluster low-income families together, vouchers in this field offer them the possibility to participate in the general housing market. These explicit vouchers are generally designed such that they provide for the difference between actual rent paid, up to a limit based on family size and local housing market conditions, and a certain percentage of the recipient's salary. The amount of the housing voucher is then adjusted regularly based on housing market trends.

Examples include the "Section 8" vouchers in the United States (launched in the mid-1970s), which provide benefits to about 2 million low-income households and had a total cost of $21.2 billion in 2003. A report by the independent congressionally-chartered Millennial Housing Commission strongly endorsed the voucher programme in its May 2002 report, describing the programme as "flexible, cost-effective, and successful in its mission."[5] Another prominent example is the "accommodation supplement" in New Zealand (launched in 1993), which provides benefits to 250 000 people. The New Zealand voucher programme does not differentiate between rent or mortgage payments. Similarly, tax credits for the reimbursement of mortgage interest expense can be viewed as a type of "reimbursement" voucher as described above.

Vouchers are most often discussed in terms of primary and secondary education. Figure 5.2 shows the percentage of total public expenditure for primary and secondary education that goes to private institutions in selected OECD member countries.

Most strikingly, over 70% of public funding for primary and secondary education in the Netherlands goes to private schools. There is a provision in the constitution (since 1917) which guarantees equal government funding for students in public schools and private schools. Most of the private schools have some linkages to churches. There is a standard minimum national curriculum, which applies for both public and private schools. Public schools are not permitted to charge additional fees whereas private schools can. In practice, the private schools limit their charges to financing smaller class sizes

---

Box 5.2. **United States food stamps programme**

The United States food stamps programme is the largest and oldest explicit voucher programme in OECD member countries. Started in 1961, it provides 19.1 million low-income individuals with an electronic card they can use like cash at most grocery stores to ensure that they have access to a healthy diet. The programme cost $23.9 billion in 2003. Interestingly, the programme is operated by the Department of Agriculture rather than a social services body.

---

and to the funding of "fringe" benefits such as excursions and sports facilities. The government funding is provided through an implicit voucher in that each school – whether public or private – receives an equal amount per student enrolled.

In 1992, Sweden embarked on a policy that also guarantees equal government funding to public and private schools. The share of students attending private schools has grown to 4%. Unlike the Netherlands, these schools are for the most part not affiliated with any religious group but rather differentiate themselves according to teaching methods or a focus on specialised subjects. Some schools use a foreign language as the main teaching language and/or cater to specific ethnic populations. The private schools are not allowed to charge tuition fees and must accept all pupils from their immediate geographic area. The government funding is also provided through an implicit voucher.

The use of explicit vouchers for primary and secondary education is most documented in the United States but its use is very limited. They have met with strong resistance from public school teachers and their allies. Explicit vouchers are indeed used in some cities but they generally provide funding to relatively few students to opt out of the public school system and enrol in private schools. They cater mainly to students from disadvantaged backgrounds. The programmes are so small in aggregate that their overall impact is minimal as can be seen from Figure 5.2.

A related development in the United States is the creation of charter schools, which operate on an implicit voucher basis, i.e. the government provides funding for them in the same manner as public schools. In fact, most of the schools are part of the normal public school system but cater specifically to students from disadvantaged backgrounds. A few of these schools can however be viewed as private in nature.

Vouchers are also used for the provision of child care (nursing care) services.[6] The most comprehensive of such reforms have been implemented in Australia. Those reforms aimed at equalising the level of public funding per child across public and private institutions by channelling all public funding through users, replacing the previous system based on grants to non-profit organisations and local governments. Now, public funding is distributed to families via the "child care benefit" earmarked for childcare provided in government-approved services. As a result, the public subsidy is equal across different institutional settings, including for-profit and non-profit community-based day-care centres and to some extent family-based day care. The Netherlands and Norway are currently considering similar comprehensive reforms. In the United States, childcare vouchers have gained ground in federal family support programmes since the early 1990s. Whereas

Figure 5.2. **Public expenditure on private institutions**

(Percentage of total public expenditure on education)

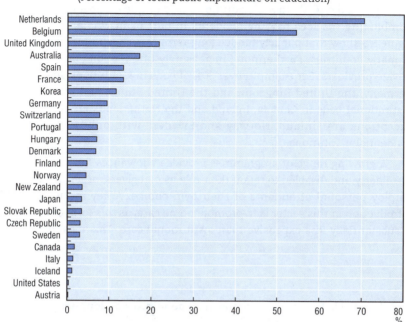

Source: OECD Education Database.

previously under this programme services were provided through direct funding to public institutions or through grants or contracts with selected private childcare institutions, recipients are now entitled to a voucher or cash benefit giving access to a wider range of care facilities.

Tax credits and cash benefits conditioned on documented expenses for private childcare, however, exist in many OECD countries. In some cases these subsidies and tax credits are targeted at low-income and working families to improve their work incentives. This is the case in Canada, Germany, the United Kingdom and the United States. Indirect public funding through tax credits and other support for employer contributions to childcare expenses play a role in some countries including Belgium, Italy, the Netherlands and the United States.

Vouchers have also been used for the long-term care for the elderly where publicly-funded provision is growing relatively rapidly in OECD countries. Care may take place in public and private residential institutions or at home, and there are often tax credits and income support for the (informal) employment of personal attendants acting as carers.

Providing publicly funded long-term care in private nursing homes and residential institutions typically takes the form of vouchers – either implicit vouchers paid directly to the institution based on the number of residents, or reimbursing the fees paid by residents in part or in whole. Table 5.2 and Figure 5.3 show that publicly funded long-term care expenditure is significant in many countries. Furthermore, increasingly often, public finance goes to private providers. For example, over 80% of beds in institutions are private in Germany, the United Kingdom, and the United States, and around half of institutional beds in Canada, Ireland and the Netherlands are privately run. Exceptions are Finland, Norway and Sweden, with only 10-15% private residential institutions.

A growing range of programmes provides allowances for the families of the elderly and disabled to retain their role as caregivers, or for the elderly to employ personal attendants of their own choice. A key motive for their introduction in this sector is to promote home care, as this form of assistance is substantially less expensive than institutional care. This most often takes

Table 5.2. **Public and private expenditures on long-term care as a percentage of GDP**

	Public expenditure			Private expenditure		
	Home care	Institutions	Total	Home care	Institutions	Total
Australia[1]	0.31	0.57	0.88	0.08	0.26	0.34
Austria	0.81	0.51	1.32		n.a.	
Canada	0.25	0.83	1.08	0.00	0.17	0.17
Germany	0.42	0.50	0.93	0.05	0.17	0.22
Hungary			< 0.2			< 0.1
Ireland	0.19	0.33	0.52	0.00	0.10	0.10
Japan	0.25	0.51	0.75		n.a.	
Korea	< 0.1	< 0.1	< 0.2		n.a.	
Luxembourg	0.15	0.37	0.52		n.a.	
Mexico			< 0.1			< 0.1
Netherlands	0.56	0.78	1.34	0.05	0.02	0.07
New Zealand	0.11	0.39	0.50	0.00	0.27	0.27
Norway[1]	1.03	1.08	2.10			0.11
Spain[1]	0.05	0.11	0.17	0.18	0.26	0.44
Sweden[1]	0.82	2.06	2.89			0.14
Switzerland	0.17	0.53	0.70	0.04	0.85	0.89
United Kingdom	0.32	0.58	0.89	0.03	0.20	0.23
United States	0.25	0.50	0.74	0.13	0.38	0.52

1. Data is for age group 65+.

Source: Pearson and Martin (2005, forthcoming).

Figure 5.3. **Public and private institutions in long-term care for the elderly, late 1990s**

(Share of beds in nursing homes and residential care institutions)[1]

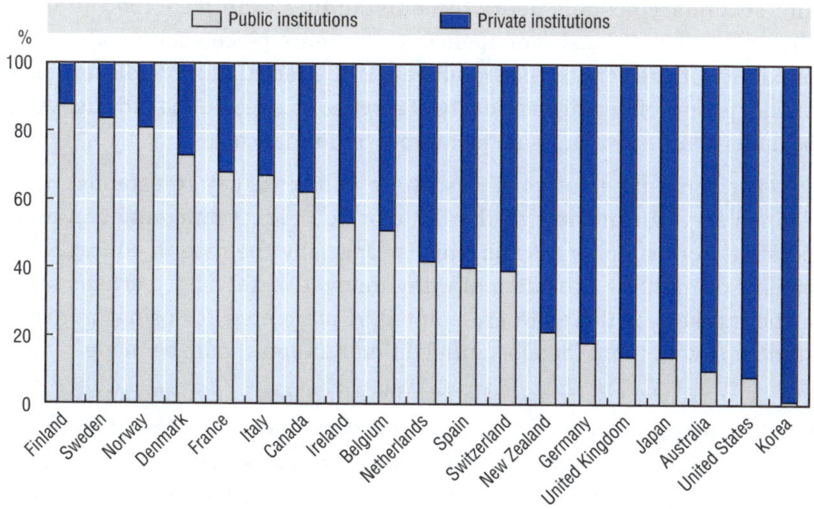

1. This figure is based on collection of available national material where the exact definitions may vary. Generally only staffed homes providing nursing care and/or practical help with activities of daily living are included while long-stay hospital sections are not included.
Source: OECD based on national sources.

the form of an explicit voucher or the use of tax credits. The French scheme, introduced in 1997, allows the user to choose among different forms of care, including employing a personal attendant, with the restriction that family members can only be hired if currently unemployed. Likewise, the Finnish informal carer's allowance introduced in 1993 allows the user to employ a personal attendant, with the allowance being paid directly to that person. The German scheme introduced with the separate mandatory insurance for long-term care in 1995 allows users a choice from a menu of service provision and cash benefits.

This shows the wide range of sectors where vouchers can be utilised. Some of the areas are in their infancy or development phase, and the use of vouchers can be expected to increase in future years.

5.2. Key issues

An analysis of OECD member countries' experience with the use of vouchers shows that there are several critical design and contextual factors associated with the successful use of vouchers.

As with all market-type mechanisms, the need for competitive markets is paramount – the voucher-holders must be able to exercise a genuine choice of suppliers. Some of the areas where vouchers are most commonly used – primary and secondary schools being the outstanding example – tend to exhibit characteristics of local monopolies. Consumers place such a value on the proximity of the service that it outweighs the fact that more distant service providers may offer a higher quality of service. As a result, the provider will not be under competitive pressure to improve performance.

For some types of vouchers, there is a tendency to establish rigidly defined service standards so that little or no product differentiation may be possible from suppliers. Again, this is especially the case in education. The benefit of multiple providers offering innovative services, perhaps serving niche markets, is therefore pre-empted. A preference for using "minimum" standards with room for substantial differentiation should be made.

A short-term shortage of attractive suppliers is not uncommon. Many services where vouchers are used require a heavy investment in order to expand the supply of services by individual providers. For housing vouchers, a tight housing market may also make their use difficult since the built-in adjustment mechanisms for market conditions tend to lag.

It may also be difficult for users of services to make informed judgments about individual service providers. This undermines the competition mechanism. Many public services are not "search goods", with the characteristic that an individual can find out everything about the service before making a choice. Rather, they are "experience goods" where the consumer only finds out about the service in the course of using it. This problem is accentuated by the fact that many public services are not consumed repeatedly, or that it is costly to switch from one provider to another.[7] League tables of performance of individual providers, such as test scores for schools or quality ratings by current and past users, can serve to alleviate this problem. Users, however, have much greater ownership of decisions they make themselves and this itself has a positive impact on their experience of the goods.

The capacity of individuals to assess the services offered by different providers may also be impaired in some instances, long-term care for the elderly being a prime example. This calls for a stronger role for the government in certifying suppliers and guiding the choice of users. Although it can mitigate the competition mechanism inherent with vouchers, the information provided by the government can lead to more informed (and more competitive) choices.

Voucher programmes often entail a prohibition of top-up payments whereby recipients can use their own resources to supplement the voucher.

These are seen as unfair by some observers since they allow richer recipients to enjoy higher quality public services. On the other hand, such payments will facilitate a better match of the quality of services offered and the users' capacity to pay, and can lead to increased product differentiation which is a key benefit of the voucher concept. Such prohibitions therefore need to be reviewed carefully.

The payment structure of the voucher can have perverse incentives. If a voucher offers a uniform payment level irrespective of the costs associated with servicing different categories of users – such as disabled children in childcare, lower-score students in education or weaker persons in long-term care – this can accentuate cream-skimming behaviour from suppliers. In such conditions there is an incentive for private suppliers to screen voucher recipients for those who cost less than others and to exclude higher-cost recipients. A payment structure that recognises such differences is key to alleviating this potential problem.

The extent of voucher use in OECD member countries is significant. They are, however, subject to unique challenges in terms of design and contextual factors. An inappropriately designed voucher can simply accentuate pre-existing problems with the delivery of public services.

A major concern raised about vouchers is that they exert an upward pressure on public expenditure. Vouchers are generally available to all who meet a certain eligibility criteria. They are therefore demand-driven entitlement programmes. Previously, the expenditure associated with these programmes could generally be controlled by limiting supply. Similarly, vouchers that are based on formulas for the calculation of the benefit, for example rental assistance vouchers that are related to developments in wages and the cost of housing, can lead to significant and sudden expenditure increases. Both of these factors demonstrate the strength of vouchers from a consumer point of view, but they are sources for concern from a budgetary point of view. The rental vouchers in the United States are coming under strain for these reasons.

6. Findings and future challenges

There are several key messages emerging from this chapter concerning the use of market-type mechanisms and their implications.

The diversity of experiences among OECD member countries shows that market-type mechanisms can be applied to a very wide range of government functions.

There are strong entry barriers to adopting market-type mechanisms. This is a function of the public's view of "the role of government" and also a function of the resistance by government staff affected by their introduction.

This explains, for example, why the resistance is greatest to outsourcing and vouchers which directly challenge existing government service provision but less pronounced with other market-type mechanisms.

Box 5.3. **Other market-type mechanisms**

This chapter has surveyed the experience in OECD member countries with outsourcing, public-private partnerships and vouchers. This box briefly highlights two other market-type mechanisms.

User charges assign to the specific consumers the full or partial cost of providing the respective services. User charges thereby create a direct link between the benefits and costs of consuming public services and thus aim at removing excess demand for previously "free" public services. Three types of user charges can be observed. The first concerns internal charges among government agencies. Previously common service agencies may have received direct appropriations for services which they then supplied "free" to other agencies. With user charges, it is the agencies that consume the services that are given the budget. They now have an incentive to limit their use of common services – or seek them from alternative sources if permitted – since any savings accrue to them. The second form of user charges concerns services delivered to business and industry. These may include various regulatory services. Such charges are generally full cost recovery and the primary motive is to relieve the general taxpayer of services benefiting specific users. The line between user-charging and taxation is especially thin in this case. The third type is charges to individual citizens. These may include various education, health care and social services. These charges are usually partial and the primary motive is to discipline user demand.

Transferable permits are mainly used for the allocation of scarce resources instead of regulatory measures such as comparative hearings ("beauty contests") and lotteries. The government establishes a maximum amount of the resource that can be used, then allocates it in the first instance by grandfathering current/past users or auctioning the permits to the highest bidder, and then allows a secondary market in the permits to operate whereby they can be sold to the highest bidder. This is the optimal economic allocation. This has been used for fisheries (where the allocation is the percentage of each year's allowable catch), airport landing and take-off slots, and the radio spectrum (3G mobile phone licenses). It is much discussed for greenhouse gas emissions as well since one ton of greenhouse gas emitted anywhere in the world has the same effect, and an international system of transferable permits would allow the reductions to take place at lowest cost.

The efficiency gains associated with market-type mechanisms can be substantial. These can be either in the form of decreased costs, improved service quality levels, or improved resource allocation economy-wide. The discussion showed, however, that care needs to be taken in their design to achieve these efficiency gains.

It is perhaps most surprising that market-type mechanisms are not more widely used in OECD member countries considering their potential for efficiency gains. Again, this highlights the strong entry barriers for their adoption.

The ability to maintain key governance principles needs to be considered as an inherent part of the decision to adopt market-type mechanisms. These include accountability, regularity, transparency, and the availability of avenues for redress.

Finally, there is always the risk that governments have the capacity to appropriately introduce market-type mechanisms only once in a sector, and then become beholden to that provider due to loss of capacity. Governments need to ensure that they continue to have the operational knowledge to make good policy and to choose – and alter – service delivery options in such a dispersed (or networked) environment and actively promote competitive supplier markets.

Notes

1. Financial support for the research on which this chapter is based was generously provided by the IBM Center for the Business of Government.

2. PPPs can also involve the private sector purchasing already existing infrastructure assets and redeveloping them.

3. This categorisation of risks and discussion draws on Eurostat's ruling on the treatment of PPP in the context of deficits and debt (STAT/04/18, 11 February 2004). See European Union (2004) and http://europa.eu.int/comm/eurostat.

4. A private partner may enjoy lower borrowing costs than the government in certain non-member countries, or than certain lower levels of government.

5. Report available at www.mhc.gov/MHCReport.pdf.

6. This discussion draws on Pearson and Martin (forthcoming, 2005).

7. This discussion draws on Cave (2001).

ISBN 92-64-01049-1
Modernising Government: The Way Forward
© OECD 2005

Chapter 6

Organising and Motivating Public Servants: Modernising Public Employment

1. Introduction

When it comes to the nuts and bolts of government, all OECD countries have one thing in common: a core public service. In other words, a centrally controlled bureaucracy made up of people working in ministries, departments and government agencies to carry out the business of government. Public service structures have evolved around the idea that public employment is different from other types of work and therefore requires a special employment system and structure. It has traditionally offered a high level of job security, or even "jobs for life", coupled with a special set of employment regulations.

However, over the past two decades, the pressures to reduce the size of government and improve its performance and responsiveness have called into question a lot of the assumptions about the appropriate structure and operation of a public service. Governments of OECD countries have reformed their public service employment either as part of a wider reform effort or as their main lever of reform.

Since the late 1980s, the nature of public employment in OECD countries has changed significantly. Many areas of public employment have lost their distinctiveness, not least because some traditional public sector functions have moved into the private sphere. Furthermore, reformers have aimed to make the employment arrangements of public servants more like those of employees in the private sector. This meant changing the employment status of civil servants by reconsidering guaranteed lifelong employment in some countries, increasing competition at entry into the civil service, moving from collective bargaining to site or individual wage bargaining, and also engaging in periodic cutback management.

In addition, there has been a desire to increase managerial flexibility and freedom by deregulating human resource management (HRM), reducing the role of central agencies, delegating more HRM authority to line departments, and enhancing and individualising accountability and performance.

As a result of these changes, in many OECD countries a lot of the assumptions about the way the public service works are no longer true. This chapter contends that these changes have placed the traditional basic models of the core public service – position-based and career-based systems – under pressure and that it is becoming increasingly difficult to fit countries into either category.

This chapter uses the term "public servants" or "civil servants" to refer to government employees of central government organisations under core public service rules and paid from public funds. The scope is confined mainly to the civil service of the central (or federal) government for comparative purposes. The terms civil service and core public service are used interchangeably.

This chapter looks at changes in the nature of employment in the core public service in OECD countries over the past two decades as well as issues and challenges for the future. There has been a variety of reform initiatives across OECD member countries, but the major trends examined in this chapter are: the attempts to reduce public employment (Section 3); the changing nature of civil service systems (Section 4); the increase in managerial flexibility through decentralisation of human resource management responsibilities (Section 5); the individualisation of employment contract, accountability and pay (Section 6); and the management of senior civil servants (Section 7). Before looking at these, this chapter discusses the distinctive nature of the public service and the traditional models for core public employment.

2. What is special about the public service?

2.1. What is the civil service?

Historically, the adjective "civil" connoted the non-military function of civil servants. In recent times, the original contrast with military personnel has been displaced by the distinction between holders of permanent posts and those elected officials whose posts changed hands when there was a change of government (Drewry and Butcher, 1991, pp. 15-17).

In many OECD countries, the term "civil servants" is used in a much more limited sense than "public servants" and is limited to core central public employment, i.e. employees in the central executive and legislative administration, in departments directly dependent on the Head of State or the Parliament, together with all other ministries and administrative departments of central government, including autonomous agencies paid by central government.

Instead of "civil service" or "civil servants", many countries use the terms "public service" or "public servants", in which the scope of coverage seems to be much wider. For example, teachers and doctors in publicly owned schools and health facilities may or may not be civil servants legally, but they are always public servants if employed by government-funded organisations. Some countries (such as Ireland, the Slovak Republic and the United Kingdom) clearly differentiate civil servants (service) from public servants (service), where civil servants are only the employees working in central government, thus excluding the other category (public servants) who work in local governments, public schools, health services, social security, etc.

But in most OECD member countries, the term "civil servants" is used interchangeably with "public servants" without any conscious distinctions between the two terms.

2.2. Why is the civil service distinctive?

All OECD countries have special arrangements for employees in the core public service designed to promote or preserve values that societies consider important for those engaged to enforce the law or otherwise carry out the collective will. The main architecture of public employment has traditionally been built around the idea of a system distinct from that of other sections of society, and this distinctiveness has been justified in terms of wider governance values. For example, such values might include the idea that public servants should not operate in a politically partisan manner. While such arrangements exist in all OECD member countries, they have produced radically different results and ways of governing because of variations in national context, institutional and constitutional arrangements, culture, leadership, and management.

In the past 20 years, many areas of public employment have lost this uniqueness and have become quite similar to the general employment system. Does this mean that the idea of a civil service as a constitutional or quasi-constitutional device for maintaining confidence in the government system is outdated, at least in some countries?

As of yet there is no definitive answer to that question, but one thing is clear: if countries look to the private sector for models in modernising public employment they must not forget that the fundamental purpose of the public service is government, not management. This means paying attention to fundamental values such as fairness, equity, justice, and social cohesion to maintain confidence in the governmental and political system as a whole. Managerial considerations, while important, in most cases can be considered secondary.

Also, the traditional, centrally controlled bureaucracy is still a workable and robust system for public management where there has been disruption or discontinuity in the constitutional institutions of society, and/or where the other institutions in society are not particularly well ordered. It is also a system that has proven more enduring in countries where national culture attaches importance to the existence of a strong and all-embracing concept of the State and therefore a need for strong cultural consistency across the core public service.

160

Although trends to modernise public service employment are moving fast, most governments still share the main elements of the traditional system of public administration. In many countries, civil servants were highly regarded and considered to be amongst the effective groups in society, and their distinctive employment arrangements were seen as important in the creation of a public-spirited group ethic and in preventing a politicisation of the civil service.

But there can be no ideal type of public employment because different societies face very different risks and problems. While one government may have a pressing need to make the public sector adaptive and innovative, for another it may be more urgent to improve discipline and co-ordination.

3. Attempts to reduce civil service employment

3.1. Staff reductions: an uneven picture[1]

The 1980s and 1990s saw many governments make deliberate efforts to reduce civil service employment, as part of the effort to contain or reduce public expenditure and the pay bill. Table 6.1, which is based on data from the OECD survey on public sector pay and employment trends, shows the changes in total public employment in a selection of OECD countries over the past ten years. This includes central, regional and local administration. Data show that the number of public servants decreased in a number of countries, a few relatively drastically. At the same time, some countries such as Ireland and Luxembourg continuously recruited public servants. However, in these countries, the structural need for public servants in order to follow the growth of the working population mainly accounts for these changes.

In many OECD countries, the reduction in total public employment has been mostly due to staff reductions at the central/federal administrative level. In some countries, staff levels at regional or local levels increased

Table 6.1. **Evolution of total public employment[1] from 1990/91[2] to 2000/01**

Percentage change in public employment	Countries
Significantly increased (>5%)	Ireland, Korea, Luxembourg, Netherlands (1996), Spain, Turkey (1997)
Moderately increased (1% ~ 5%)	Poland (1994)
Slightly changed (-1% ~ 1%)	Austria, Belgium, Japan
Moderately decreased (-5% ~ -1%)	Canada, Hungary (1997)
Significantly decreased (>- -5%)	Australia, Finland, Germany, New Zealand, Sweden (1995)

1.   This is based on total public sector employment in terms of headcount and full-time equivalents. This includes central, regional and local administration. For more details see OECD (2002b).
2.   For some countries the data set does not go back as far as 1991. In these cases the year from which the percentage change is calculated is indicated in brackets.

Source: OECD (2002b). The interpretation of these data should be subject to caution as the definitions of total public employment differ from one country to another. The results of a decrease or an increase in total public employment can be due to changes across government organisational forms rather than to employment levels in the public sector.

simultaneously – particularly, for example, in Japan, Spain, and the United States.

Table 6.2 shows the annual percentage change in central or federal administration employment in OECD countries over the past decade.

While the changes in total public employment vary significantly across countries, overall, in the late 1990s, the comparative number of public employees against the total labour force generally decreased with a few exceptions, albeit slightly in most cases. Two factors may account for this: first, downsizing policies; and second, the economic booms resulted in the

Table 6.2. **Annual change in central or federal administration employment**

	1990/ 1991	1995/ 1996	1996/ 1997	1997/ 1998	1998/ 1999	1999/ 2000	2000/ 2001	Annual percentage change	
Australia[1]	0.9%	-4.8%	-23.3%	-8.7%	-7.8%	2.4%	-1.2%	1990-2001	-4.4%
Austria[2]	-0.3%	1.0%	-0.2%	-0.2%	-1.1%	-2.4%	-2.2%	1990-2001	-0.1%
Belgium[2]		-3.1%	-0.7%	-0.1%	0.4%	4.0%		1992-2000	0.0%
Canada[3]	2.2%	-4.2%	-5.4%	-2.0%	0.2%	2.3%	5.0%	1990-2001	-1.2%
Czech Republic[2, 4]		2.2%	-5.1%	-2.4%	-6.4%				
Denmark[2]				-1.2%	-5.8%	-0.2%	0.3%		
Finland[3]	-0.7%	-1.9%	0.7%	1.4%	0.4%	-1.4%	-2.6%	1990-2001	-1.8%
France				1.4%	1.0%	1.1%			
Germany		-2.5%	-1.3%	-2.0%	-1.1%	-1.6%		1991-2000	-2.9%
Greece				3.6%					
Hungary				1.7%	-0.2%	-2.4%	-0.9%		
Ireland[2]	2.8%	-0.8%	-0.6%	2.2%	3.6%	3.9%	5.6%	1990-2001	2.3%
Italy				-0.3%	-0.8%				
Korea[2]	2.4%	0.4%	0.3%	-1.0%	-1.3%	-0.3%	0.4%	1990-2001	0.2%
Luxembourg	7.3%	1.2%	5.8%	-0.4%	2.4%	6.2%	9.1%	1990-2001	4.5%
Netherlands[2]			1.6%	3.3%	1.3%	2.5%			
New Zealand		2.0%	-3.7%	1.7%	3.7%	-5.4%	3.6%	1991-2001	-0.2%
Poland[2]		9.8%	4.1%	4.5%	-15.8%	-8.8%		1994-2000	0.3%
Spain	-4.8%	0.6%	-2.2%	-1.1%	0.1%	-7.7%	-11.7%	1990-2001	-2.3%
Sweden[2]		-1.8%	-1.8%	-1.4%	0.0%	-2.8%	-3.4%	1995-2001	-1.8%
Switzerland					1.8%	3.2%	4.3%	1991-2001	-0.5%
Turkey				1.0%	1.7%	0.4%			
United States	-4.3%	-2.1%	-2.3%	-1.2%	0.2%	3.1%		1990-2000	-1.2%

1. Excluding permanent defence forces.
2. Full-time equivalent.
3. Excluding government business enterprises.
4. Excluding permanent defence forces and police.

Source: OECD (2002b). The interpretation of these data should be subject to caution as the definitions of total public employment differ from one country to another. The results of a decrease or an increase in total public employment can be due to changes across government organisational forms rather than to employment levels in the public sector.

creation of a large number of jobs in the private sector which in turn reduced the proportion in the public sector.

3.2. *Diverse approaches to downsizing*

Different approaches have been adopted for workforce reduction. In some countries, policies focused on more passive measures to curb growth in the public service workforce, such as hiring freezes and natural attrition as a way to stabilise or reduce employment levels, rather than on actively making significant reductions in the number of existing staff.

In more flexible systems, such as in Australia, Canada, Finland, Norway, Portugal and the United States, or in transition economies such as Poland and Hungary, more active workforce reduction programmes were introduced with various levels of intensity. Some were implemented on a national scale, as in Canada where a 16% reduction in federal staffing levels was planned for the period 1995-98. In other cases such as Australia, policies were more devolved. In a number of countries throughout the 1980s and 1990s and continuing in some cases into the new millennium, staff reductions were achieved through the privatisation of government activities or the change of status of public institutions. In fact, in doing so, countries attempted to re-define the role of government. For example in Finland, six major public enterprises changed their status from 1989 to 1990, resulting in a 10% decrease in total public employment.[2] Such actions have been important in reducing civil service employment and may have brought significant benefits to the conduct of the enterprises. However, from a management perspective, these are one-off decisions that do not provide a basis for ongoing public sector reform.

In other cases, such as in Germany in recent years, jobs were cut within the existing public service. This type of cutback tends to occur in response to a fiscal problem resulting in some political crisis. Such downsizing episodes are often associated with public management re-engineering of different kinds, and indeed any resultant reduction in the public workforce is often cited as evidence of the success of the management reforms.

OECD research suggests that what these cutback episodes have in common is a sense of political crisis and a political and administrative imperative to take action. What particular kind of management reform is introduced at the time of the cutback is secondary to whether the cutback occurs. This suggests that these periodic major staff cutbacks owe more to political conditions than to management ideas, and explains why some cutbacks were made without strategic forethought, causing the loss of key competencies (Blair, 2002). However, these problems at the micro level do not obviate the larger reasons for taking action to control aggregate public employment. There is scope, however, for developing better downsizing strategies.

Policies for workforce adjustments are difficult because they are politically sensitive and because they face a number of obstacles. In many OECD countries, rigid career systems by their very nature limit the scope of workforce adjustments.

Overall, large-scale staff reductions have generally been linked to organisational restructuring and redirecting programmes, whereas small-scale staff reductions (linked to efficiency-type gains) have occurred without substantial organisational reform. When downsizing has been part of a larger reform agenda, such as fiscal consolidation, it has not always been linked explicitly to organisational reforms aimed at redirecting the scope and organisation of work. In this context, downsizing tends to be "numbers-driven" and focused on achieving staff reduction targets through means such as hiring freezes. These numbers-driven reductions carry risks for good management and organisational capacity, and produce rigidities that hinder rather than contribute to efficiency gains. How can government keep pace with new skills if recruitment is frozen? How can redundancies be spread sensibly to allow new staffing needs to be realised?

Faced with such questions, some countries have adopted a more "managerial" approach to workforce adjustments that seek to balance the need to achieve staffing targets with the need to ensure that organisations maintain the needed skills and capacities to carry out their work. In this latter case, staff reductions flow from broader policies to reorient or restructure public service organisations, allowing organisations to better target workers, occupations or particular departments for re-training, redeployment, reduction or other staffing adjustments. The idea is less about focusing on the overall size of the public sector workforce, but more toward facilitating change in the context of achieving greater organisational efficiency and effectiveness.

4. The changing nature of civil service systems

4.1. *What type of civil service systems?*

There are two basic models for core public service employment in OECD countries, "career-based" or "position-based". The choice of one system or the other has a profound effect on a country's public service culture.

In career-based systems, public servants are expected to stay in the public service more or less throughout their working life. Initial entry is based on academic credentials and/or a civil service entry examination. Once recruited, people are placed in positions at the will of the organisation. This may include moving staff from one ministry to another and from one area of specialisation to another. Promotion is based on a system of grades attached to the individual rather than to a specific position. A public servant's progress depends to a large extent on how he/she is viewed by the organisational hierarchy, a powerful lever for moulding behaviour to conform to group norms. This sort of system is characterised by limited possibilities for entering the civil service at mid-career and a strong emphasis on career development.

Position-based systems focus on selecting the best-suited candidate for each position, whether by external recruitment or internal promotion. They allow more open access, and lateral entry is relatively common. In contrast to career-based systems, for position-based systems technical considerations are likely to be more important.

France, Greece, Japan, Korea, Luxembourg, and Spain seem to have the strongest characteristics of a career service system, while position-based tendencies are the most evident in countries which have been more active in reforming their public service over the past two decades such as Finland, New Zealand, Sweden, Switzerland, and the United Kingdom. It is interesting to note that Eastern European countries adopted different models of civil service systems in their transitional period from the early 1990s. Hungary and the Slovak Republic have adopted a career-based system; the Czech Republic and Poland have chosen a more position-based system. There may be much to learn from a comparison of how these radically different choices are affecting governance and civil service culture in those four countries.

Career-based systems tend to promote collective values at entry in specific sub-groups of the civil service (*e.g.* the notion of "corps" in France), with relatively weaker cross-hierarchical and cross "corps" values. The downside is a weaker emphasis on individual performance and accountability. More position-based systems tend to have weaker cross-government values at entry than career-based systems, but tend to be less deferential and may create stronger links across levels of hierarchy and status.

4.2. A changing picture

The career-based system is under pressure in developed economies because it runs against trends in the wider job market, and because it is seen as less able to deliver specialised skills and flexibility than the position-based approach. But there is little evidence that OECD countries with a career-based system wish to abandon it altogether. The challenge for career-based systems is how to have a civil service that is responsive to the needs and specialised skill demands of contemporary society. The challenge for position-based systems is how to ensure that the collective interest is served.

While the traditional distinction between position-based and career-based systems remains interesting in terms of the overall tendency of each civil service system, more and more countries do not fit into one of the two categories. Increasingly, no current civil service in the OECD area is a pure example of either the career-based or position-based type. There seems to be

Table 6.3. **Main strengths and weaknesses of civil service systems in the promotion of collectivity and ethical behaviours**

	Classic career-based system		Classic position-based system	
	Relative strengths	Weakness	Relative strengths	Weakness
Entry into the civil service	• Fairness ensured by competitive examination/diplomas. • Whole-of-government collective values ensured by similar pre-entry training for different categories of civil servants.	• Weak cross-hierarchical values: different values and culture depending on hierarchical level of the groups. • Weak assessment at entry of individual's drive for results. • Collective values and culture weakened by division of staff in coherent but closed groupings with different statuses.	• Fairness ensured by open and competitive processes for each position. • More collective values across staff with different statuses.	• Possible biases at entry, when lack of transparency in recruitment process. • Weak common values at entry into the core public service.
Promotion	• Limited possibilities of unfair management by separation of the grade (acquired with time in the civil service) and the specific post.	• Lack of transparency on appointment to different posts (due to weak individual staff assessment).	• Fairness ensured by strong individual performance assessment.	• When processes are not transparent, possible patronage in promotion (grades and posts being mixed). • More difficult cross-departmental appointments.

Source: OECD (2003h).

a tendency for each to adopt some processes from the other to mitigate the weaknesses to which each system is prone.

Position-based systems are trying to make up for their difficulties in maintaining government coherence and collective culture through a rather more centralised system of management for senior management than before, and through emphasis on post-entry training. On the other hand, traditional career-based systems are tending to increase the number of posts open to external competition, delegate HRM practices to line ministries and lower hierarchical levels, and increase the individual accountability for performance. As a result, it seems that the overall picture is more that of a continuum of systems rather than clearly differentiated categories of systems.

This blurring of the systems is compounded by the existence of several parallel systems, most particularly in two areas. First, behind the formal civil service architecture there is increasingly a "contractual shadow" which is significantly position-based even in the most strongly career-based systems. At the same time, there is an increasing tendency to create a distinctive set of employment arrangements for the senior civil service which are increasingly career-based even in the most strongly position-based systems.

There are countries with a relatively high level of delegation and which tend to emphasise a lifelong career in the civil service with minimum lateral entry. The OECD has coined the term "department-based systems" to characterise these hybrid systems which give a lot of HRM responsibilities to line ministries in the definition and practices of HRM policies, but where civil servants make a career mostly in a single ministry.

5. Delegation of human resource management responsibilities: Increasing managerial flexibility[3]

While the scope and pace of delegation has varied from one country to another, most OECD member countries have moved towards decentralising control of HRM responsibility in order to increase managerial flexibility and to improve performance and responsiveness. In general, three methods of delegation were used in OECD countries, either jointly or separately:

- Transferring responsibilities for human resource management from central bodies to line ministries/departments/agencies.

- Simplification of rules and procedures. Where devolution has concerned the operational aspects of HRM, with responsibility for determining policy remaining at the centre, there is a tendency towards making policy frameworks much less detailed than before by simplifying rules and procedures.

- Developing more flexible HRM policies. Even where devolution of authority is very limited in some countries, central HRM bodies have developed different types of flexible policies and less cumbersome procedures. Although pay determination has remained centralised in most countries, various types of pay flexibilities are given to the line ministry/department.

5.1. Changing role of central HRM bodies

The delegation of HRM has had a major impact on central HRM bodies. However, these bodies still play a significant role especially in policy formulation.

Across OECD member countries, the organisation and structures of central HRM bodies vary significantly from one country to another. These bodies may be stand-alone or may be located within finance ministries, public management departments or prime minister's departments. Table 6.4 summarises structures in selected OECD member countries.

Two countries (Belgium and Sweden) do not have such a body, reportedly because the government has delegated most of the responsibility for its employer policy to the line ministries/departments/agencies. In these countries the responsibility for HRM policies is decentralised and rests with each independent government agency. In Denmark, Finland, Portugal and Spain, HRM functions are performed by one or two directorates within the finance ministry. In other countries such as Australia, Austria, France, Germany, New Zealand, Norway, and the United States, a separate ministry/department takes charge of management including HR policies. These countries seem to view HRM functions as an important tool for government management and policy co-ordination.

There is no obvious answer regarding which type of institutional arrangement would be most appropriate for organising central HRM bodies. It seems very dependent on countries' management priorities and their context. It appears that where countries see HRM in a wider management context linked to public expenditure, they usually establish a central HRM body within the ministry of finance. In contrast, if countries put more emphasis on policy co-ordination or departmental performance, they seem to set up such units under the prime minister or cabinet.

5.2. Relationship between central human resource management bodies and line ministries/agencies

It appears that central HRM bodies are still playing a significant role in policy formulation. In most countries, they retain legal responsibility and play an initiating role in reforming HRM policies, introducing new HRM policies, and processing HRM-related laws. In over two-thirds of countries they have legal responsibility for determining the pay level of civil servants, negotiating with trade unions on wage determination, and reforming the pension system

Table 6.4. **Structure and location of central HRM bodies in OECD member countries**

Structure	Location in government	Countries
No central HRM bodies		Belgium, Sweden
Single ministry/ department/agency	Finance ministry	Denmark, Finland, Portugal, Spain
	Separate ministry/department/agency	Australia, Austria, France, Germany, New Zealand, Norway, United States
	Prime minister's office or cabinet office	Czech Republic, Mexico, Slovak Republic, United Kingdom
Two agencies	Commission + management ministry	Japan, Korea
	Commission + finance ministry	Canada, Ireland

Source: OECD (2003h).

for civil servants. They also play a key role in managing and developing the senior civil service system (SCS) and in setting up basic terms and conditions of SCS. However, most countries appear to delegate the authority of recruiting and selecting candidates for SCS to line departments.

In essence, the central human resource management body retains legal authority for formulating policy and development in more than two-thirds of OECD member countries. In some countries such as Greece, Ireland, Japan, Norway, and the Slovak Republic, the central authority is responsible not just for setting policy but also for implementing it. In these systems, line departments have very little discretion or autonomy.

However, while the HRM policies are set centrally in half of OECD countries, the implementation of these policies is now decentralised. In those countries where the function is not strongly centralised – Australia, New Zealand and Sweden are the outstanding examples – the functions of the central human resource management body are limited, but in quite different ways. The contrast in approach between New Zealand and Sweden is particularly striking, especially as both are countries with low corruption and a high level of cultural cohesion. In New Zealand, although the State Services Commissioner formally carries wide human resource management authority over the public service, in practice he/she carries out this function only for chief executives of ministries and departments and relies on them to manage their staff properly. In Sweden the core function of the human resource management agency is consultancy, not only for HRM but also for management generally. A good indicator of freedom to manage is the degree to which departments, rather than central agencies, control the personnel budget. The devolution of budgetary authority is essential before central control over key human resource management aspects such as staff numbers, classification, grading and pay can be relaxed. Such devolution of budgetary authority for personnel took place between 1986 and 1993 in Canada, Denmark, Finland, the Netherlands, New Zealand, Sweden and the United Kingdom.

The degree of delegation in human resources management across OECD countries has been assessed through an index compiling different answers from the survey on strategic human resources management (OECD, 2004g).[4] Results of the index indicate that Australia, Finland, Iceland, New Zealand and Sweden appear to have the highest degree of managerial delegation of personnel matters, while Greece, Japan, Luxembourg and the Slovak Republic are the most centralised. It is also noteworthy that, in general, position-based systems seem to go hand in hand with wider freedom to manage. In many countries this freedom has been accompanied by a focus on holding managers accountable for results through systems of corporate and personal performance management.

It is not clear from the evidence to date that further decentralisation of human resource management is the trend of the future. What is clear is that if the trend towards more formal directions to departments in the form of performance agreements and contracts continues, management will take on a more strategic aspect at the centre of government than it has had to date. However it seems more likely that this role will be exercised by finance ministries or prime minister's departments than by central HRM agencies.

Table 6.5. **Index of delegation in human resources management**

Low delegation	Fairly low delegation	Fairly high delegation	High delegation
Greece	Austria	Belgium	Australia
Japan	Canada	Czech Republic	Finland
Luxembourg	France	Denmark	Iceland
Slovak Republic	Hungary	Germany	New Zealand
	Ireland	Mexico	Sweden
	Italy	Norway	
	Korea	Portugal	
	Poland	Switzerland	
	Spain	United Kingdom	
	United States		

Source: OECD (2005e).

6. Individualising: Employment contracts, accountability, performance and pay

The assumption underlying delegation is that it will enable ministries/ departments to manage their staff to improve individual and organisational performance. This delegation enables organisations to tailor their human resource management strategies to meet their objectives as well as to individualise staff treatment and management more in accordance with the individual's performance and the organisation's changing needs.

The individualisation of HRM is a broad concept, implying the management of employees as individuals, not just as part of a collective entity or by grade classification, and different treatment of staff according to the changing needs of organisations and depending on their performance. The individualisation of HR practices is at the heart of the reforms aiming at increasing the responsiveness of the public service. The trends towards individualisation have mostly taken place around the selection process, the term of appointments, termination of employment and performance management and pay.

6.1. The individualisation of employment contracts: term contract vs. permanent employment[5]

Guaranteed lifelong employment has traditionally been the norm in OECD public sectors, with much greater job security than the private sector. Indeed, job security and retirement benefits led to a popular belief in many countries that it was a good thing for a young person to obtain a public service job. In some countries, this situation has changed significantly since the late 1980s.

Since the late 1980s, four trends have characterised employment in government, in addition to the move of some government functions to State-owned enterprise (SOEs) or other government-owned organisational forms and the subsequent changes in the rules applying to their employees:

- In some countries, the specific rules under which lifelong employment in government was guaranteed have been abolished and civil servants have been put under general labour laws.

- In other countries, while lifelong employment in government remains protected, term contracts for positions have been used to increase the individual's responsibility for performance: while civil servants remain in the public service, their stay in a position is not guaranteed anymore, but rather depends on their performance. This trend is even more acute for senior managers.

- Civil servants have been put under short-term contracts with no guarantee of further employment in the civil service.

- Finally, although the OECD lacks comparative data in this area, some countries have increasingly used various contractual arrangements for employees in positions that could theoretically be filled by regular public servants. In some cases, these arrangements are even less favourable than general labour laws, since government does not always have to abide by general labour laws applicable to private firms. A hypothesis that would need to be studied further would be the link between the use of staff under less favourable terms (consultants, contract staff, etc.) and the rigidity of HR systems.

Table 6.6 gives a detailed description of civil service status development in 12 countries.

In some countries which are not included in Table 6.6, such as Austria and Spain, although lifelong employment has not been replaced by temporary (or contract) employment in general, this trend has occurred partially or in some specific sectors. In Austria, unlimited employment for senior civil servants was replaced by limited appointment in 1995. New employees tend to be employed under contracts rather than under civil service status. In Spain, there have been transformations of the legal framework of public employment in specific sectors such as national airports and ports, where statutory employment was replaced by contract employment. The differences between public service and private sector employment are lessening; legislation is becoming more flexible and fixed-term contracts are becoming more prevalent.

The move towards more temporary employment and away from lifelong careers appears to be driven mainly by the realities of the contemporary labour market. There are new attitudes and values among new entrants to the

Table 6.6. **Changing civil service status**

Countries	Development of civil service status
Australia	The ratio between "ongoing" and "non-ongoing" employees is more or less the same since 1996. Neither ongoing nor non-ongoing employees are guaranteed lifelong employment. Ongoing employees may be retrenched if they are not needed following a change in workplace needs.
Belgium	Six-year "mandate" system for managers (Director General, and two levels below).
Canada	The ratio of term/casual employees is increasing against employees on indeterminate terms.
Denmark	Significant reductions are to be expected in the number of civil servants. Civil service employment is being replaced by collective agreement employment. Temporary employment is becoming more popular in hiring at the managerial level. In 2001, about 19% of all heads of division had fixed-term employment contracts.
Finland	In jobs of a permanent nature, permanent contracts/employment relationships are used. But there is no tenure, *i.e.* there is always a possibility to give notice if there are legal grounds. There is also a possibility to use fixed-term contracts if needed on operational grounds.
Hungary	In 2001, 18 930 administrators and blue collar workers were placed under the scope of the Labour Code. Following a 2003 new amendment to the Civil Service Act, administrators have been placed back under the rules of the civil service act, but lower ranking officials remain under the scope of the general labour code.
Ireland	Contractualisation has taken place on an *ad hoc* basis and applies to a minor proportion of civil or indeed public service staff and affects only lower grade staff.
Korea	Since 1998, 20% of senior posts in central government have been open for competition. Those recruited from non-government sectors are appointed under a fixed-term contract.
New Zealand	In the public service, 93% of staff are on open-term contracts, 7% are on fixed-term contracts.
Sweden	With the exception of very few positions (such as judges), all lifelong employment in the Swedish Government administration has been replaced by employment on a permanent contract basis. This means that government employees are under the same legislation for employment protection as any employee in Sweden. Today, more than 95% of government staff are employed under a permanent contract basis.
Switzerland	As from 1 January 2002, there are no more civil servants. All federal staff have employee status except only a small category of personnel such as members of federal appeals commissions.
United Kingdom	The civil service makes use of both fixed-term and casual appointments alongside its permanent staff in order to give managers flexibility to meet genuine short-term needs sensibly and economically.

Source: OECD (2003h).

work force, a greater variety of competing jobs in the wider market, and new pressures for labour flexibility as governments are not generally in a growth phase and new jobs tend to appear at the expense of existing jobs. Governments are also increasingly anxious about the long-term financial liabilities which accumulate, particularly for health care and pensions, and the future need to reallocate staff across government sectors.

6.2. Organisational and individual performance management[6]

One of the immediate consequences of the move towards the monitoring of organisational performance (see Chapter 2) is the closer monitoring of individual performance. The emphasis on performance within various national administrations has taken a number of forms, in many cases inspired directly by private sector management methods. Individual performance management should imply a lightening of *ex ante* controls in terms of process and inputs, but a strengthening of the controls around establishing what has been accomplished – including making managers accountable for performance.[7] This requires efforts to establish a close link between organisational and personal performance through the performance management system. Performance-oriented management involves linking the targets of the unit to the strategic goals of the organisation.

Most OECD member countries have introduced individual performance appraisal systems for civil servants, which rely largely on job objectives as defined in an employee/management performance agreement rather than on standard, generalised criteria for a given job (a job description established by management irrespective of the aims for the position at a given point in time). Some countries have further developed formal contractual relationships between the most senior officials and ministries in order to reinforce accountability but also to bridge the political/administrative interface. This has occurred in some position-based systems and in countries with a long agency tradition, such as Australia, Denmark, New Zealand, Norway or Sweden. More recently, some long standing career-based systems have moved in that direction for top managers, for example, France and Korea.

The process of performance management is usually an annual cycle, where the line manager identifies key objectives for the year with his/her employee(s), generally in line with organisational goals. After a period of time (the "appraisal period", generally one year), the employee's performance is assessed by his/her manager. The evaluation can be based on a detailed grid or list of criteria or can be much more informal.

Performance appraisal systems can exist on their own, as strategic and planning management tools. They are usually linked to promotion and advancement, especially in career-based systems.

Box 6.1. **Performance agreement for senior civil servants in the United Kingdom**

The annual performance agreement for senior civil servants contains both of the following:

- Up to four key personal business objectives or targets which clearly reflect departmental priorities for the year ahead and define the in-year deliverables and the way in which performance against these targets will be measured. Objectives should as far as possible derive from published strategic or operational priorities, taking account of the department's Performance Partnership Agreement. They do not cover the whole job. Personal business objectives or targets should be stretching, tightly defined and SMART (Specific, Measurable, Agreed, Realistic and Time-related) with measures for achievement. Where targets extend beyond the appraisal year, appropriate in-year milestones should be devised. Objectives should anticipate foreseeable change. Amendments in-year should only be made in the event of significant shifts in business priorities.

- How the job is to be performed identifying the key competencies, standards and behaviours expected for the individual's current responsibilities in the year ahead, especially in relation to leadership and broader corporate objectives, including diversity. These should take into account the individual's development needs.

Source: United Kingdom (2004).

With experience and distance, the performance management systems have evolved. Ten to fifteen years ago, the most advanced countries in this field tried to implement a scientific approach to individual staff performance management, with detailed and scientific rating systems mostly looking at individuals' outputs and outcomes. Today, performance appraisals tend to rely more on the assessment of pre-identified objectives and on dialogue with line management than on strictly quantifiable indicators. Other criteria than measurable outputs also seem to have more importance such as improvement of competencies and behavioural criteria. In addition, performance rating systems are less standardised and less detailed than ten years ago.

6.3. Linking pay to performance[8]

Twenty years ago, nearly all civil servants in the central government of OECD member countries were paid according to incremental salary scales. By the turn of the millennium, an increasing number of civil servants were covered by performance-related pay (PRP) schemes of one kind or another in most OECD member countries – particularly senior managers, but increasingly also non-managerial employees. The introduction of PRP in OECD public sectors is only one facet of a wider movement towards increased pay flexibility and individualisation.

Two-thirds of OECD member countries report having implemented PRP for government employees or being in the process of doing so. However, there are wide variations in the degree to which PRP is actually applied throughout an entire civil service. In many cases, PRP concerns only managerial staff or specific departments/agencies. In addition, there is often a gap between the stated existence of a so-called performance-related pay scheme and the fact that some of these schemes are just variable pay that is not formally linked to performance.

In fact, only a handful of countries can be considered to have an extended, formalised PRP policy for civil servants and they include countries such as Denmark, Finland, Korea, New Zealand, Switzerland, and the United Kingdom.

Countries that have developed the strongest links between performance appraisals and pay are those that have the highest delegation of responsibility for human resources and budget management – usually position-based systems. However, PRP policies have recently been introduced into some career-based systems like in France, Hungary, and Korea.

There is no single model of PRP across OECD member countries. Models vary according to the nature of the civil service system, the pay determination system and the degree of centralisation or delegation in financial and human resources management. However, common trends are clearly emerging across groups of countries and in the OECD area as a whole:

- PRP policies have spread from the management level to cover many different categories of staff in the past ten years.

- Among PRP policies, there has been some increase in the use of collective or group performance schemes, at the team/unit or organisational level.

- Long-running standardised PRP schemes have evolved into more decentralised systems which facilitate delegation of managerial functions.

The size of performance payments is generally a fairly modest percentage of the base salary, especially among non-managerial employees. PRP bonuses, which tend to supplement or replace merit increments, usually represent less than 10% maximum of the base salary. At the management level, performance payments are generally higher, approximately 20% of the base salary.

Performance pay is an appealing idea, but experience indicates that its implementation is complex and difficult. Performance measurement in the public sector requires a large element of managerial judgement. The notion of performance itself is complex, owing to the difficulty of finding suitable quantitative indicators and because performance objectives often change with government policy. The impact of PRP on motivation is ambivalent: while

---

Box 6.2. **PRP in Denmark**

The Danish Government introduced performance-related pay in 1987 by establishing a local pay scheme with the intention of individualising the wage payment. In 1997 however, these local pay schemes only represented about 2% of the total wage payment in Denmark, and the budget dedicated to these policies was fairly low. As from 1997, a new pay system was introduced progressively. By collective agreement, in 2002 most of the unions entered the new pay system.

The salary policy normally includes: i) functions-related allowance; ii) quali-fication-related allowance; iii) performance-related pay. The final ambition of the new pay system is that up to 20% of the total salary payment should consist of allowances and performance-related pay. PRP applies to all staff in Denmark, but is not necessarily compulsory. PRP can be applied at the individual level or at the team/unit level.

Performance-related payments are decided on the basis of individual appraisals, based on a dialogue between the employee and the line manager. The agreements are agreed and signed by the manager and the union representative/liaison. Some institutions use a kind of balanced scorecard for this appraisal, but normally the rating is much more informal and the salary discussion is only based on the local salary policy. There are no centrally determined levels of pay reward. Top managers are assessed on the basis of organisational results (result contracts).

In 2001, the Ministry of Finance and the Danish Central Federation of State Employees' Organisations conducted an evaluation of the experiments on the new pay system in 111 government institutions. Some key results of this survey are that PRP leads to better acceptance of individual goal setting and feedback, is an incentive for staff development and the development of new competencies, and leads to improved possibilities for recruitment. Among the most negative effects was the fact that PRP represents too much administration and that the motivating effect of PRP is limited. A key lesson mentioned by Denmark is that it is crucial to pursue the HR and pay delegation within each institution/agency by empowerment of the line management to achieve the full effect of PRP.

Source: OECD (2005e).

---

it appears to motivate a minority of staff, it seems that a large majority often do not see PRP as an incentive. In fact, while base pay as it relates to the wider "market" is important, supplementary pay increases for performance are a second-rank incentive for most government employees, especially those in non-managerial roles. Job content and career development prospects have been found to be the strongest incentives for public employees. PRP is unlikely to motivate a substantial majority of staff, irrespective of the design.

However, experience shows that PRP facilitates other organisational changes. These include an improved and stronger focus on effective appraisal and goal-setting processes as well as clarification of tasks, a better attention to the acquisition of skills and team work, the improvement of employee-manager dialogue, and increased flexibilities in work organisation. Introducing PRP can be the catalyst that allows organisational changes to occur and, at the same time, facilitates a renegotiation of the "effort bargain" thus assisting in recasting the culture at the workplace. These dynamics have positive impacts on work performance.

To conclude, it appears that it is not through the financial incentives it provides that PRP can contribute to improving performance, but rather through its secondary effects – that is, the changes to work and management organisation needed to implement it. As a consequence, it is crucial not to have a narrow focus on the pay incentive aspects of PRP as the way of addressing the range of factors needed to improve performance management. The significance and impact of PRP on motivation should not be overestimated, and PRP should be seen as the catalyst for far-reaching organisational and managerial changes which then lead to improved performance.

7. Managing senior public servants

In addition to better incentives mechanisms for staff and the general monitoring of individual staff performance, most OECD countries – whether they have a career orientation or a position orientation – have put an important emphasis on better managing their senior civil service. These reforms have been seen as core in an environment where countries have delegated increased managerial responsibilities to line managers.

The senior civil service is in many instances seen as a corporate cadre whose aim, both individually and collectively, is to give a clear sense of direction to policy formulation and improve performance and effective delivery of services, both within and across departmental boundaries. Reforms of the management of senior civil servants have aimed at inducing a performance-oriented culture within the public service, enhancing personnel

Figure 6.1. **The overall impact of performance-related pay on performance**

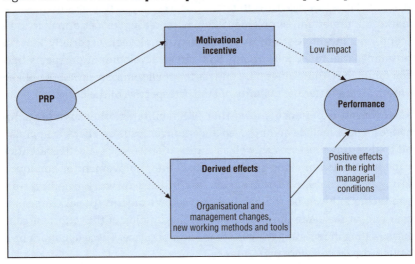

Source: OECD (2005e).

mobility between ministries or departments within the government, and developing "leadership".

Reforms can be categorised into four main trends:

● Many countries are putting a strong emphasis on developing "leaders", i.e. recruiting or nurturing staff who will be in a position to make their organisation change. This trend is very much linked to the wider trend of monitoring organisational performance. Countries would like to recruit staff at senior management level who have a proven record of achieving change in their organisation towards more efficiency and effectiveness. For countries the leadership profile includes: focusing on delivery of results, challenging assumptions, being open to learning from the outside, understanding the environment and its impact, thinking and acting strategically, building new patterns and ways of working, and developing and communicating a personal vision of change.

● Several countries have created or restructured the senior civil service and started to manage their top officials as a distinct group. Most of the countries operating a Senior Executive Service system have unique recruitment and selection procedures, which differ from those for other civil servants. Recruitment and selection of SCS are more collectively managed in most cases. And many countries have a pre-defined competency framework for selecting SCS candidates.

Box 6.3. **Policies for developing leadership: country cases**

United Kingdom

In the United Kingdom, the civil service has been undergoing major reform since 1999. The Cabinet Office has defined the leadership skills required for the 21st century, in order to establish programmes to ensure that these skills are obtained and maintained. To this end, two projects have been instituted with the aim of defining leadership: (1) to identify a set of core competencies; and (2) the Senior Civil Service Leadership Project. Leadership seminars and workshops attended by most senior civil servants have been conducted in order to canvass opinion and establish the parameters of these projects.

United States

Leadership development in the United States has been supervised by the Office of Personnel Management (OPM), established over twenty years ago. One of their first strategies was to draw up a list of Executive Core Qualifications (ECQs) which are continually monitored and adjusted to suit current requirements. Training schemes are based on these ECQs, which are designed to foster creative thinking, the ability to negotiate, relate with staff, handle increasingly complex information technology, improve business acumen, and aid in recognising particular talents amongst staff, etc. The OPM established the Office of Executive and Management Development (OEMD) to organise assessment programmes, training seminars and continuous learning opportunities. The OEMD also engages in partnerships with agencies and departments within the federal administration to examine and improve leadership skills according to their specific requirements. Another division, the Office of Resource Management, also offers leadership symposiums and seminars for networking and exchanging ideas.

Germany

In the aim of providing a more efficient and citizen-oriented civil service, almost all ministries and departments in the German federal administration have formulated their own strategies to develop and improve leadership. Newcomers to the civil service take part in compulsory introduction and induction programmes organised by the Federal Academy for Public Administration. This academy was established in 1968 for the precise purpose of training staff in the higher civil service. It also offers ongoing training during the first three years of appointment. The German public administration of today also favours generalists, and increasingly needs leaders with international skills and competence in European matters. Control of leadership is by performance dialogues at least once a year, established evaluation criteria for appointment and advancement, and a new technique introduced recently: evaluation of performance by one's own staff. The latter technique was recommended by a working group set up by the

Box 6.3. **Policies for developing leadership: country cases**
(cont.)

federal government to manage the development and implementation of leadership programmes for the future.

Sweden

In Sweden most of the recruitment decisions and management training are handled by agency managers. This provides greater flexibility to the individual departments in their staff policies, but central government maintains its control by appointing those who manage the agencies. It also maintains control in its formal recruitment policy, adopted in the mid-1990s, which emphasises professional open recruitment, increased number of women in managerial positions, the importance of induction programmes, the continuous development of managers' skills, performance dialogues and mobility between appointments.

In 1999, the Swedish government set up the National Council for Quality and Development, a body responsible for overall control of management in agencies and public administration, which offers a range of management training programmes. Amongst these is a programme for female managers and a mentor programme which has proved particularly popular.

Mexico

Recent and major reform in the Mexican civil service recognises the importance of training leaders suitable for a more efficient and people-oriented administration. This will institute recruitment policies which were previously non-existent as well as professional development programmes and performance appraisals. A compulsory training scheme for civil servants was introduced in July 2000. The Civil Service Unit (USC) within the Ministry of Finance has set up a Directive Committee on Quality, and an Executive Committee on Quality, both designed to improve the performance of leaders of the USC and to ensure that the wider society receives the services it requires.

Source: OECD (2001e).

- Many position-based countries, which traditionally are decentralised and favour lateral entries into their human resources systems, are putting an emphasis on the very early identification of future leaders and the creation of "pools" of future leaders who are given special opportunities for development, *de facto* creating more of a "career" system within an otherwise very flexible and open human resource management system.

This is the result of the recognised loss of whole-of-government values and cultural cohesion following devolution of authority, fragmentation of policy making, and changes to the recruitment and status of public servants.

● At the same time, more career-oriented systems have used reforms of the management of their senior civil service as a priority for cultural change towards more flexibility and individual accountability for performance. In recent years, Korea has opened up the recruitment of senior management to the private sector instead of only nurturing staff from within. In addition, many career-based systems have focused increasingly on the individual monitoring of senior management performance and, in some cases, have implemented PRP at senior management level.

In summary, many countries have given a renewed attention to leadership in pursuit of two somewhat conflicting goals – the use of the individual leader to spearhead better performance, and the desire to replace the collective civil service cultural glue that has been weakened by the strong individualising tendencies of other management changes. New and more demanding schemes of performance management and the implementation of performance-related pay have often been applied to senior civil servants in priority and, having decentralised human resource management generally, a good number of countries have recentralised the management of their senior civil servants by designing whole-of-government profiles and whole-of-government management schemes for senior civil servants.

8. Findings and future challenges

Over the past two decades, the majority of OECD member countries' public employment has changed significantly. The scope and pace of change has varied greatly, with some countries strongly embracing New Public Management doctrines while other countries adopted a slower pace of reform. There is evidence to suggest that these reforms have been generally successful in managing people better, sharpening the focus on government performance, providing better quality public services, and creating a managerial culture.

Nevertheless, this chapter concludes that the early reformers did underestimate the complexity of introducing private sector style HRM arrangements to the public service in spite of the fact that staying with traditional public employment arrangements was not a viable option for most countries.

It turned out that the most important issue was not whether traditional public service arrangements were good or bad as a system but that wider changes in the government sector and in the labour market required an adaptation of the management of the civil service.

The two main traditional ways of organising civil service systems, career-based and position-based, are both under pressure: the former because it lacks adaptivity, and the latter because it lacks collectivity. The modern government environment needs both, but each system has a distinctive set of formal and informal incentives and culture with its own integrity. So, simple instrumental transfers are unlikely to work. For instance, career-based civil service systems tend to generate a greater sense of collectivity and a more coherent workforce but at the expense of their capacity to adapt to changing outside circumstances. Reforms from position-based systems are often not directly transferable; they tend to emphasise individual accountability for results which is hard to implement in career-based systems. The challenge is to establish new forms of accountability for results that emphasise the responsibility of the group rather than the individual. Similarly, career-based systems opening up to lateral recruitment from outside the civil service may increase patronage or politically partisan appointments because their traditional recruitment processes do not have well-embedded competitive mechanisms for lateral entry.

Governments should understand the structural strengths and weaknesses of their existing systems and build on their strengths rather than be counter cultural. There are no easy solutions. OECD work on the management of the senior civil service demonstrated the trade-off between the individualisation and delegation of HR practices to improve the adaptivity of the civil service, and the sense of collectivity, shared values and language amongst senior civil servants and across hierarchical levels. Strongly individualised performance management has not always achieved its expected results in government, and it can sometimes be counter productive if it is done in bad managerial conditions. Overall, governments are juggling three variables. First, they are balancing between changing career-based and position-based systems for their core staff. Second, they are managing an increasing contractual workforce which is designed to improve flexibility and cover critical skill gaps. Finally, they are also, in many settings, reinforcing common values and enhancing strategic capacities through the establishment of a distinctive senior civil service body.

It is also important to give more attention to systemic issues and in particular to what can be expressed as three fundamental dilemmas:

- The increasing knowledge and skill demands of modern government and the increasing difficulty of government in attracting and keeping high-quality staff.
- The interconnectedness of key public problems, and the fragmentation and individualisation of public service responsibilities, incentives and capacities.

- How to attract and motivate senior executives who meet the high performance demands of a modern ministry, while keeping them in a wider cross-government culture bound by the public interest.

In the medium term, it appears that countries with systems tending towards the career-based end of the continuum will emphasise ways to bring more market pressures to bear, while those tending towards the position-based end of the continuum will be looking for ways to strengthen cultural cohesion. What is unclear in the longer run is how effective the current modifications to both kinds of system will be in changing the deeper cultural characteristics.

It is interesting that despite a looming crisis due to an ageing civil service and the staff reallocation needed to face the new demands on the public service as a consequence of the ageing population, not many countries seem to have addressed this issue in a systemic manner. This is probably a sign that despite fundamental changes, strategic resource allocation remains difficult in the public service. The OECD will be conducting research in this area.

Notes

1. All data are available in OECD (2002b).

2. The six enterprises include post and telecommunications, railways, national printing service, national geographical institute, public catering service, and the national data processing centre.

3. OECD (2004d).

4. The index gathers responses to 27 questions in the HRM survey, weighed according to the importance and relevance of the question. Two countries have been excluded from the index, due to lacking data (Netherlands and Turkey).

5. Based on OECD (2004d).

6. This section is based on OECD (2005e).

7. See Chapter 3 for a more detailed discussion of this approach.

8. This section is based on OECD (2005e).

ISBN 92-64-01049-1
Modernising Government: The Way Forward
© OECD 2005

Chapter 7

Modernisation: Context, Lessons, and Challenges

1. Introduction

All governments are to varying degrees engaged in public sector modernisation. It is no longer an option, but a necessity, if governments are to respond to changing societal needs and to maintain a competitive economy in an uncertain international environment.

What has become apparent from this review is that modernisation is context dependent. The national context creates opportunities and constraints that influence the nature of both the reform problem and the solution. It is important for governments to understand the risks and dynamics of their own systems of public administration and to design reforms that are not only calibrated to these specific dynamics but also adopt a whole-of -government approach. In designing reform strategies and incentives, it is important to realise that achieving objectives requires changes in behaviour from many interrelated actors in the system.

This chapter provides a general overview of the technical lessons learned about the different levers of reform, and discusses the key strategic lessons, mainly the importance of context.

2. Technical lessons learned from the different levers of reform

The modernisation review has examined the key levers that can and have been used by governments to reform their public sectors, including: open government; performance budgeting and management; accountability and control systems; restructuring organisations and reallocation; introducing market-type mechanisms; and changing public employment. Broadly, these levers seek to change the behaviour and culture of public servants and organisations through changing rules, incentives, norms and values, and structures. It is not just a question of examining how well these levers performed in helping governments adapt to the changing needs of society but also how they influenced public governance in OECD countries, and whether they had intended or unintended effects on other attributes of modern government such as responsiveness, responsibility, and legitimacy.

There is a wide variation in the pace and degree to which governments of OECD countries have pursued public sector reform. For example, New Zealand introduced performance-based budgeting and management nearly twenty years ago. In contrast, France will be fully implementing this approach across central government during 2006. Some countries have used a combination of all levers; others have concentrated on two or three.

This section examines briefly what has been learned about the trends in each of the levers of reform and their influence on governance more widely.

2.1. Open government

One of the most important changes in the period reviewed has been a move towards more open government. This trend reflects the changing nature of the relationship between citizens and the State. In the past decade, the majority of OECD countries have undertaken initiatives to make government more open. These initiatives have included the creation of new institutions and the passage of new laws. Today, 90% of OECD countries have a Freedom of Information Act and an Ombudsman office.

Transparency has unquestionably strengthened modern public governance across the board. Open government, however, goes beyond transparency. This review examines the components of open government including accessibility, public consultation on policies, and participatory decision making.

Both government services and information on government activities are more readily accessible to citizens today than twenty years ago. Governments are more user-friendly, helped by cutting through "red tape" and expanding online service delivery. Over 50% of OECD member countries have some form of customer service standards. The challenge is to meet ever-higher expectations from citizens and businesses for tailored services, universal access and streamlined transactions.

There is a greater public demand for officials not only to give a public account, but to bear personal consequences of any misuse of power or resources. Citizens increasingly expect to be informed in advance and consulted about decisions that affect them. Today, public consultation on law making and rule making is increasingly accepted as a valuable means of improving the quality of public policy while strengthening its legitimacy.

Consultation, and even active participation in decision making, does not mean that elected and appointed officials should surrender their responsibility for making final decisions (OECD, 2001b). To do so would undermine the established ministerial accountability mechanisms of representative government, which is a key pillar of governance.

Openness in itself does not necessarily improve governance, nor does it override all other public values. It should be balanced against other values of efficiency, equity, and responsibility. A significant challenge facing governments today is balancing the need to ensure greater national security with the need to preserve openness.

2.2. Enhancing performance and control

The view that public management should be judged on its performance is here to stay. In today's increasingly complex society, performance and control are essential for successful government. One of the most common approaches to improving public sector performance has been the introduction of performance budgeting and management. For example, 72% of OECD countries include non-financial performance data in their budget documentation, although most countries continue to struggle with integrating this information into their budgeting decision-making processes.

There has been greater success with introducing performance information into management systems. This approach has generally advocated relaxing input controls and devolving authority from central agencies to the actual service providers. The idea is to give managers the authority, and the incentive, to make decisions and manage resources in the way that they judge best suited to producing the desired outcomes. This requires government to focus on performance, to clarify organisational objectives and to motivate public officials to achieve them. At the same time, budgetary controls will continue to be used to drive the search for efficiency. However, governments should be wary of overestimating the potential of performance-oriented approaches to change behaviour and culture, and of underestimating the limitations of performance-based systems.

For OECD countries, a key issue that has emerged from the use of this reform lever is how to integrate performance measurement systems with the particular country's traditional accountability system, and how to balance the need for control with managerial flexibility.

Devolving management and focusing on performance can create problems of control. Public sector agencies and managers must have clearly defined responsibilities. If devolved agencies do not know where they stand vis-à-vis central agencies or government, and if their new responsibilities are combined with many of the old practices of accountability, of interference and of political uncertainty, then the potential benefits of devolved authority will be lost. The efficient use of resources in such a system requires a willingness to manage risk in a way that does not fit comfortably with an adversarial political environment (and media) that seeks to identify and punish every apparent failure of service delivery or financial control. Central agencies dealing directly with government are vulnerable to political pressure and may find it difficult to give genuine authority to devolved managers. At the worst, central agencies may view output controls and measures as an additional level of control rather than a replacement for input controls.

In addition, in OECD countries with highly delegated systems, managers have heavy responsibilities for performance, strategy, reputation, the deployment of human and financial resources, internal control and accountability. This burden can defeat managers unless central agencies develop risk assessment and management processes to ensure that the control, while effective, is not unnecessarily restrictive. Failing this, government can be left exposed to risk, which relatively free agents are meant to manage. A handful of countries encourage or require departments to have formal risk management techniques in place.

Across OECD countries, internal control systems do not appear to be keeping pace with change, as there is no tendency to cover performance information in any depth. While there have been improvements in external performance reporting, especially with the increased auditing by SAIs, this area is still underdeveloped. Most results information provided to parliaments and the public lacks independent verification. In the majority of OECD countries, parliament does not use the performance information provided to it.

Governments have always struggled with finding a balance between flexibility and control in their administrative systems. Too much discretion for public servants may result in abuse of authority, distortion of policies, self-interested judgement, or even increased corruption. Limiting discretion extensively through rules and regulations can result in inefficiency, ineffectiveness and an unresponsive public service. Indeed, reformers who call for greater autonomy and flexibility have argued that the problem is not that there are too few checks on the public sector, but too many. The rules designed to ensure accountability and control may create inefficiency and become ends in themselves. Formal compliance with regulations can be a feature of the modern devolved, performance-oriented public service just as it was in the centralised, process-driven public sector of old.

Reform initiatives, in theory, seek to delegate authority, increase flexibility and relax input controls. Across OECD countries in general, however, there is no clear pattern of input controls being lightened as performance indicators are strengthened. The delegation of authority and the relaxation of input controls have happened quickly or have not been accompanied by adequate risk management techniques, resulting in problems of scandals and misuse of funds. At the other extreme, some countries have not relaxed input controls at all, but have imposed additional reporting requirements on top of existing ones. There is a continuing struggle to find the right balance between control and flexibility, which is dependent on the individual country context.

2.3. Reallocation and restructuring

In response to pressures for change, governments must continually adjust their structure and reallocate resources. Structural change, however, should not be undertaken lightly. For reforms that have emphasised the creation of agencies, there is a danger of fragmenting government into a series of autonomous agencies lacking a common purpose or ethos. Such bodies should still operate within the main body of administrative law, and their autonomy should not be at the expense of the capacity for whole-of-government policy making and accountability.

Nor should established organisations be dismantled lightly. They provide stability and continuity in policy advice and administration, and allow officials to build up the reputation, capacity, knowledge and relationships necessary for addressing complex public policy problems. Once lost through radical restructuring, it takes a long time for them to be rebuilt and, in the interim, governments run the risk of under-performance. To retain a functioning public service, governments should understand the structural strengths and weaknesses of their existing systems and build on their strengths.

Nonetheless, the capacity to make timely adjustments to organisational form is essential for a modern government. The development of modern accounting and information technology has made arm's-length management of public agencies more possible and allows for a greater range of agency types, better tailored to their specific responsibilities. The adoption of innovative administrative structures, the decentralisation of management responsibility and the introduction of market-style methods of service delivery should improve the quality of outcomes. Nevertheless, these actions may not reduce the size of central agencies. Governments that have introduced these types of changes have also found that they need to invest in strengthened co-ordination mechanisms and core government steering capacities.

As governments move forward in deciding on future organisational change, the case for adopting a whole-of-government perspective is overwhelming. How new structures will relate to government's overall purposes and interests, to general government rules and processes, and to the existing process for oversight and democratic accountability must be thought through before the implementation of structural change.

The deeply ingrained disposition towards coping with change by increasing the budget is no longer unsustainable. The strategic use of the budget process emerged as a powerful management tool in the period under review, both for resource reallocation and as a driver for management changes. Thus, the budget process, which has been used to force cutbacks, has also helped to push a wider administrative focus on efficiency and effectiveness. The need for reallocation will continue as governments respond to changing pressures and political priorities.

2.4. Changing public employment

A key element for keeping pace with change is to reorient the incentives and attitudes of public servants. National differences in this area are less to do with management theory than with underlying beliefs about the role of the State and its relationship to the individual. With the diversification of public employment systems through the increasing use of contracts and casual staff, the use of consultancy services and, in some countries, the creation of arm's-length public bodies with distinctive employment conditions, the logic of a single overriding public employment system is not compelling.

The public interest continues to be paramount but it is clear that it can be promoted through a variety of employment systems. Systems tending towards the position-based end of the continuum will tend to have a weaker sense of collective values and may lack coherence. In contrast, systems in which the career-based approach predominates tend to generate a greater sense of collective purpose and a more coherent workforce but may be less adaptable to changing outside circumstances. The lateral recruitment of specialists into such systems may also be problematic, disrupting hierarchies and salary differentials and posing problems of patronage or politicisation as government tries to buy in expertise it believes is lacking within the established structure. Position-based systems tend to emphasise individual responsibility and accountability for results, which can be hard to implement in career-based systems.

Reforms appropriate to one system are often not directly transferable to the other. Administrative efficiency may require the adoption of a range of agency structures and career options for individuals, both characterised by greater individual autonomy and responsibility. However it is vital that a common public service ethos and commitment to a wider cause be fostered. There are no easy solutions, but what clearly stands out is that governments need to give more attention to whole-of-government human resource management policies. Social controls on behaviour will always be of particular importance in the complexity of government. Without the willing commitment of staff to a wider cause, modern public management is impossible.

2.5. Market-type mechanisms

Market-type mechanisms of various kinds have become more common across OECD countries. After stopping direct delivery of utilities and other services, governments have in many cases constructed markets to ensure competition. Outsourcing has also grown significantly over the past two decades and has become a mainstream element of modern public administration in most OECD member countries. Its introduction however is sometimes controversial. The controversy can arise from the displacement of public servants, the opposition of unions, and the mistrust of the public. It will continue to be important for governments to manage these factors because it is inevitable, with the demands on government and the further development of private sector services, that there will be more outsourcing in the future.

The value of outsourcing depends on the nature of the service, the market of suppliers and the governance risks. In societies where corruption is a live issue or, more specifically where ensuring that contracts are managed in the public interest is problematical, outsourcing can be risky. If the risks of non-delivery are such that government has to put a huge effort into detailed specification, monitoring and enforcement, the advantages of outsourcing will be eroded. These risks vary by the nature of service, by sector and by country.

Public-private partnerships (PPPs) appear to have a significant but limited role in public management. They are most appropriate for large-scale projects such as highways that involve extensive maintenance and operating requirements over the project's life. The larger the maintenance and operating components, the greater the potential for efficiency gains. Conceptually, PPPs are a specialised form of outsourcing. Their strength appears to come from the internalisation of incentives for ultimate project success. It could well be that these advantages could be achieved without the debatable dimension of private financing.

Vouchers and voucher-like mechanisms are significant in OECD member countries and their use is likely to increase, especially in social services. However, their impact on the flexibility of public finance will be a limiting factor in the period ahead when most governments will be under heavy pressure to reallocate funds to meet the rising costs of pensions and health. The governance limitations on the use of vouchers are threefold. First, they may allow consumer choice at the expense of equity; second, as an expenditure system geared directly to demand, they can create problems for containing public expenditure; and finally, care must be taken to ensure that suppliers do not focus only on higher yield consumers.

Vouchers are a useful means of allocating social services in a manner sensitive to demand. Their application, while significant, will be limited to areas where there are clearly delineated and reasonably standard services. Context is relevant to compliance costs. In a society with a highly compliant culture, it is easier to have reasonable assurance of the genuineness of demand.

Looking forward, a key challenge for government is how to use these levers in an individual country context and from a systemic perspective in order to promote the public sector's overall capacity to adapt to changes while maintaining core values and public confidence.

3. Context matters: Can governments learn from each other?

In view of the differences in national context, the most challenging question in any study of public administration that takes an internationally comparative approach is: What are the relevance and the applicability of such a study to individual countries?

The characteristics of governments and their administrative systems arise from their history and circumstances. Figure 7.1 illustrates how national context can flow through to contemporary governance and public management policy.

Figure 7.1 also illustrates the complexity of the factors and inter-relationships that must be considered before embarking on any programme of public sector management reform and the implication of the range of directions in which reform may go. Whether public management systems will evolve in the direction of devolution and delegation of authority and the use of markets; whether they will embrace openness; to what degree they need formalisation or more or less diversity of government arrangements – these questions are strongly influenced by structural factors and historical momentum. Factors such as population diversity, size, and social and economic cleavages affect the level of trust within a society and society's trust

Figure 7.1. **Factors and interrelationships underpinning public sector management**

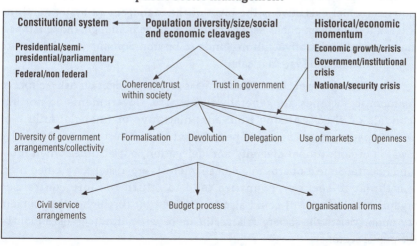

in government. These in turn affect the capacity to devolve, delegate, diversify, open up or formalise public management. The security or economic situation will also affect both the capacity of government to reform public administration and the direction in which public administration evolves. The broad constitutional system, itself a product of history, shapes the general management rules and processes, and sets the political threshold for change in specific areas (e.g. the capacity to change labour relations) but only marginally affects the capacity to reform public administration.

3.1. Organisational structures

Changing organisational structure is context dependent. Both the overall institutional structure of the public sector and the culture which informs attitudes to it, among staff and the general public, are unique products of each country's history, constitutional structure and current political, social and economic circumstances. For example, countries that have successfully created semi-autonomous agencies to administer large areas of the public sector tend to have had a well-embedded culture of disinterested public service and a history of relatively low corruption at either the political or administrative levels. These would appear to be essential pre-conditions, and their absence may explain why agency-style reforms have not worked well in developing countries.

The appropriate methods for exercising control over core government agencies are also highly sensitive to the prevailing ethos of each individual country. Control methods sit along a continuum from the explicit contractual relationships, for example in New Zealand, to the implicit controls derived from the general societal ethos and the specific culture of the public sector, as in Japan. Perhaps the former corresponds better in a culture where the individual chief executive is the pivot of the management system and the latter in a collectivist public service culture. It is clear enough, though, that if the wider administrative culture tends to be non-compliant and prone to corruption, a formal system is safer.

The desirability of certain structures is also dependent on risk. Politics in democratic societies are generally risk averse. Governments do not like scandals or shocks arising from administrative or financial failure or unanticipated crises. In stable periods, the public sector tends to evolve towards organisational diversity and delegation, but at times when more fundamental State (or partisan political) interests are at stake, e.g. when there is a threat to security, countries tend to return to more centralised organisational forms. It could also be argued that the higher the ambient corruption risk in the society at large, the more vertically integrated should be the public sector.

3.2. Budgeting

By contrast with changing structures, budgeting (and reporting) is becoming a common international practice characterised by a high level of mutual learning and benchmarking. Budgeting is also subject to an international context that demands openness and the adoption of common standards and practices. Governments whose fiscal position is unsound, unpredictable or obscure pay a penalty in terms of borrowing costs and low investment. Furthermore, governments are increasingly linked in a common global business cycle. Much of the pressure on individual governments to address issues such as the size of budget deficits, levels of public debt and the overall size of government has come from external economic and market forces.

However, when the budget process is also the platform for introducing management and other microeconomic changes to the whole-of-government process, context dependency is important. The merits of policies such as individualising performance incentives, more use of market-type mechanisms and private providers, or setting up arm's-length delivery structures cannot be judged *a priori*. How they will work varies according to the underlying institutional structures.

3.3. Employment

Employment arrangements tend to have deep roots in the society in question. There are differences in values and attitudes including those with regard to trust in government and the role of government, the role of trade unions, the responsibilities of firms for their employees, the ability to achieve consensus, attitude to authority, disposition to obey the law, sense of fairness, and level of tolerance for inequalities in society. However there do seem to be clusters of countries with generally similar human resource management dynamics. Where these can be identified there could be systems learning amongst the more similar countries.

3.4. Accountability and control

OECD member countries are not converging in the accountability and control techniques used in the public sector. Such systems complement the constitutional architecture of the country in question. Key constitutional differences are the relative influence of the executive, the legislature and the judiciary, and the relationship to them of the machinery for external invigilation. Whether the locus of external control is the court of accounts, the ministry of finance, the parliament, the auditor general or a general accounting office derives directly from deeper governance arrangements. There are also differences in the processes and priorities of public management. Countries face different risks – both from their external environment and from the ambient culture. To be effective, control and accountability must be calibrated to those risks. Approaches to management predicated on high social control cannot, for example, be expected to work where the ambient culture has strong features of clientelism.

3.5. Performance

At the rhetorical level, measuring and improving the performance of the public sector is of interest to all OECD member countries, but the choice of performance-related instruments is highly context dependent. A country seeking to devise a strategy for enhancing system-wide performance must consider a range of issues.

At the outset, it is important to define the characteristics of the performance problem. For example, are the culture and structure of the public sector ones that emphasise process and compliance over outcomes or do the main weaknesses appear to be in aligning individual with corporate objectives, motivating individuals, or obtaining credible feedback? The answers to these questions will determine the extent and direction of reform. If a system is seeking to move to a more performance-focussed approach to public management, it must address the nature of the control environment. For a performance orientation to work, managers need some freedom to make managerial choices, and central agencies such as the ministry of finance need to be confident that the tools for reliable measurement and evaluation are available. The effectiveness and level of compliance with existing controls is a good indicator that greater autonomy will be used responsibly.

4. Strategic lessons: Improving the empirical basis

The question may arise as to whether, given the unique nature of each society and the importance of context in designing any reform programme, learning from other countries or developing common international standards are likely to be productive or even possible. However, there are clearly factors at work that support the transfer of ideas, policies and even institutional designs across borders.

The attempt to establish international principles and standards has a long history. Core principles related to the protection of the rights of individuals, regarded as universal, have been articulated in international law since the 19th century. Universally applicable standards in matters such as the law of the sea have similarly long histories. With globalisation, the volume and scope of international standard setting is increasing rapidly – and is an important function of bodies such as the OECD. There are also wider governance principles that are held in common by many countries and that in some cases are codified into standards and good practices. There is a high degree of agreement across OECD member countries on the underlying principle of open government, regardless of national context. Increasingly, OECD member countries are also agreeing to codification and international and national disclosure in specific areas such as economic reporting, national statistics and fiscal policy. As globalisation proceeds, the range of international principles and standards on issues relating to public management will increase. The OECD has a role in brokering such agreements via guidelines on conflicts of interest, budget transparency, etc., and the scope for this will increase.

The "best practice" movement – the attempt to improve by emulating successful techniques from others in the same business – has also had a strong influence on spreading standards and practices across international boundaries. It is an attractive idea, partly because it is easy and inexpensive to apply. It has been particularly influential in areas such as manufacturing, where similar processes in different countries can be measured and compared. The "best practice" approach has been a strong element in comparative public administration over the entire review period. Particular instruments and policies developed in one jurisdiction have been copied in others (for example, the United Kingdom Next Steps agency model and the Swedish institution of Ombudsmen have both been widely copied). The OECD publicised best practices on a wide range of public administration topics amongst all OECD member countries. The weakness of the best practice approach is that governments may be very differently structured and the components of their systems are interdependent. Therefore, the usefulness of introducing a particular technique – say, performance-related pay – will be heavily influenced by the institutional culture and the quality of other managerial factors.

Such borrowings have had successes and failures. The successes tend to be amongst countries with strong similarities, for example, amongst the Nordic countries, and amongst the Westminster-derived countries. However, there is much less interest in exchanges across different jurisdictional types within the OECD area. For example, in international development assistance there have been many instances of practices that were developed in OECD member countries being transferred to jurisdictions of quite different types and different stages of development. Sometimes such transfers have been harmful, and a strong body of professional opinion has now turned decisively against such transfers.

The major problem with "best practice" transfer is not the principle of practical mutual learning, but the "unit of exchange". The transfer of a specific process depends on the new organisational setting being similar to the old. In a healthy well-managed organisation, performance-related pay may well strengthen the organisational sense of purpose. However, in a hierarchical, non-transparent and "political" organisation, it may have adverse impacts. If the exchange was not of a specific technique, but of an understanding of the dynamics of a healthy, well-performing organisation, it is more likely to be worthwhile.

A final problem with "best practice" learning can be poor problem definition and universal application of the favoured remedy. As mentioned above, the application of any new practice, structure or management technique should be preceded by a thorough analysis of the problem being addressed and the outcome sought.

Learning across jurisdictions is more likely at the level of systems than instruments. The analysis of systems encourages those involved to see what is feasible, to identify differences, and to avoid trying grafts that will be rejected.

One area of successful systemic learning has been around national budgeting systems and particularly the move across OECD countries towards top-down budgeting. Principles of good budgeting are applicable regardless of national context because budgeting policies are of wide interest to international markets and therefore governments want to present their policies in a credible way. Budgeting also involves areas of internationally agreed principles such as statistical reporting, accounting and transparency.

A variation on "best practice" is the adoption of policies on an *a priori* basis. Where best practice seeks to generalise from the success of a proven technique, this approach argues that because a technique is based on and conforms to strong intellectual principles, it is universally applicable. A number of ideas entered public administration from New Institutional Economics – for example, the separation of policy agencies from implementing agencies on the basis of agency theory. The strength of the approach is that it is inexpensive and apparently intellectually rigorous. The weaknesses are that the principle may be untried and gives little guidance on implementation (should government have two policy agencies or a hundred?), and reality usually involves the balancing of contending principles. A *priori* management policies are marketed and adopted as if they are not context dependent when, in fact, they usually are.

Relativists might argue that each public management system is unique because of its history, culture and circumstance, and that improvements can only be home grown. There are areas of government where this viewpoint is justifiable. Where cultural and social influences are dominant, for example in the political-administrative interface, it is often difficult to isolate the determining factor – and then almost impossible to replicate it elsewhere. This is not an area for direct borrowing of techniques. While the principle of public service professionalism in advice to politicians is widely shared, instilling it at the local level depends heavily on informal factors. However, as a general proposition, relativism is untenable and is sometimes misused as a defence against the application of well-established international principles and standards.

4.1. Improving mutual learning at the international level

An important issue for the OECD Public Governance Committee is to know how transferable public management policies are. This section discusses the considerations contributing to a framework in which to make such judgements.

It is assumed that for issues that are or will soon be covered by internationally accepted principles or standards, context dependency is low. The problems of context arise at the practical level when the principle is being applied. For instance, it might be generally accepted that political parties should be funded in a way that does not make them vulnerable to improper influence. Whether this is best dealt with by banning private funding or by making all donations transparent is a contextually sensitive choice.

The borrowing or fostering of specific instruments as "best practice" is appropriate only between very similar situations. General principles and an understanding of the dynamics of management and governance systems are more widely transferable. Taking a systemic as opposed to an instrumental approach to public sector change requires an analysis of the reasons for the current unsatisfactory state of affairs, a focus on the major behavioural change desired and finally the development of an integrated plan for the instrumental changes that have to be made to bring about the desired behavioural change. Reform processes that select the reform instrument before diagnosing the underlying problem stand a high risk of failure.

All public management instruments need to be tested in the kind of environment in which they are expected to operate, including those with strong a priori appeal. Evaluation of such instruments tends to be expensive and difficult but, given that instruments, once in place, tend to endure, the benefit-to-cost ratio can be very high indeed.

Insight into the dynamics of a country's public management system can be assisted by the study of other governments with similarities in respect of the area being addressed. In assessing the degree of similarity between systems, this study highlights the following important areas, each of which should be seen as a continuum:

- Collectivised vs. individualised human resource management (both nationally and in government);
- Unified vs. diverse national culture;
- High vs. low compliance risk (both nationally and in government);

- Centralised *vs.* delegated management;

- High prestige *vs.* low prestige public service;

- Dominant *ex ante vs. ex post* controls;

- Strong *vs.* weak parliamentary scrutiny;

- Open *vs.* secretive administrative cultures (including degree of public accountability);

- Unified *vs.* distributed public agencies;

- Strong *vs.* weak unionisation;

- Co-operative *vs.* confrontational industrial relations (nationally as well as in government);

- Career-based *vs.* position-based public service systems;

- High *vs.* low tendency to use market-type mechanisms and private agents.

Findings from the review brought to light that the position of a particular system along each of these continuums creates a different dynamic in public management processes. The first temptation in managing knowledge transfer across national contexts is to group geographically or historically related countries together. However, that would be limiting: it would underestimate differences within culturally similar countries and fall short of the true potential of comparative public management. From the criteria in the list above, there may be more similarities between Japan and France than between, say, France and Italy. Understanding how these factors affect different national settings is a potentially rich source of inter-governmental learning. The elaboration of this approach is a subject for future work.

5. Conclusion

Twenty years of reform have seen significant changes in public sector management in OECD member countries. Compared with two decades ago, today the governments of most OECD countries are more transparent, accessible and customer-aware, more devolved, more efficient, and more performance-focused. Also, the mode of government intervention has changed significantly from direct provision of services to regulation of markets.

The extent of change, however, should not be overstated. The pace and extent of reform ranges from the sudden shock experienced by Finland in the early 1990s, to the slower incremental pace of change in France. Fiscal crisis has generally, but not always, been the trigger. East European accession countries introduced change in order to meet the European Union entry criteria. The latest modernisation initiative in the Netherlands was launched in reaction to recent political and societal tensions. The approaches and objectives have differed as have the changes themselves, varying from wholesale transformation of government to mere tinkering at the margins.

The reforms have produced positive benefits. However, in many countries they have not lived up to expectations or have had unintended consequences such as negative effects on underlying governance values and capacity. The process of change also showed that public administrative arrangements are inextricably linked to deeper institutions of public governance, and that managerial changes which affect the role of government can be intensely political. The values of responsiveness, responsibility, and legitimacy are in ascending order of governance importance. Public management policy makers need to be aware of possible impacts at all three levels.

OECD countries' experiences highlight that the same reform instrument/technique functions differently in different country contexts and produces different results. In addition, management techniques used and developed in the private sector have proven problematic when transferred to the public sector.

There is no single generic solution to the problems of public administration. Countries come from different starting points, each with a unique context, and face different problems. Therefore, modernisation is not just a matter of applying new techniques and instruments that can easily be transferred from one country to another. That would ignore the complexity of public sector reform and the fact that reformers are not beginning with a blank slate – they are introducing instruments into an existing system, with its own set of institutions, rules, cultural values, incentives and relationships, all of which have formal and informal dimensions.

The main lesson that emerges from this review is that modernisation is context dependent: the nature of the problem and the solution are strongly influenced by the national country context. The design of reform strategies must be calibrated to the specific risks and dynamics of the national public administration system and take a whole-of-government approach.

Traditional thinking on public sector reform has often seen policy, people, money, and organisations as if they were independent components of public management. This study has made it clear that they are closely interlinked. It is important for reform strategies to take account of the interlinked nature of these components of government. This can help reduce potential tensions and contradictions in reform initiatives.

Furthermore, when designing new reform strategies it is vital to engage in thorough analysis of the problems to be addressed and the desired outcomes. It is also important to engage in honest and independent evaluations of what has been achieved. All too often, countries impose one reform on top of another without evaluating the results and effects of the previous initiatives.

Reform requires focus, the mobilisation of resources, incentives, and persistence. Developing a modernisation strategy encompasses understanding the nature of the problems and devising solutions that can be applied in the given country context. Successful reform also requires a strategy that puts reform on the political agenda and obtains and maintains the support of those necessary to implement the new initiatives and make them work.

MODERNISATION: THE WAY FORWARD

Twenty years ago some public sector reformers had the ambition to refurbish or replace what they saw as an outdated set of institutions. Others resisted these ideas, fearing that commercial and economic notions were intruding on the complex domain of government and putting the public interest at risk. Representatives from different countries were aligned for or against. Practitioners in many countries began to experiment with the new approaches.

The year 2005 brought a different perspective. Both points of view still had some validity, but the driver of change was not new ideas about public management. The impetus came from the political, social, technological, and economic developments in the latter half of the 20th century, which put pressure on all governments in every part of the world to adapt to new problems, new capacities and new relationships between citizens and governments.[1] It was essential to bring in new ideas about public management. Even more important was to incorporate them within the core institutions and values that form the governance architecture of OECD member countries.

Strategic Findings

To help countries go forward, this review identifies some areas for attention in public management policy design and implementation:

- Public management policy now has a much higher political profile than twenty years ago. This is good where it offers sustained leadership for difficult changes. However, there are dangers of politicising arrangements which should be managed in the light of long-term governance, or of introducing politically attractive but ineffective short-term solutions to entrenched problems.

- There is no clear line between governance and public management – any significant public administrative change has governance consequences. There is a hierarchy of such consequences, described in ascending order of importance as responsiveness, responsibility, and legitimacy.

MODERNISATION: THE WAY FORWARD (cont.)

● Public management policies need to be designed and adjusted from a whole-of-government perspective. Knowledge of possible new instruments of public management is readily available. Much more difficult is building the capacity to understand a specific social and administrative environment to the point of being able to make effective changes.

● A feature of the reform period has been measures that, individually and in their totality, tailor government structures, processes and services to the needs of target groups and individuals. This puts delivery at a remove from central control, and creates a micro-political constituency in support of the service that can become a problem if the service has to be reduced or withdrawn. Governments will increasingly need to respond to new demands by taking resources from existing services to invest in new ones. Responsiveness to organised public opinion may make reallocation more difficult in the medium term.

● The politics of persuading the general public of the need to reduce expenditure has tended to give an exaggerated ideological edge to "Big Bang" reforms. The rhetoric of change can be excessively critical of existing public management and over-optimistic about the capacity of new instruments. Given that the need for periodic fiscal reallocation is not diminishing, there is a need to de-politicise these adjustments.

● The ambitions of the modern public sector are attainable only insofar as agencies and their staff internalise the necessary motivation, values and discipline. Instrumental change alone cannot transform behaviour. There is a need for an investment in building a more principled and empirically based public management policy capacity in governments.

● A by-product of the reform period is public management terminology designed for persuasion rather than analysis. This encourages a fixation on instruments and a tendency to lurch from one reform to another. The capacity of government to adapt would be strengthened by more sober analysis and appraisal, notwithstanding the need for persuasion in implementing change.

● While all countries in the OECD area are subject to similar pressures, their responses are heavily influenced by individual context. Mutual learning has never been so important, but mimicry of others' management techniques has little value. There needs to be better means to analyse the distinctive dynamics and priorities of public administrative structures in each country, and better hypotheses for appropriate intervention. International learning in public management would be enhanced if the focus were more on system dynamics than instruments, and if there were a stronger empirical base for claims of success and failure.

MODERNISATION: THE WAY FORWARD (cont.)

Findings on key public management policy levers

- Privatisation, the move from service delivery to regulation, the creation of quasi-markets, and the contracting in and out of services are essential tools for modern government as it responds to changing needs and capacities in society. Whether they are appropriate in a particular case should be decided not as a matter of general principle, but in terms of the benefits and risks to the policy area, bearing in mind the longer-term collective and governance interests of the society in question.

- The budget process has emerged as a key strategic management instrument for resource reallocation and as a platform for management changes. The need to reallocate funds to new services requires a stronger top-down budgeting process. While governments would like major resource reallocation to be smooth and timely, it has been observed that such changes occur stochastically, with stability punctuated by short politically dramatic episodes of reform and adjustment. These periods of adjustment also open the system up to new ideas.

- In all dimensions of management, individuals' motivation, values and attitudes are more important than formal systems. Strategies to strengthen control and accountability must take account of this or they will fail. Performance-oriented management can and should allow a lightening up of input and process controls, not because formal performance planning and reporting becomes the control system, but rather because formal controls can be partly replaced by social controls as staff internalise organisational goals. The cost of this is that senior officers must give much more attention to management than was necessary in a traditional bureaucracy.

- The adaptation of public service employment systems is of key importance. While countries tend to favour either a more individualised system (position-based systems) or a more collective system (career-based systems), in practice most countries have drawn on both systems to meet particular needs. These changes have tended to be made piecemeal and risk undermining the overall coherence of civil service systems. The two systems have different strengths, all of which are desirable in modern public administration. Combining them in a coherent public management system is a major challenge.

- The selection, management, development and holding to account of senior public servants has been given high priority in a very wide range of countries. "Leadership" is seen as the key to leading change, inspiring staff, increasing performance, and strengthening values. There is conflict within these objectives and governments need to be clear on their specific priorities.

MODERNISATION: THE WAY FORWARD *(cont.)*

- The performance orientation of public management is here to stay. Societies are now too complex to be managed only by rules for input and process and a public-spirited culture. However, there has been a tendency to overestimate the potential of performance-oriented approaches to change behaviour and culture, and to underestimate the limitations of performance goals and results in the public management process. External performance reporting and auditing are still underdeveloped – most results information provided to parliaments and the public lacks independent verification. Much of the information provided to parliaments is unused by them.

- Performance, though important, is not government's only concern. Governments have a limited attention span, and too strong an emphasis on performance can distract necessary attention from underlying governance values such as equity.

- A growing number of countries assign accountability to individuals rather than to groups or organisations; for the straightforward areas of public service, this works well. In challenging policy areas, it is difficult to individualise accountability for policies which must be collaborative and in which the impact of actions is difficult to isolate. There is a Hobson's choice between individualising accountability but missing full policy intent and perhaps discouraging teamwork, or collectivising accountability but making it hard to assign individual reward or gain.

- Governments must keep adjusting their structure to remain relevant. The long-standing tendency in many governments to accept structural arrangements as a "given" will be difficult to sustain in the future. However, structural change creates serious discontinuities and should be considered only after management remedies are exhausted. Governments need a whole-of-government perspective on how structure relates to overall purposes and interests, and they need rules and processes for the oversight and democratic accountability of all government bodies.

Citizens' expectations and demands of governments are growing, not diminishing: they expect openness, higher levels of service quality delivery, solutions to more complex problems, and the maintenance of existing social entitlements. Reforms to the public sector in the past 20 years have significantly improved efficiency, but governments of OECD countries now face a major challenge in finding new efficiency gains that will enable them to fund these growing demands on 21st century government. For the next 20 years, policy makers face hard political choices. Since most governments cannot increase their share of the economy, in some countries this will put pressure

MODERNISATION: THE WAY FORWARD (cont.)

on entitlement programmes. These new demands on builders of public management systems will require leadership from officials with enhanced individual technical, managerial and political capacities who think and plan collectively and who can work well with other actors.

1. The authoritative review by Pollitt and Bouckaert (2004) concludes with the statement "…a crucial ingredient of a successful reform strategy is that it should create and sustain conditions in which 'small improvements' – many of them unforeseen and unforeseeable – can flourish."

Bibliography

Campbell Public Affairs Institute (2003), *National Security and Open Government: Striking the Right Balance*, Campbell Public Affairs Institute, Syracuse University, Syracuse, New York.

Canadian Government (2003), "InfoSource Bulletin 2003 – Privacy Act and Access to Information Act", Bulletin No. 26, December, Ottawa, *www.infosource.gc.ca*.

Cave, M. (2001), "Voucher Programmes and their Role in Distributing Public Services", *OECD Journal on Budgeting*, Vol. 1, No. 1, OECD, Paris.

Christensen, Tom, and Per Laegreid (eds.) (2002), *New Public Management: The Transformation of Ideas and Practice*, Ashgate Publishing Limited, Burlington, Vermont.

Clark, Frances, *et al.* (2001), *Long-Run Costs and Performance Effects of Competitive Sourcing*, Center for Naval Analysis (CNA), Alexandria, Virginia.

Committee of Sponsoring Organizations of the Treadway Commission (COSO), *www.coso.org*.

Commonwealth Secretariat (2002), *Commonwealth Public Administration Reform 2003*, The Stationery Office, Norwich, United Kingdom.

Condrey, Stephen E., and Robert Maranto (eds.) (2001), *Radical Reform of the Civil Service*, Lexington Books, Lanham, Maryland.

Coplin, William D., Astrid E. Merget, and Carolyn Bourdeaux (2002), "The Professional Researcher as Change Agent in the Government Performance Movement", *Public Administration Review*, Vol. 62, No. 6, American Society for Public Administration, Washington DC.

Curristine, Teresa (2002), "Reforming the U.S. Department of Transportation: Challenges and Opportunities of the Government Performance and Results Act for Federal-State Relations", *Publius: The Journal of Federalism*, Vol. 32, No. 1, Center for the Study of Federalism, Temple University, Philadelphia, Pennsylvania.

Dilger, R.J., *et al.* (1997), "Privatization of Municipal Services in America's Largest Cities," *Public Administration Review*, Vol. 57, No. 1, Blackwell Publishing, Oxford, United Kingdom.

Drewry, Gavin, and Tony Butcher (1991), *The Civil Service Today* (2nd edition), Blackwell, London.

Eggers, William, and Stephen Goldsmith (2003), "Networked Government", *Government Executive*, Vol. 35, Issue 7, Executive Publications, Washington DC.

Euro-barometer (2004), *Euro-barometer Spring 2004: Public Opinion in the European Union*, Commission of the European Communities, Brussels.

European Investment Bank (2004), *The EIB's role in public-private partnerships*, European Investment Bank, Luxembourg, *www.eib.eu.int*.

European Union (2004), "New decision of Eurostat on deficit and debt: Treatment of public-private partnerships", Eurostat Press Office, Luxembourg, *http://europa.eu.int/comm/eurostat*.

Farazmand, Ali (ed.) (2002), *Administrative Reform in Developing Nations*, Praeger, Westport, Connecticut.

Feldman, Martha S., and Ann M. Khademian (2002), "To Manage is to Govern", *Public Administration Review*, Vol. 62, No. 5, American Society for Public Administration, Washington DC.

Finer, S.E. (1997), *The History of Government from the Earliest Times,* Vol. 3, Oxford University Press, New York.

Finland Government (2004), "Civil Participation Policy Programme", Helsinki, *www.valtioneuvosto.fi/vn/liston/base.lsp?r=40242&k=en.*

Geva-May, Iris (2002a), "Comparative Studies in Public Administration and Public Policy", *Public Management Review*, Vol. 4, No. 3, Routledge, London.

Geva-May, Iris (2002b), "From Theory to Practice: Policy Analysis, Cultural Bias and Organizational Arrangements", *Public Management Review*, Vol. 4, No. 4, Routledge, London.

Gianakis, Jerry A. (2002), "Planning for Strategic Planning: What's Next?", *Public Performance and Management Review*, Vol. 25, Issue 4, Sage Publications, Thousand Oaks, California.

Gilardi, Fabrizio (2003), "Spurious and Symbolic Diffusion of Independent Regulatory Agencies in Western Europe", paper presented at a workshop on The Internationalization of Regulatory Reforms, Center for the Study of Law and Society, University of California, 25-26 April.

Gill, Derek (2002), "Signposting the Zoo – From Agencification to a More Principled Choice of Government Organisational Forms", *OECD Journal on Budgeting*, Vol. 2, No. 1, OECD, Paris.

Grizzle, Gloria A. (2002), "Performance Measurement and Dysfunction: The Dark Side of Quantifying Work", *Public Performance and Management Review*, Vol. 25, Issue 4, Sage Publications, Thousand Oaks, California.

Hagen, Rune Jansen (1997), "Political Instability, Political Polarisation, and Public Sector Institutional Reforms", paper provided by Norwegian School of Economics and Business Administration, *http://ideas.repec.org/s/fth/norgee.html.*

Halachmi, Arie (1998), *Performance and Quality Measurement in Government: Issues and Experiences*, Chatelaine Press, Burke, Virginia.

Halachmi, Arie (2002a), "Performance Measurement, Accountability, and Improved Performance", *Public Performance and Management Review*, Vol. 25, Issue 4, Sage Publications, Thousand Oaks, California.

Halachmi, Arie (2002b), "Performance Measurement and Government Productivity", *Work Study*, Vol. 51, Issue 2, MCB University Press, London.

Halachmi, Arie (2002c), "Performance Measurement: A Look at Some Possible Dysfunctions", *Work Study*, Vol. 51, Issue 5, MCB University Press, London.

Hall, Peter A. (1993), "Policy Paradigms, Social Learning, and the State: The Case of Economic Policymaking in Britain," *Comparative Politics*, Vol. 25, No. 3, Political Science Program of the City University of New York, New York.

Hatry, Harry P. (1999), *Performance Measurement: Getting Results*, Urban Institute Press, Washington DC.

Hatry, Harry P. (2002), "Performance Measurement: Fashions and Fallacies", *Public Performance and Management Review*, Vol. 25, Issue 4, Sage Publications, Thousand Oaks, California.

Healy, Thomas, and Jane Linder (2003), *Outsourcing in Government: Pathways to Value*, Accenture.

Heinrich, Carolyn J. (2002), "Outcomes Based Performance Management in the Public Sector: Implications for Government Accountability and Effectiveness", *Public Administration Review*, Vol. 62, No. 6, American Society for Public Administration, Washington DC.

H.M. Treasury (2003), *PFI: Meeting the Investment Challenge*, H.M. Treasury, London.

H.M. Treasury (2004), *The United Kingdom's Public Service Agreement*, H.M. Treasury, London, *www.hm-treasury.gov.uk/spending_review/spend_sr04/psa/spend_sr04_psaindex.cfm.*

H.M. Treasury and the Prime Minister's Office of Public Services Reform (2002), *Better Government Services: Executive agencies in the 21st century*, H.M. Treasury and the Prime Minister's Office of Public Services Reform, London.

Holkeri, Katju (2002), "Public Scrutiny and Access to Information in Finland", in *Public Sector Transparency and Accountability: Making it Happen*, OECD, Paris.

Holley, Lyn M., Donna Dufner, and B.J. Reed (2002), "Got SISP? Strategic Information Systems Planning in U.S. State Governments", *Public Performance and Management Review*, Vol. 25, Issue 4, Sage Publications, Thousand Oaks, California.

Hood, Christopher (1986), *Administrative Analysis: An Introduction to Rules, Enforcement, and Organizations*, Wheatsheaf Books, Brighton, United Kingdom.

Hood, Christopher (1998), *The Art of the State: Culture, Rhetoric, and Public Management*, Clarendon Press, Oxford, United Kingdom.

Hood, Christopher (2001), *The Government of Risk: Understanding Risk Regulation Regimes*, Oxford University Press, New York.

Hood, Christopher, et al. (eds.) (2004), *Controlling Modern Government: Variety, Commonality, and Change*, Edward Elgar Publishing, Inc., Cheltenham, United Kingdom.

Huber, John D. (2000), "Delegation to Civil Servants in Parliamentary Democracies", *European Journal of Political Research*, Vol. 37, Issue 3, Elsevier, Amsterdam, The Netherlands.

Ingraham, Patricia W., James R. Thompson and Ronald P. Sanders (eds.) (1998), *Transforming Government: Lessons from the Reinvention Laboratories*, Jossey-Bass Inc., San Francisco, California.

International Monetary Fund (2001), *Government Finance Statistics Manual 2001*, International Monetary Fund, Washington DC.

International Monetary Fund (2004), *Public-Private Partnerships*, International Monetary Fund, Washington DC.

International Organization of Supreme Audit Institutions (INTOSAI) (1977), *Lima Declaration of Guidelines on Auditing Precepts*, INTOSAI, Vienna, *www.intosai.org/Level2/2_LIMADe.html*.

Islam, Roumeen (2003), *Do More Transparent Governments Govern Better?*, World Bank Policy Research Working Paper 3077, The World Bank, Washington DC.

Joint Standing Committee on Foreign Affairs, Defence and Trade (1998), *Funding Australia's Defence*, Parliament of Australia, Canberra.

Jones, Lawrence R., and Fred Thompson (1999), *Public Management: Institutional Renewal for the Twenty-First Century*, JAI Press Inc./Elsevier Science Inc., New York.

Joyce, Philip G. (1996), "Jesse Burkhead and the Multiple Uses of Federal Budgets: A Contemporary Perspective", *Public Budgeting and Finance*, Vol. 16, Issue 2, Blackwell Publishing, Oxford, United Kingdom.

Kaufman, Herbert (2001), "Major Players: Bureaucracies in American Government", *Public Administration Review*, Vol. 61, No. 1, Blackwell Publishing, Oxford, United Kingdom.

Kaufmann, D. (2003), "Rethinking Governance: Empirical Lessons Challenge Orthodoxy", Discussion draft, 11 March, The World Bank, Washington DC.

Kearney, Richard C., and Evan M. Berman (eds.) (1999), *Public Sector Performance: Management, Motivation and Measurement*, Westview Press, Boulder, Colorado.

Kettl, Donald F. (2000), *The Global Public Management Revolution: A Report on the Transformation of Governance*, Brookings Institution, Washington DC.

Kickert, Walter J.M. (ed.) (1997), *Public Management and Administrative Reform in Western Europe*, Edward Elgar Publishing, Inc., Cheltenham, United Kingdom.

Kitchener, Martin, Malcolm Beynon, and Charlene Harrington (2002), "Qualitative Comparative Analysis and Public Services Research: Lessons from an Early Application", *Public Management Review*, Vol. 4, No. 4, Routledge, London.

Kuuttiniemi, K., and P. Virtanen (1998), "Citizen's Charters and Compensation Mechanisms: A Study on Citizen's Charters Compensation Mechanisms in OECD Countries", *Research Reports 11/98*, Public Management Department, Ministry of Finance, Helsinki.

Lane, Jan-Erik (2000), *New Public Management*, Routledge, London.

Lawyers Committee for Human Rights (2003), *Assessing the New Normal: Liberty and Security for the Post-September 11 United States*, Lawyers Committee for Human Rights, New York, New York.

Light, Paul (2002), *The Troubled State of Federal Public Service*, Center for Public Service, The Brookings Institution, Washington DC.

MacDonell, Roderick (2003), "Access to Information: The Commercial Side", *Development Outreach*, World Bank Institute, Washington DC.

Madison, James (1822), Letter to W.T. Barry, 4 August.

Marcella, R., and G. Baxter (2000), "Information needs, information seeking behaviour and participation", *Journal of Documentation*, Vol. 56, No. 2, Bradford, United Kingdom.

Mascarenhas, R.C. (1996), "Searching for Efficiency in the Public Sector: Interim Evaluation of Performance Budgeting in New Zealand", *Public Budgeting and Finance*, Vol. 16, Issue 3, Blackwell Publishing, Oxford, United Kingdom.

McCall, Lorraine (2002), "Social Capital, Civic Engagement, and Civic Literacy: Reviewing, Refining, and Defining the Concepts", *Public Performance and Management Review*, Vol. 25, Issue 4, Sage Publications, Thousand Oaks, California.

McDonald, Robert, and George Teather (2000), "Measurement of S&T performance in the government of Canada: From outputs to outcomes", *Journal of Technology Transfer*, Vol. 25, Issue 2, Springer, Dordrecht, The Netherlands.

Millennial Housing Commission (2002), *Meeting Our Nation's Housing Challenges*, Millennial Housing Commission, Washington DC.

Moon, M. Jae (2002), "The Evolution of Policy Analysis", *Public Administration Review*, Vol. 62, No. 4, American Society for Public Administration, Washington DC.

MORI (Market and Opinion Research International) (2003), *Trust in Public Institutions: Topline Results*, 19 March, London.

Muramatsu, Michio, and M. Matsunami (2003), "The late and sudden emergence of New Public Management reforms in Japan", in Hellmut Wollmann (ed.), *Evaluation in Public Sector Reform*, Edward Elgar Publishing, Inc., Cheltenham, United Kingdom.

Nunberg, Barbara (2000), *Ready for Europe: Public Administration Reform and European Union Accession in Central and Eastern Europe*, The International Bank for Reconstruction and Development/The World Bank, Washington DC.

OECD (1995a), "Recommendation of the Council of the OECD on Improving the Quality of Government Regulation", OCDE/GD(95)95, OECD, Paris.

OECD (1995b), *Governance in Transition: Public Management Reforms in OECD Countries*, OECD, Paris.

OECD (1996a), *Performance Management in Government: Contemporary Illustrations*, OECD, Paris.

OECD (1996b), *Ministerial Symposium on the Future of Public Services*, OECD, Paris.

OECD (1997), *Administrative Procedures and the Supervision of Administration in Hungary, Poland, Bulgaria, Estonia, and Albania*, SIGMA Papers no. 17, OECD, Paris.

OECD (1998), "Best Practice Guidelines for Evaluation", *PUMA Policy Brief* No. 5, May, OECD, Paris.

OECD (1999), *Improving Evaluation Practices: Best Practice Guidelines for Evaluation*, OECD, Paris.

OECD (2000a), "OECD Report on Parliamentary Procedures and Relations", PUMA/LEG(2000)2/REV1, OECD, Paris.

OECD (2000b), *Trust in Government: Ethics Measures in OECD Countries*, OECD, Paris.

OECD (2001a), "Best Practices for Budget Transparency," *OECD Journal on Budgeting*, Vol. 1, No. 3, OECD, Paris.

OECD (2001b), *Citizens as Partners: Information, Consultation and Public Participation in Policy-making*, OECD, Paris.

OECD (2001c), "Integrating Financial Management and Performance Management", *OECD Journal on Budgeting*, Vol. 1, No. 2, OECD, Paris.

OECD (2001d), *An Overview Report, Public Sector: An Employer of Choice?*, OECD, Paris.

OECD (2001e), *Public Sector Leadership for the 21st Century*, OECD, Paris.

OECD (2002a), *Distributed Public Governance: Agencies, Authorities, and Other Government Bodies*, OECD, Paris.

OECD (2002b), "Highlights of Public Sector Pay and Employment Trends", PUMA/HRM(2002)7, OECD, Paris.

OECD (2002c), *OECD Journal on Budgeting*, Vol. 1, No. 4, OECD, Paris.

OECD (2002d), "Overview of Results-focused Management and Budgeting", PUMA/SBO(2002)1, OECD, Paris.

OECD (2002e), "Public Service as an Employer of Choice", *OECD Policy Brief*, OECD, Paris.

OECD (2002f), *Public Sector Transparency and Accountability: Making it Happen*, OECD, Paris.

OECD (2002g), "Recent privatisation trends in OECD countries", *Financial Market Trends* No. 82, June, OECD, Paris.

OECD (2002h), *Regulatory Policies in OECD Countries: From Interventionism to Regulatory Governance*, OECD Reviews of Regulatory Reform, OECD, Paris.

OECD (2002i), *Relations between Supreme Audit Institutions and Parliamentary Committees*, SIGMA Papers no. 33, OECD, Paris.

OECD (2003a), *The e-Government Imperative*, OECD, Paris.

OECD (2003b), *From Red Tape to Smart Tape: Administrative Simplification in OECD Countries*, OECD, Paris.

OECD (2003c), "The Learning Government: Introduction and Draft Results of the Survey of Knowledge Management Practices in Ministries/Departments/Agencies of Central Government", GOV/PUMA(2003)1, OECD, Paris.

OECD (2003d), *Privatising State-owned Enterprises: An Overview of Policies and Practices in OECD Countries*, OECD, Paris.

OECD (2003e), *Promise and Problems of e-Democracy*, OECD, Paris.

OECD (2003f), "Public Sector Modernisation", *OECD Policy Brief*, OECD, Paris.

OECD (2003g), *Recommendation on Guidelines for Managing Conflict of Interest in the Public Service*, OECD, Paris.

OECD (2003h), "Public Sector Modernisation: Modernising Public Employment", GOV/PUMA (2003)18, OECD, Paris.

OECD (2004a), *Enhancing the Effectiveness of Public Spending: Experience in OECD Countries*, OECD, Paris.

OECD (2004b), "Public Sector Modernisation: Changing Organisational Structures", *OECD Policy Brief*, OECD, Paris.

OECD (2004c), "Public Sector Modernisation: Governing for Performance", *OECD Policy Brief*, OECD, Paris.

OECD (2004d), "Public Sector Modernisation: Modernising Public Employment", *OECD Policy Brief*, OECD, Paris.

OECD (2004e), "Regulatory Authorities in OECD Countries", GOV/PGC/REG(2004)5, OECD, Paris.

OECD (2004f), "Modernising Government: The Synthesis", GOV/PGC(2004)17, OECD, Paris.

OECD (2004g), "Trends in Human Resources Management Policies in OECD Countries: An Analysis of the Results of the OECD Survey on Strategic Human Resources Management", GOV/PGC/HRM (2004)3/FINAL, OECD, Paris.

OECD (2005a), *E-government for Better Government*, OECD, Paris (forthcoming).

OECD (2005b), "Public Sector Modernisation: Modernising Accountability and Control", *OECD Policy Brief*, OECD, Paris.

OECD (2005c), "Performance Information in the Budget Process", GOV/PGC/SBO(2005)6, OECD, Paris.

OECD (2005d), *Reallocation: The Role of Budget Institutions*, OECD, Paris.

OECD (2005e), *Performance-related Pay Policies for Government Employees*, OECD, Paris.

OECD (2005f), *Independent Regulators, Political Challenges and Institutional Design*, OECD, Paris (forthcoming).

OECD (2005g), "Regulatory Authorities: Summary and Conclusions of the Expert Meeting", GOV/PGC/REG (2005)5, OECD, Paris, January.

OECD (2005h), *Long-term Care for Older People*, OECD, Paris.

OECD (2005i), "Public Sector Modernisation: Open Government", *OECD Policy Brief*, OECD, Paris.

OECD and World Bank (2003), "OECD/World Bank Budget Practices and Procedures Database", *www.oecd.org/gov/budget*.

O'Neill, Onora (2002), "A Question of Trust", Reith Lectures 2002, London, *www.bbc.co.uk/radio4/reith2002*.

Osborne, David, and Peter Plastrik (2000), *The Reinventor's Fieldbook: Tools for Transforming Your Government*, Jossey-Bass, San Francisco, California.

Pallot, June (2001), "A Decade in Review: New Zealand's Experience with Resource Accounting and Budgeting", *Financial Accountability and Management*, Blackwell, Oxford, United Kingdom, pp. 383-400.

Pallot, June (2002), "Government Accounting and Budgeting Reform in New Zealand", *OECD Journal on Budgeting*, Vol. 2, Supplement 1, OECD, Paris.

Pearson, M., and J.P. Martin (2005), "Should we extend the role of private social expenditure?", OECD, Paris (forthcoming).

Perrin, Butt (2002), "Implementing the Vision: Addressing Challenges to Results-Focused Management and Budgeting", presented at the OECD meeting on

Implementation Challenges in Results Focused Management and Budgeting, 11-12 February, Paris.

Peters, B. Guy, and Donald J. Savoie (eds.) (2000a), *Taking Stock: Assessing Public Sector Reforms*, Canadian Centre for Management Development/McGill-Queen's University Press, Montreal.

Peters, B. Guy, and Donald J. Savoie (eds.) (2000b), *Governance in the Twenty-first Century: Revitalizing the Public Service*, Canadian Centre for Management Development/ McGill-Queen's University Press, Montreal.

Pfiffner, James P., and Douglas A. Brook (eds.) (2000), *The Future of Merit: Twenty Years after the Civil Service Reform Act*, The Woodrow Wilson Center Press, Washington DC.

Pierce, John C., Nicholas P. Lovrich Jr., and C. David Moon (2002), "Social Capital and Government Performance: An Analysis of 20 American Cities", *Public Performance and Management Review*, Vol. 25, Issue 4, Sage Publications, Thousand Oaks, California.

Piotrowski, Suzanne J., and David H. Rosenbloom (2002), "Nonmission Based Values in Results Oriented Public Management: The Case of Freedom of Information", *Public Administration Review*, Vol. 62, No. 6, American Society for Public Administration, Washington DC.

Polidano, Charles (2001), "Why Civil Service Reforms Fail?", *Public Policy and Management Working Paper* no. 16, Institute for Development Policy and Management, Manchester, United Kingdom, *www.man.ac.uk/idpm/idpm_dp.htm*.

Pollitt, Christopher, *et al.* (1999), *Performance or compliance?: Performance Audit and Public Management*, Oxford University Press, New York.

Pollitt, Christopher, and Geert Bouckaert, (2004), *Public Management Reform: A Comparative Analysis*, Oxford University Press, New York, 2nd edition.

Pope, Jeremy (2002), "Access to Information: Whose Right and Whose Information?", in *Global Corruption Report 2003*, Transparency International, Berlin.

Rivenbark, William C., and Carla M. Pizzarella (2002), "Auditing Performance Data in Local Government", *Public Performance and Management Review*, Vol. 25, Issue 4, Sage Publications, Thousand Oaks, California.

Roberts, Nancy C. (2002), "Keeping Public Officials Accountable Through Dialogue: Resolving the Accountability Paradox", *Public Administration Review*, Vol. 62, No. 6, American Society for Public Administration, Washington DC.

Rutledge, Eric (2002), "Some Unfinished Business in Public Administration", *Public Administration Review*, Vol. 62, No. 4, American Society for Public Administration, Washington DC.

Schiavo-Campo, Salvatore, and Pachampet Sundaram (2001), *To Serve and to Preserve: Improving Public Administration in a Competitive World*, Asian Development Bank, Manila.

Schick, Allen (1996), *The Spirit of Reform: Managing the New Zealand State Sector in a Time of Change*, a report prepared for the State Services Commission and The Treasury, New Zealand, Crown Copyright, *www.ssc.govt.nz/spirit-of-reform*.

Schick, Allen (2001), "Reflections on the New Zealand Model", based on a lecture at the New Zealand Treasury, August, *www.treasury.govt.nz/academiclinkages/schick/ paper.asp*.

Schick, Allen (2002), "Redemocratizing the Budget", paper prepared for the conference on The State Budget: Transparency and Democracy, 22 October, Foundation for the Modernisation of Spain, Madrid.

Schick, Allen (2003), "The Performing State: Reflection on an Idea Whose Time Has Come but Whose Implementation Has Not", *OECD Journal on Budgeting*, Vol. 3, No. 2, OECD, Paris.

Schultz, David (2002), "Civil Service Reform", *Public Administration Review*, Vol. 62, No. 5, American Society for Public Administration, Washington DC.

Schwartz, R., and J. Mayne, (2005), *Quality Matters: Seeking Confidence in Evaluation, Auditing and Performance Reporting*, Transaction Publishers, New Brunswick, New Jersey.

6, Perri, *et al.* (2002), *Towards Holistic Governance: The New Reform Agenda*, Palgrave Publishers Ltd, Houndmills, Basingstoke, United Kingdom.

Soper, Nancy (2002), "What's Wrong and What Should be Done? Comments on the Case Study", *Public Performance and Management Review*, Vol. 25, Issue 4, Sage Publications, Thousand Oaks, California.

Stiglitz, Joseph (2002), "Transparency in Government", in *The Right to Tell: The Role of Mass Media in Economic Development*, The World Bank Publications, Washington DC.

United Kingdom (2004), *Senior Civil Service: Guide to Performance Management and Reward in the SCS*, London, March.

United Kingdom Cabinet Office (2002), *Consultations Index*, London, *www.consultations.gov.uk*.

United Kingdom Cabinet Office (2004), *Code of Practice on Written Consultation*, London, *www.cabinet-office.gov.uk/regulation/consultation*.

United Kingdom Office of the Deputy Prime Minister (2002), *The Business Case for Communications: Why Investing in Good Communications Makes Sense*, Office of the Deputy Prime Minister, London.

United Kingdom Office of Government Commerce (2003), *Increasing Competition and Improving Long-Term Capacity Planning in the Government Market-Place*, Office of Government Commerce, London.

United States Office of Management and Budget (2004), *Program Assessment Rating Tool (PART)*, Washington DC, *www.whitehouse.gov/omb/part*.

Van Oosteroom, R. (2002a), "The Netherlands" in *Distributed Public Governance: Agencies, Authorities and Other Government Bodies*, OECD, Paris, pp. 113-131.

Van Oosteroom, R. (2002b), "Nationwide evaluation of the departmental agency in the Netherlands", report prepared for the OECD experts meeting on Monitoring Agencies, Authorities and Other Government Bodies: How to Best Balance Autonomy and Control?, 14-15 November, Paris.

Walker, Richard M., Emma Jeanes, and Robert Rowlands (2002), "Measuring Innovation – Applying the Literature-Based Innovation Output Indicator to Public Services", *Public Administration*, Vol. 80, No. 1, Blackwell Publishing, Oxford, United Kingdom.

Washington, Sally (1998), "Pieces of the Puzzle: Machinery of Government and the Quality of Policy Advice", *Working Paper No. 4*, State Services Commission, New Zealand, *www.ssc.govt.nz/working-papers*.

Wilson, J.Q. (1989), *Bureaucracy: What Government Agencies Do and Why They Do It*, Basic Books, New York.

Wise, Lois Recascino (2002), "Public Management Reform: Competing Drivers of Change", *Public Administration Review*, Vol. 62, No. 5, American Society for Public Administration, Washington DC.

Wollmann, Helmut (2000), "Comparing Institutional Development in Britain and Germany: (Persistent) Divergence or (Progressing) Convergence?", in Helmut Wollmann and Eckhard Schröter (eds.) *Comparing Public Sector Reform in Britain and*

Germany: Key Traditions and Trends of Modernisation, Ashgate Publishing Ltd., Aldershot, United Kingdom.

Wollmann, Helmut (2001), "Germany's Trajectory of Public Sector Modernisation: Continuities and Discontinuities", *Policy and Politics*, Vol. 29, MacMillan Journals, London.

Wollmann, Helmut (2003), *Evaluation in Public Sector Reform*, Edward Elgar Publishing, Cheltenham, United Kingdom.

Wollmann, Hellmut, and Eckhard Schröter (eds.) (2000), *Comparing Public Sector Reform in Britain and Germany: Key Traditions and Trends of Modernisation*, Ashgate Publishing Ltd., Aldershot, United Kingdom.

ANNEX A

Table A.1. **Share of the public employment over the labour force (%)**

	1990	1991	1992	1993	1994	1995	1996	1997	1998	1999	2000	2001
Australia[1]	20.8	20.5	19.9	19.6	18.3	17.9	17.5	16.4	15.9	15.6	15.2	15.2
Austria[2]	12.4	12.3	12.3	12.3	12.1	12.0	12.0	11.4	11.4	11.3	11.2	
Canada[3]	18.7	18.9	19.0	18.7	18.3	18.0	17.3	16.7	16.3	16.0	15.8	15.7
Czech Republic[4]								14.4	14.2	13.9		
Denmark[2]								22.6	22.8	22.6	22.6	23.1
Finland[3]	22.4	22.7	22.3	21.3	21.4	20.9	21.3	21.8	21.6	21.0	20.8	20.8
France								18.1	18.3	18.3		
Germany		13.3	13.2	12.8	12.5	12.2	11.9	11.6	11.3	11.0	10.7	
Greece								6.4	6.1			
Hungary								20.4	20.5	19.5	19.2	19.3
Ireland	15.2	15.2	15.3	15.1	15.1	15.0	14.6	14.4	14.0	13.9	14.1	
Italy								13.4	13.5	13.2		
Luxembourg	8.8	8.8	8.7	7.5	7.4	7.3	7.2	7.5	7.1	7.0	6.9	6.7
Netherlands							10.4	10.5	10.5	10.4	10.5	
New Zealand		14.6	13.8	13.7	13.5	12.6	12.4	11.8	11.9	12.2	11.6	11.8
Norway										5.7	5.7	
Poland[2]					12.2	12.3	12.4	12.5	12.6	12.8	12.4	
Spain	11.8	11.4	11.4	11.6	11.6	11.8	11.9	11.9	12.0	12.1	11.2	12.0
Turkey								8.9	8.8	9.1	10.0	
United States	14.1	14.1	14.1	14.1	14.1	14.0	14.0	13.8	13.9	13.9	14.1	

1. Public Employment excludes Permanent Defence Forces.
2. Public Employment Data in Full Time Equivalent.
3. Public Employment excludes Government Business Enterprises.
4. Public Employment excludes Permanent Defence Forces and Police.

Source: Labour Force: OECD Labour Force Statistics, 2002. Public Employment: OECD Public Management Service, 2002. Copyright OECD 2002. All rights reserved.

ANNEX B

Table B.1. General government total outlays
Per cent of nominal GDP

	1986	1987	1988	1989	1990	1991	1992	1993	1994	1995	1996	1997	1998	1999	2000	2001	2002	2003	2004	2005
Australia	40.3	38.9	36.3	35.5	36.2	37.8	39.6	39.7	39.1	39.1	38.2	37.1	36.8	35.7	35.6	37.1	36.3	36.4	36.2	36.2
Austria	55.8	56.1	55.2	53.6	53.1	54.2	54.9	57.9	57.4	57.1	56.6	53.9	54.0	54.0	52.3	51.6	51.3	51.2	50.5	50.2
Belgium	58.9	57.0	55.1	53.4	53.4	54.4	54.7	55.7	53.4	52.9	53.0	51.4	50.7	50.1	49.4	49.5	50.5	51.4	49.9	50.0
Canada	47.5	46.1	45.4	45.8	48.8	52.3	53.3	52.2	49.7	48.5	46.6	44.3	44.4	42.5	41.0	41.4	40.6	40.1	40.1	39.9
Czech Republic[a]	:	:	:	:	:	:	48.0	69.9	50.4	57.2	45.5	45.0	46.0	45.9	46.1	47.3	49.9	50.8	50.6	50.2
Denmark	53.3	55.0	57.2	57.3	57.0	57.8	59.0	61.7	61.6	60.3	59.8	58.0	57.6	56.3	54.9	55.3	55.8	56.1	55.7	54.7
Finland	47.9	48.5	47.0	45.2	48.6	57.7	63.0	64.2	62.9	59.6	59.7	56.4	52.8	52.1	49.1	49.2	50.1	50.6	50.9	50.2
France	52.7	51.9	51.4	50.4	50.7	51.5	53.0	55.3	54.9	55.1	55.4	54.9	53.7	53.5	52.5	52.5	53.4	54.5	53.8	53.4
Germany[b]	45.4	45.8	45.3	44.0	44.5	47.1	48.1	49.3	49.0	49.4	50.3	49.3	48.8	48.7	45.7	48.3	48.5	48.9	48.2	47.1
Greece	45.2	45.1	44.0	45.4	50.2	46.7	49.4	52.0	49.9	51.0	49.2	47.8	47.8	47.6	49.9	47.8	46.8	47.2	47.4	47.1
Hungary	:	:	:	:	:	56.7	60.3	59.8	63.4	56.9	53.9	51.8	52.8	50.0	48.0	48.5	53.4	50.1	50.6	49.9
Iceland	40.6	37.5	42.6	45.2	42.4	43.8	44.7	44.6	44.4	43.8	43.3	41.7	42.4	43.5	43.2	44.1	46.2	47.9	46.5	45.3
Ireland	53.7	52.1	48.6	42.2	43.3	44.9	45.3	45.1	44.4	41.5	39.6	37.2	35.0	34.6	32.1	33.8	33.3	35.2	35.8	35.8
Italy	51.4	50.8	51.5	52.8	54.4	55.5	56.7	57.7	54.5	53.4	53.2	51.1	49.9	48.9	46.9	48.7	48.0	48.9	48.7	49.0
Japan[c]	31.0	31.5	30.9	30.2	31.7	31.5	32.5	34.2	34.8	35.8	36.3	35.1	36.1	37.7	38.2	37.7	38.2	37.7	36.9	36.6
Korea	18.0	17.1	18.0	:	18.5	19.6	20.7	20.2	19.8	19.5	20.5	21.2	23.5	22.5	22.0	24.0	22.2	24.3	24.2	23.9
Luxembourg	:	:	:	:	43.2	44.4	46.0	45.7	44.5	45.5	45.6	43.3	42.0	41.3	38.5	39.1	44.3	46.9	46.6	47.2
Netherlands[d]	56.9	58.4	56.6	54.5	54.8	54.8	55.8	56.0	53.6	51.4	49.6	48.2	47.2	46.9	45.3	46.6	47.5	48.9	47.7	46.9
New Zealand	:	53.6	52.7	52.0	53.3	51.5	49.5	46.0	43.0	41.9	41.0	41.6	42.9	41.4	40.2	39.0	38.6	38.5	38.7	38.5
Norway	48.3	50.5	52.6	52.2	52.8	54.9	56.3	55.1	54.1	51.6	49.2	47.3	49.7	48.3	43.4	44.8	47.6	48.4	47.6	47.6

Table B.1. **General government total outlays** (cont.)

	1986	1987	1988	1989	1990	1991	1992	1993	1994	1995	1996	1997	1998	1999	2000	2001	2002	2003	2004	2005
Poland	..	..	..	..	..	49.9	51.4	50.8	46.1	49.4	48.7	48.1	46.4	46.1	44.5	45.3	45.9	46.2	46.6	46.0
Portugal	41.3	40.0	38.5	38.8	42.1	45.1	46.2	47.8	46.0	45.0	45.8	44.8	44.1	45.3	45.2	46.3	46.1	47.9	47.0	46.2
Slovak Republic	..	..	..	..	..	..	..	..	57.8	54.1	61.5	65.0	61.9	59.2	63.6	54.3	49.5	46.6	44.7	43.4
Spain	42.6	41.0	40.9	42.2	43.4	44.9	45.9	49.4	47.3	45.0	43.7	41.8	41.4	40.2	40.0	39.6	39.9	39.5	39.3	39.1
Sweden	63.3	59.5	59.9	59.8	60.7	62.7	67.6	72.9	70.9	67.6	65.2	62.9	60.7	60.3	57.3	57.0	58.2	58.2	58.3	57.9
United Kingdom	45.6	43.6	41.1	40.5	42.2	44.0	45.7	45.7	45.0	44.6	42.7	41.0	39.8	39.2	37.0	40.3	40.9	42.6	42.6	43.3
United States[a]	36.9	36.7	35.9	35.7	36.6	37.4	38.1	37.5	36.6	36.5	36.1	34.9	34.2	33.8	33.7	34.6	35.3	35.7	35.2	35.2
Euro area	49.3	48.9	48.5	47.9	48.7	50.1	51.3	53.0	51.8	51.4	51.5	50.2	49.3	48.9	47.1	48.1	48.3	49.0	48.4	47.9
Total OECD	40.5	40.2	39.5	39.2	40.1	41.4	42.5	43.1	42.1	42.1	41.7	40.5	40.1	39.8	39.0	39.9	40.3	40.7	40.3	40.1

Note: Total outlays are defined as current outlays plus capital outlays. Data refer to the general government sector, which is a consolidation of accounts for the central, state and local governments plus social security. One-off revenues from the sale of mobile telephone licenses are recorded as negative capital outlays for some countries. See OECD *Economic Outlook Sources and Methods* (*www.oecd.org/eco/sources-and-methods*).

a) The data for 1993 and 1995 reflect large scale privatisation of public enterprises. From 2003 onwards the projections are based on the GPS data profile.
b) The 1995 outlays are net of the debt taken on this year from the Inherited Debt funds.
c) The 1998 outlays would be 5.3 percentage points of GDP higher if account were taken of the assumption by the central government of the debt of the Japan Railway Settlement Corporation and the National Forest Special Account. The 2000 outlays include capital transfers to the Deposit Insurance Company.
d) The 1995 outlays would be 4.9 percentage points of GDP higher if capital transfers to a housing agency offering rentals to low income people were taken into account.
e) These data include outlays net of operating surpluses of public enterprises.

Source: OECD *Economic Outlook-Volume 2004/1, No. 75,* June 2004.

ANNEX C

Table C.1. **OECD recommendations and guidelines on open government**

Dimensions of openness	OECD Council Recommendations	OECD guidelines and checklists
I. Transparency	• OECD 1998 *Recommendation on Improving Ethical Conduct in the Public Service including the Principles for Managing Ethics in the Public Service* (§6) • 1997 *Ministerial Report on Regulatory Reform* (§3) • OECD 1995 *Recommendation on Improving the Quality of Government Regulation* (§8)	• OECD 2001 *Best Practices for Budget Transparency* (§3.4) • OECD 2001 *Guiding Principles for Engaging Citizens in Policy-making* (§2 and 8)
II. Accessibility		• OECD 2003 *Guiding Principles for Successful E-Government* (§5 and 6) • OECD 2001 *Guiding Principles for Engaging Citizens in Policy-making* (§5)
III. Responsiveness	• OECD 2003 *Recommendation on Guidelines for Managing Conflict of Interest in the Public Service* (§ 2.4.1.b) • OECD 1995 *Recommendation on Improving the Quality of Government Regulation* (§9)	• OECD 2003 *Guiding Principles for Successful E-Government* (§7) • OECD 2003 *Guiding Principles for Successful Online Consultation* (§2 and 7) • OECD 1998 *Best Practice Guidelines for User Charging for Government Services* • OECD 1998 *Best Practice Guidelines for Evaluation*

ANNEX D

Table D.1. **Legislation and policy measures for open government**[1]

Country	Law on Access to Information and Documents	Law on Administrative Procedure	Law on Ombudsman/ Commissioner	Law on Privacy and Data Protection	Law on Electronic Data and Signatures	E-government policy
1. Australia						
Year	1982	2000 (1977, 1975)	1976	1988	2000; 1999	2000
Date				Nov-88	25-Nov-00	Apr-00
Title	Freedom of Information Act	Administrative Reform Act	Ombudsman Act	Privacy Act	Electronic Signature Act Electronic Transaction Act	Government Online Strategy
2. Austria						
Year	1987	1991	1977	1999 (1987, 1978)	1998	2000 (1997)
Date	15-May-87			Dec-99		Spring (Oct-97)
Title	"Auskunftspflichtgesetz" obliges federal authorities to answer citizens' questions – does not give rights of access to documents	General Law on Administrative Procedure	"People's Attorney" introduced	Data Protection Act	Digital Signature Act	Information and Communication Project (Strategy & Action Plan for Information Society)
3. Belgium						
Year	1994		1995	1992	2001	1997
Date	11-Apr-94		22-Mar-95	8-May-92	09-Jul-01	30-May-97
Title	Law on Openness of the Administration At the regional level: Parliament of Flanders Act on the Public Nature of Government (18 May 1999)		Federal Ombudsmen Act At the regional level: Parliament of Flanders Act on the Flemish Ombudsman Service (1998)	Law on the Protection of Private Life Regarding the Processing of Personal Data	Law establishing certain rules related to the juridical framework for electronic signatures and certification services	Federal Action Plan for the Information Society At the regional level: Government of Flanders decree on e-government (8-Dec-00)

Table D.1. **Legislation and policy measures for open government**[1] (cont.)

Country	Law on Access to Information and Documents	Law on Administrative Procedure	Law on Ombudsman/Commissioner	Law on Privacy and Data Protection	Law on Electronic Data and Signatures	E-government policy
4. Canada						
Year	1982			1982	2000	2000
Date					Apr-00	25-Feb-00
Title	Access to Information Act		Information Commissioner	Privacy Act	The Personal Information Protection and Electronic Document Act	Government On-Line: Serving Canadians in a Digital World
5. Czech Republic						
Year	1999	1967	1999	1992	2000	1999
Date	11-May-99	29-June-67	8-Dec-99	4-Apr-92	29-Jun-00	31-May-99
Title	Act on Free Access to Information (No.106/1999 Coll.)	Act on Administrative Procedure (No. 71/1967 Coll)	Act on the Ombudsman (No. 349/1999 Coll.)	Data Protection Act (No. 101/2000 Coll.)	Act on Digital Signature (No. 227/2000 Coll.)	State information policy
6. Denmark						
Year	1998 (1993,1991,1985, 1970)	1985	(1953)	2000 (1987, 1978)	2000	1999 (1995)
Date	(30-Jun-93, 6-Jun-91, 19-Dec-85, 10-Jun-70)	Dec-85		Jul-00 (Jun-87, Jun-78)	Mar-00	Dec-99
Title	Act on Access to Public Administration Files (Law No. 276, No. 504, No.572, No. 280)	Law on Administrative Procedures (Law No. 571)	(Under the Constitution)	Law on Processing Personal Data (Law No. 429)	Law on Electronic Signatures	IT Policy Strategy: "Realigning to a Network Society" (IT Policy Action Plan "From Vision to Action")
7. Finland						
Year	1999 (1951)	1982	(1919)	1999 (1987)	2000, 1999	1998 (1995)
Date	9-Feb-51				01-Jan-00	Dec-98 (Jan-95)
Title	Act on Openness of Government Activities (Publicity of Official Documents Act)	Administrative Procedure Act	(Under the Constitution)	Data Protection Act (Personal Data Act)	– Act on Electronic Services in the Administration – Act on Electronic Transaction	Second Strategy "Quality of Life, Knowledge and Competitiveness" ("Finland towards the Information Society")

MODERNISING GOVERNMENT: THE WAY FORWARD – ISBN 92-64-01049-1 – © OECD 2005

Table D.1. **Legislation and policy measures for open government**[1] (cont.)

Country	Law on Access to Information and Documents	Law on Administrative Procedure	Law on Ombudsman/ Commissioner	Law on Privacy and Data Protection	Law on Electronic Data and Signatures	E-government policy
8. France						
Year	1979 (1978)	1979	2000 (1973)	1978	2000	1998
Date	(17-Jul-78)	11-Jul-79	12-Apr-00 (03-Jan-73)	06-Jan-78	29-Feb-00	Jan-98
Title	Law No. 79-583 (Law No. 78-753 on access to administrative documents)	Law on the justification for administrative acts	(Law No. 73-6 establishing the Mediator of the Republic)	Act on Processing, Data Files and Individual Liberties (Law of 6.01.1978 on IT, files and freedoms)	Law on Electronic Signatures No. 2000-230	Governmental Action Programme "Preparing for the Information Society" (PAGSI); Ministerial Action Programmes (PAMSI)
9. Germany						
Year		1976	1975	1990 (1977)	1997	1999 (1996)
Date		25-Jul-76		20-Dec-90 (27-Jan-77)	13-Jun-97	Nov-99 (Feb-96)
Title	(No general freedom of information law)	Act on Administrative Procedure	No Ombudsman at the federal level. The Parliament's (Bundestag) petitions committee	Federal Data Protection Act (last amended in 2000)	Digital Signatures Act enacted as Art. 3 of the Information and Communication Services Act (last amended 2001)	Action Programme "Innovation and Jobs in the Information Society of the 21st Century" (Info-2000: Germany's way to the Information Society)
10. Greece						
Year	2000 (1986)	1999	1997	1997	1998	1999 (1995)
Date				Apr-97		Feb-99
Title	Right of Access to Administrative Document (Act No. 1599/1986 on Access to Information)	Law No. 2690/1999 Code on Administrative Procedure	Law No. 2477/1997 establishing the Ombudsman	Law No. 2472/1997 on the Protection of Individuals with Regards to the Processing of Personal Data	Law No. 2672/1998 on Information by E-mail	2nd White Paper "Greece in the Information Society: Strategy and Actions" (White Paper "Greek Strategy for the Information Society")

Table D.1. **Legislation and policy measures for open government**[1] (cont.)

Country	Law on Access to Information and Documents	Law on Administrative Procedure	Law on Ombudsman/ Commissioner	Law on Privacy and Data Protection	Law on Electronic Data and Signatures	E-government policy
11. Hungary						
Year	1992	1991 (1957)	(1990)	1992	2001; 2003	2003
Date	**(Combined FOI and Data Protection Act)**		**(Under the Constitution)**	**(Combined FOI and Data Protection Act)**	29-May-01, 24-Nov-03	Nov-03
Title	Act LXIII of 1992 on the Protection of Personal Data and the Publicity of Personal Data of Public Interest	General Rules of State Administration Procedures Act XXVI (Act IV of 1957)	(3 Parliamentary Commissioners for civil rights; ethnic and national minorities; data protection)	Act LXIII of 1992 on the Protection of Personal Data and the Publicity of Personal Data of Public Interest	Act on Electronic Signature Act on Electronic Communications	Hungarian Information Society Strategy (MITS) 1126/2003. (XII. 12.)
12. Iceland						
Year	1996	1993	1988	1989		2004
Date				Dec		Apr-04
Title	Information Act	Administrative Act	Office of Ombudsman was established	Act Concerning the Registration and Handling of Personal Data		Resources to Serve Everyone: Policy of the Government of Iceland on the Information Society 2004 - 2007
13. Ireland						
Year	1997	1990	1980	1988	2000	1999 (1997)
Date	21-Apr-97		14-Jul-80		10-Jul-00	Jan-99 (Mar-97)
Title	Freedom of Information Act No. 13	n.a.	Ombudsman Act	Data Protection Act	Electronic Commerce Act	Implementing the Information Society in Ireland: An Action Plan (Information Society Ireland: Strategy for Action)

Table D.1. **Legislation and policy measures for open government**[1] (cont.)

Country	Law on Access to Information and Documents	Law on Administrative Procedure	Law on Ombudsman/ Commissioner	Law on Privacy and Data Protection	Law on Electronic Data and Signatures	E-government policy
14. Italy						
Year	1990	1999 (1990)		1997; 1996	2001; 1997	2000
Date	7-Aug-90			1-Jan-97; 31-Dec-96	31-Oct-97	23-Jun-00
Title	Act No. 241 on Access to Administrative Documents	Administrative Procedure Law	No Ombudsman at national level (only sub-national level). Since 1990, a government "Commission for access to administrative documents" ensures oversight.	– Processing of Personal Data Act – Protection of Individual and Other Subjects with regard to the Processing of Personal Data Act No. 675	– Law on Electronic Signature and Data – Digital Document Regulations	E-Government Action Plan
15. Japan						
Year	1999	1994	1984 (1966)	2005	2000	2003 (2001)
Date	14-May-99	01-Oct-94		1-Apr-05	24-May-00	Jul-03 (29-Mar-01)
Title	Law Concerning Access to Information Held by Administrative Organs	Administrative Procedure Act	No parliamentary ombudsman [Administrative Inspection Bureau (Administrative Counsellor's Law) functions as a point of appeal]	Act for Protection of Personal Information Held by Administrative Organs	Law Concerning Electronic Signatures and Certification Services	eJapan strategy II 2003 (E-Japan Priority Policy Programme)
16. Korea						
Year	1996	1996	1994	1999	2001	2002 (1999)
Date	31-Dec-96	31-Dec-96	Apr-94	8-Feb-99	27-Feb-01; 5-Feb-99	Apr-02
Title	Act on Disclosure of Information by Public Agencies	Administrative Procedure Act	Ombudsman of Korea	Act on Promotion of Utilisation of Information System and Protection of Information	Electronic Government Act; Digital Signature Act	E-Korea Vision 2006 (E-Government Project; Cyber-Korea 21)

Table D.1. **Legislation and policy measures for open government**[1] (*cont.*)

Country	Law on Access to Information and Documents	Law on Administrative Procedure	Law on Ombudsman/ Commissioner	Law on Privacy and Data Protection	Law on Electronic Data and Signatures	E-government policy
17. Luxembourg						
Year		1978	2003	1979	1999	2001
Date		1-Dec-78	22-Aug-03	Mar-79		26-Jan-01
Title	(No general freedom of information law)	Act on Administrative Procedures	Law establishing an ombudsman	Act of 30 March on the Identification of Physical and Legal Persons by Number; Act of 31 March on Use of Nominal Data in Data Processing	Draft law on Digital Signatures	E-Luxembourg
18. Mexico						
Year	2002	1995	1992		2000	2001
Date	Jun-02	01-Jun-95	23-Jun-92		7-Jun-00	
Title	Federal Transparency and Access to Public Government Information Law	Federal Law on Administrative Procedure Act	Law of the commission of human rights	No specific privacy law (in the Constitution, Penal Code Article 214)	E-Commerce Act (covers privacy, e-signature and e-documents)	The National e-Mexico System
19. Netherlands						
Year	1998 (1992, 1980, 1978)	1998	1999 (1981)	2001 (1988)	2003	1999
Date	18-Jun-98	01-Jan-98	12-May-99 (4-Feb-81)	01-Sep-01	08-May-03	Mar-99
Title	Government Information Act Stb. 356 (9-Nov-78 St. 581)	General Administrative Procedural Law Act	National Ombudsman Act	Personal Data Protection Act (Data Registration Act)	Law on Electronic Signatures	Electronic Government Action Programme
20. New Zealand						
Year	1982	2001 (1969)	2003 (1975, 1962)	1994 (1993)	2002	2003 (2001)
Date			21-Oct-03			Jun-03
Title	Official Information Act	Administration Amendment Act (Administration Act)	Ombudsmen Act	Privacy Amendment Act (Privacy Act)	Electronic Transactions Act	government.nz@your.service

Table D.1. **Legislation and policy measures for open government**[1] (cont.)

Country	Law on Access to Information and Documents	Law on Administrative Procedure	Law on Ombudsman/Commissioner	Law on Privacy and Data Protection	Law on Electronic Data and Signatures	E-government policy
21. Norway						
Year	1970	1970	1962	2000 (1978)	2001	2002 (1999)
Date	19-Jun-70	10-Feb-70		14-Apr-00 (9-Jun-78)	15-Jun-01	May-02
Title	Freedom of Information Act	Public Administration Act	Act on the Parliamentary Ombudsman for Public Administration	Act N° 31 on the Processing of Personal Data (Act on Personal Data Registers)	Act 2001/81 on Electronic Signature	eNorway 2005 Action Plan (E-Government Action Plan)
22. Poland						
Year	2001	1999 (1960)	1987	1997	2001	2004
Date	6-Sep-01	01-Jan-99 (14-Jun-60)	15-Jul-87	29-Aug-97	18-Sep-01	Jan-04
Title	Law on Access to Public Information	Act on Administrative Proceedings Code	Act on the Ombudsman	Law on the Protection of Personal Data	Act on Electronic Signatures	The Strategy on the Development of the Information Society in Poland
23. Portugal						
Year	1993	1976	1996 (1991, 1975)	1998	2003	2003 (2000)
Date	26-Aug-93		14-Aug-96 (9-Apr-91)	Oct-98	3-Apr-03	Feb-03 (22-Aug-00)
Title	Law n° 65/93	Code of Administrative Procedure	Statute of the Ombudsmen	Law N° 67/98 on the Protection of Personal Data	Electronic Signatures Decree-Law (Decree-Law n° 62/2003)	e-Government action plan (Internet Initiative RCM No. 110/2000)
24. Slovak Republic						
Year	2000		2001	2002 (1998)	2002	2001
Date	17-May-00		23-Feb-01	3-Jul-02 (Feb-98)	15-Mar-02	
Title	Act on Free Access to Information		Constitutional Statute No. 90/2001 Coll. (constitutional amendment creating a Public Defender of Rights)	Act n. 428/2002 on Personal Data Protection	Act n. 215/2002 on Electronic Signatures	Policy for the Development of the Information Society in the Slovak Republic

Table D.1. **Legislation and policy measures for open government**[1] (cont.)

Country	Law on Access to Information and Documents	Law on Administrative Procedure	Law on Ombudsman/Commissioner	Law on Privacy and Data Protection	Law on Electronic Data and Signatures	E-government policy
25. Spain						
Year	1998 (1992)	1999 (1992, 1958)	(1981)	1999 (1992)	2003	2003 (1999)
Date	13-Jul-98 (26-Nov-92)	(26-Nov-92, 17-Jul-58)		13-Dec-99 (Oct-92)	19-Dec-03	Dec-99
Title	Law No. 29/1998 (Law No. 30/92 on Public Administration and Common Administrative Procedures)	Act on Administrative Procedure	(Under the Constitution)	Personal Data Act (Law on the Regulation of the Automatic Processing of Personal Data)	59/2003 Law on digital signature	Plan de Choque para el impulso de la Administración Electrónica (Strategic Investment Plan for IT)
26. Sweden						
Year	1994 (1766)	1998	1986 (1809)	1998 (1994, 1973)	2000	2002 (2000)
Date			13-Nov-86	29-Apr-98	Apr-00	Nov-02
Title	Freedom of Information Act (Freedom of Press Act now part of the Constitution)	Government Public Administration Bill	The Act with Instructions for the Parliamentary Ombudsmen	Personal Data Act (Personal Data Protection Act)	Act on Qualified Electronic Signature (2000:832) (Regulation on Services concerning Electronic Certifications)	The Swedish e-Government Strategy (National Strategy for Information Society)
27. Switzerland						
Year	2004	1968		1992	2003	2002 (1998)
Date	17-Dec-04	20-Dec-68		19-Jun-92	19-Dec-03	13-Feb-02 (18-Feb-98)
Title	Freedom of Information Act	Federal Act on Administrative Procedure	(Creation of a federal ombudsman was rejected by parliament on 16 June 2004)	Data Protection Act	Federal Act on Digital Signatures	E-Government Strategy (Strategy for an Information Society in Switzerland)
28. Turkey						
Year	2003				2004	1999
Date	9-Oct-03				15-Jan-04	Jun-99
Title	Law on the Right to Information (Law No 4982)				Law on Electronic Signature	Project on Restructuring Management

Table D.1. Legislation and policy measures for open government[1] (cont.)

Country	Law on Access to Information and Documents	Law on Administrative Procedure	Law on Ombudsman/ Commissioner	Law on Privacy and Data Protection	Law on Electronic Data and Signatures	E-government policy
29. United Kingdom						
Year	2000	2000	1994 (1967)	1998 (1984)	2002 (2000)	1999
Date	31-Jan-00	Nov-00		Jul-98	14-Feb-02 (25-May-00)	30-Mar-99
Title	Freedom of Information Act	Code of practice on Written Consultation	Parliamentary Commissioner Act	Data Protection Act	The Electronic Signatures Regulations (Electronic Communication Act)	Modernising Government White Paper New: March 2000
30. United States						
Year	1996 (1966)	1946		1974	1999; 1997; 1996	2002
Date	Oct-96				Oct-96	17-Dec-02
Title	Electronic Freedom of Information Act (Freedom of Information Act)	Administrative Procedure Act	No national ombudsman	Privacy Act	– Digital Signatures Act – Electronic Data Security Act – Electronic Freedom of Information Act	The E-Government Act (H.R. 2458)
31. European Commission						
Year	1999		2000	1995	1999	2002 (1994)
Date	1-May-99		22-Jun-00			Jun-02
Title	The Amsterdam Treaty (establishing right of access to Community Institution documents)		Statute of European Ombudsman (first appointed in 1995) (Treaty of Maastricht 1992)	EC Data Protection Directive (95/46/EC)	Directive for the Electronic Signature	eEurope Action Plan (Project on Information Society in Europe)

1. Year in brackets indicates date of first passage of legislation in this field. For example: 2001 (1978). This means that the current law dates from 2001, and that legislation was first passed in 1978.

Source: • Country feedback on "Factsheet on Open Government" [GOV/PGC(2004)18/ANN] received by 15 November 2004.
• Country responses to the OECD/PUMA questionnaire on "Strengthening Government-Citizen Connections" [PUMA/CIT(2000)1], received in the Autumn of 1999.
• Country responses to the OECD/PUMA questionnaire on "Parliamentary Procedures and Relations" [PUMA/LEG(2000)1], received in the Summer of 2000.
• "Comparative Analysis of the Member States' Legislation Concerning Access to Documents", Secretariat General of the European Commission, January 2000.

Table D.2. **Oversight institutions for open government**

Country	Ombudsman	Parliamentary Commissioners[1]	Supreme Audit Institution[2]
AUSTRALIA	Commonwealth Ombudsman [est. 1976] Link: *www.comb.gov.au*	Privacy Commissioner for Human Rights and Equal Opportunity Commission Federal Privacy Commissioner Link: *www.privacy.gov.au*	The Auditor General [est. 1901] Link: *www.anao.gov.au*
AUSTRIA	The Austrian Ombudsman Board (Volksanwaltschaft) [est. 1977] Link: *www.volksanw.gv.at* Federal Children's Ombudsman (Kinder & Jugend Anwaltschaft des Bundes) [est. 1989]	Data Protection Commission (Datenschutzkommission) Link: *www.dsk.gv.at*	The Court of Audit (Rechnungshof) [est. 1761] Link: *www.rechnungshof.gv.at*
BELGIUM	The Federal Ombudsman (De Federale Ombudsman) [est. 1995] Link: *www.federalombudsman.be* At the regional level: – Flemish Ombudsman Service [est. 1998] Link: *www.vlaamseombudsdienst.be* – Wallonien Ombudsman (Le Médiateur de la Région Wallonne) [est. 1994] Link: *mediateur.wallonie.be*	Commission for the protection of privacy Link: *www.privacy.fgov.be*	The Court of Audit (Rekenhof/ Cour des Comptes) [est. 1846] Link: *www.courdescomptes.be*
CANADA	(Ombudsmen at provincial level starting in 1967)	Information Commissioner Link: *www.Infocom.gc.ca* Federal Privacy Commissioner Link: *www.privcom.gc.ca*	The Office of the Auditor General [est. 1878] Link: *www.oag-bvg.gc.ca*
CZECH REPUBLIC	The Czech Ombudsman [est. 1999] Link: *www.mujweb.cz/spolecnost/cesky-ombudsman*	The Office for Personal Data Protection Link: *www.uoou.cz* The Commissioner for Civil Rights Protection	Supreme Audit Office [est. 1993] Link: *www.nku.cz*
DENMARK	Ombudsman (Folketingets Ombudsmand) [est. 1954] Link: *www.ombudsmanden.dk*	The Danish Data Protection Agency Link: *www.datatilsynet.dk*	The National Audit Office (Rigsrevisionen) [est. 1975] Link: *www.ftrr.dk*

MODERNISING GOVERNMENT: THE WAY FORWARD – ISBN 92-64-01049-1 – © OECD 2005

Table D.2. **Oversight institutions for open government** (cont.)

Country	Ombudsman	Parliamentary Commissioners[1]	Supreme Audit Institution[2]
FINLAND	Parliamentary Ombudsman (Eduskunnan oikeusasiamies/ Riksdagens justitieombudsmans kansli) [est. 1919] Link: *www.oikeusasiamies.fi* Ombudsman for minorities Link: *www.mol.fi/vahemmistovaltuutettu/ ombudsmaneng.html* Ombudsman for equality Link: *www.stm.fi/Resource.phx/tasa-arvo/english/ authorities/ombudsman/ombudsman.htx*	Data Protection Ombudsman Link: *www.tietosuoja.fi*	The State Audit Office (Valtiontalouden tarkastusvirasto/Statens revisionsverk) [est. 1824] Link: *www.vtv.fi*
FRANCE	Ombudsman of the Republic (Le Médiateur de la République) [est. 1973] Link : *www.mediateur-de-la-republique.fr*	Data Protection Commissioner (Commission Nationale d'Informatique et des Libertés) Link: *www.cnil.fr*	The Court of Accounts (Cour des Comptes) [est. 1807] Link: *www.ccomptes.fr*
GERMANY	Petitions Committee of the German Bundestag (Petitionsausschuss) Link: *www.bundestag.de/htdocs_e/orga/03organs/ 04commit02commper/comm02.html*	The federal data protection commissioner (Bundesbeauftragten für den Datenschutz) Link: *www.bfd.bund.de*	The Federal Audit Court (Bundesrechnungshof) Link: *www.bundesrechnungshof.de/ 1024.html*
GREECE	The Greek Ombudsman [est. 1998] Link: *www.synigoros.gr/*	Hellenic Data Protection Authority Link: *www.dpa.gr/home_eng.htm*	Supreme Court of Audit
HUNGARY		– Parliamentary Commissioner for the rights of national and ethnic minorities – Parliamentary Commissioner for civil rights – Parliamentary Commissioner for data protection Link (portal): *www.obh.hu*	State Audit Office, 1868 Link: *www.asz.gov.hu/ASZ/www.nsf*
ICELAND	The Althing Ombudsman (Umboðsmaður Alþingis) Link: *www.umbodsmaduralthingis.is/english.asp* Ombudsman for Children, 1988 Link: *www.barn.is/erlent/english.html*	Data Protection Agency Link: *www.personuvernd.is/tolvunefnd.nsf/pages/ index.html*	National Audit Office (Ríkisendurskoðun) Link: *www.rikisend.is*
IRELAND	The Ombudsman [est. 1980] Link: *www.irlgov.ie/ombudsman*	Data Protection Commissioner (Coimisinéir Cosanta Sonraí) Link: *www.dataprivacy.ie*	Office of the Comptroller and Auditor General [est. 1866] Link: *www.irlgov.ie*

Table D.2. **Oversight institutions for open government** (cont.)

Country	Ombudsman	Parliamentary Commissioners[1]	Supreme Audit Institution[2]
ITALY	Italy does not have a national Ombudsman. However, it does have an extensive network of regional ombudsmen. The ombudsman of the region of Valle d'Aosta acts as coordinator. Link: *www.consiglio.regione.toscana.it/difensore*	Data Protection Commissioner Link: *www.garanteprivacy.it*	Corte dei Conti [est. 1862] Link: *www.corteconti.it/*
JAPAN	Office of Trade and Investment Ombudsman Link: *www5.cao.go.jp/access/english/oto_main_e.html*	Administrative Inspection Bureau	Board of Audit [est. 1880] Link: *www.jbaudit.go.jp*
KOREA	The Ombudsman of Korea [est. 1994] Link: *www.ombudsman.go.kr/english/index.html*		Board of Audit and Inspection [est. 1948] Link: *www.bai.go.kr/*
LUXEMBOURG	Ombudsman (Le Médiateur au service des citoyens) [est. 2004] Link: *www.ombudsman.lu*	Commission for the Protection of Personal Data	Court of Accounts (Cour des Comptes) Link: *www.cour-des-comptes.lu/*
MEXICO		National Commission for Human Rights (Comisión Nacional de los Derechos Humanos) [est. 1992] Link: *www.cndh.org.mx*	Supreme Audit Office (Auditoría Superior de la Federación) [est. 1824] Link: *www.asf.gob.mx*
NETHERLANDS	National Ombudsman (De Nationale Ombudsman) [est. 1982] Link: *www.ombudsman.nl*	Data Protection Authority Link: *www.cbpweb.nl/en/index.htm*	Court of Audit (Algemene Rekenkamer) Link: *www.rekenkamer.nl*
NEW ZEALAND	The Ombudsmen [est. 1962] Link: *www.ombudsmen.govt.nz*	Privacy Commissioner Link: *www.privacy.org.nz/top.html*	Controller and Auditor General Link: *www.oag.govt.nz*
NORWAY	Parliamentary Ombudsman for Public Administration [est. 1962] Link: *www.sivilombudsmannen.no*	Data Inspectorate Link: *www.datatilsynet.no*	Office of the Auditor General (Riksrevisjonen) [est. 1816] Link: *www.riksrevisjonen.no*
POLAND	Ombudsman for Children (Rzecznik Praw Dziecka) Link: *www.brpd.gov.pl/ang.htm*	General Inspector of Personal Data Protection Link: *www.giodo.gov.pl* Commissioner for Civil Rights Protection (Rzecznika Praw Obywatelskich), 1987 Link: *www.brpo.gov.pl/index.php?e=1*	Supreme Chamber of Control (Najwyzsa Izba Kontroli) [est. 1808] Link: *www.nik.gov.pl*
PORTUGAL	Office of Justice (Provedor de Justiça) [est. 1975] Link: *www.provedor-jus.pt/ingles*	National Commission on Data Protection Link: *www.cnpd.pt*	Court of Auditors (Tribunal de Contas) [est. 1279] Link: *www.tcontas.pt*

Table D.2. **Oversight institutions for open government** (cont.)

Country	Ombudsman	Parliamentary Commissioners[1]	Supreme Audit Institution[2]
SLOVAK REPUBLIC		The Office for Personal Data Protection Link: www.dataprotection.gov.sk Public Defender of Rights, 2001 Link: www.vop.gov.sk	The Supreme Audit Office [est. 1782] Link: www.nku.gov.sk/english/index_eng.html
SPAIN	People's Defender (Defensor del Pueblo) [est. 1981] Link: www.defensordelpueblo.es	Data Protection Agency (Agencia Espanola de Protección de Datos) Link: www.agpd.es	Court of Acccounts (Tribunal de Cuentas) [est. 1828] Link: www.tcu.es
SWEDEN	The Parliamentary Ombudsman (Riksdagens Ombudsmän) [est. 1809] Link: www.jo.se	Data Inspectorate Link: www.datainspektionen.se	National Audit Office (Riksrevisionen) [est. 2003] Link: www.riksrevisionen.se
SWITZERLAND	The creation of a federal ombudsman was rejected by parliament on 16 June 2004	Data Protection Commissioner Link: www.edsb.ch/framese.html	Federal Audit Office [est. 1852] Link: www.efk.admin.ch/englisch/index.htm
TURKEY			Court of Accounts [est. 1862] Link: www.sayistay.gov.tr/english_tca/eng.asp
UNITED KINGDOM	The Northern Ireland Ombudsman Link: www.ni-ombudsman.org.uk	Information Commissioner Link: www.dataprotection.gov.uk	National Audit Office [est. 1983] Link: www.nao.org.uk
UNITED STATES	Many regional and local ombudsmen	Small business ombudsmen (also called 'national ombudsman') Link: www.epa.gov/sbo/	Government Accountability Office [est. 1921] Link: www.gao.gov/
EUROPEAN UNION	The European Ombudsman [est. 1995] Link: www.euro-ombudsman.eu.int/home/en/default.htm	Committee of petitions for European Parliament Link: www.europarl.eu.int/committees/peti_home.htm	European Court of Auditors [est. 1977] Link: www.eca.eu.int/index_en.htm

1. Useful link: www.privacylaws.com/links/linknational.htm
2. Useful link: www.eurosai.org/direc_mien.htm

OECD PUBLICATIONS, 2, rue André-Pascal, 75775 PARIS CEDEX 16
PRINTED IN FRANCE
(42 2005 13 1 P) ISBN 92-64-01049-1 – No. 54149 2005